P9-CRU-947

PASSIONATE
DOUBTS

Passionate Doubts

DESIGNS OF INTERPRETATION IN CONTEMPORARY AMERICAN FICTION

PATRICK O'DONNELL

UNIVERSITY OF IOWA PRESS

IOWA CITY

University of Iowa Press,
Iowa City 52242

Printed in the United States of America

Jacket and book design by Richard Hendel

Typesetting by G&S Typesetters, Inc., Austin, Texas

Printing and binding by Kingsport Press, Kingsport, Tennessee

Library of Congress Cataloging-in-Publication Data

O'Donnell, Patrick, 1948–
Passionate doubts.
Includes index.
1. American fiction—20th century—History and criticism. 2. Self in literature. I. Title.
PS374.S44O36 1986 813'.54'09 85-28865
ISBN 0-87745-138-9

FOR THOMAS HANZO

"There is a project for the sun. The sun
Must bear no name, gold flourisher, but be
In the difficulty of what is to be."

CONTENTS

ACKNOWLEDGMENTS

In writing this book, I have benefited from the criticism and generosity of several friends and colleagues. I wish to especially thank Herbert Schneidau, Barbara Babcock, Douglas Canfield, Jerrold Hogle, Edgar Dryden, Susan Aiken, and John T. Matthews for the time they took to comment upon my work, often when they were heavily involved in projects of their own. Two friends from abroad, Marc Chénetier and Heide Ziegler, gave both encouragement at just the right time and the necessary insights from their own work on contemporary American fiction. For several years, Robert Con Davis and I have been talking over matters of theory and fiction. Our dialogue has been a continuous source of provocation and enrichment, and his support for my work in general has been essential to the completion of this single example.

The insights and enthusiasm of my students in English 596-G, History and Theory of Fiction, provided the final spark of energy I needed to finish this book. A grant from the Arizona Humanities Council allowed me to use the fine collections in contemporary fiction and theory at the libraries of the University of California-Irvine and the University of California–Los Angeles. Albert Geggenheimer, editor of the *Arizona Quarterly*, and Claude Richard, editor of *Delta*, have kindly allowed me to reprint revisions of the discussions of *Pale Fire* and *Travesty* which originally appeared in their journals.

Not at all finally, my family has given me the kind of consideration and support which can be properly acknowledged only in private. This book is dedicated to my teacher, Thomas A. Hanzo, who first made me aware of the pains and joys of interpretation.

PREFACE

Our doubt is our passion
and our passion is our task.
Henry James, "The Middle Years"

This book considers six important contemporary American novels in light of their concern with interpretation—both as a labor undertaken by the reader of fiction and as an activity that takes place within the text itself. We know what it is to read, but the novels that I shall discuss raise the issue of what it is *to be read*. By foregrounding a process of interpretation, by dramatizing the scene of their own writing, these novels question their begetting as texts while suggesting that the production and reading of signs, whether or not these appear between the covers of a book, correspond to the articulation of what is meaningful in human experience. In this scriptive view, to be "human" is to be a reader; to achieve an "identity" means to become a sign (of something) to others. In one sense, for these texts, the activity of interpretation is a sign of life, and its suppression or silencing a sign of death, no matter what errors may arise from the former or what silent testaments may issue from the latter.

More specifically, I am concerned to show how particular contemporary texts create a semantic field, or area of hermeneutic play, wherein various "conditions of meaning" are exposed and where the reader is engaged in the formation of these conditions.[1] The meaningful conditions of a fiction may appear in several ways. They may be observed in a theme that emerges from the protagonist's quest for the significance of his or her own existence. Often, this quest will end in an articulation of some complex but definitive relation to "reality." Alternatively, the conditions of meaning in a novel may be viewed as a matter of "narratology"—how narrative grammar, rhetoric, repetition, structure, and the labyrinthine narrative line represent a verbal world, while revealing the presuppositions that allow for its maintenance.[2] A fictional world may embody, among other things, a version of the real, the portrait of a consciousness, or a system of verbal relations that tangentially refer to an "unconscious" allegorized in the form of social, familial, and marital relations.[3] And always, since novels are inscriptions, the conditions of meaning they give rise to are a matter of their textuality, their status as texts, existing in a historical profusion of other texts which they echo, mock, distort, or dispute.[4]

The idea that literary texts create an arena for hermeneutic play, where these conditions unfold, informs my choice of the phrase "passionate doubts" to describe the sensibilities that are aroused by reading contemporary narrative. On the one hand, passion can be defined, according to the OED, as "an eager outreaching of the mind towards something, a vehement predilection." On the other hand, the artist who pronounces the epigraph from James' "The Middle Years" defines passion as the labor of doubt. The novels I address tease out this double sense of the reader's relation to the text as, simultaneously, a possession and a skeptical distancing. They do this by reflecting upon the nature of signs and the activity of interpretation while deploying the very signs that encourage this reflection.

As I use the term in this book, a sign may be thought of as something which gives with one hand what it takes away with the other, since it represents and puts off the "reality" it points to. The sign stands in relation to something else; more precisely, a sign is one thing that stands for another thing and signifies that thing as a "deferred presence."[5] Narratives are made up of signs written down as words, sentences, chapters, even individual letters; traditionally conceived as problematic representations of "reality," narratives are, rather, open-ended sign systems that exist as the nexus of other sign systems (linguistic, historical, social), which overlap in various combinations to foster individual fictions. Where is the reader to be found in this profusion of signs? Walter Benn Michaels, following Charles Sanders Peirce, has argued for a semiotic conception of the "self" as both a reader and a text, as both an interpreter of and that which is interpreted by the social reality of which the reader is a part: "For Descartes, the self is autonomous—this is simply to say again that it is primary, it exists independent of any external constraints; for Peirce, the self is a sign—it is itself 'external,' like all signs, it 'must address itself to some other, must determine some other, since that is the essence of a sign.' These others constitute the sign system, what Peirce calls 'reality,' what Royce will call the 'community of interpretation,'" a concept which yields the conclusion that "the self, like the world, is a text."[6] If this analogy holds, if it is true that the human self can be regarded as a complex interaction between "sign-reader-text," then, I shall argue, readers of fictions are put in the peculiar position of reading a text while, in some sense, *being* a text; they interpret signs while existing as a form of signification. Readers are compounded by their reading, a complexity that motivates much of the discussion in this book.

In *Passionate Doubts*, I attempt to explore the conditions of meaning that contemporary novels establish, then query, by problematizing the constitution of their own narrative signs, thus forcing upon the reader a playful confrontation with readerly self-constructions. I present readings of six novels, framed by an introductory dialogue and a closing theoretical chapter on the reader in contemporary fiction. The novels under discussion include Nabokov's *Pale Fire*, Hawkes' *Travesty*, Barth's *LETTERS*, Pynchon's *Gravity's Rainbow*, O'Connor's *Wise Blood*, and Elkin's *The Franchiser*. The choice of text is not intended to exclude the many other novels I might have selected for discussion but represents a spectrum incorporating various scenes of contemporary writing and acts of interpretation. The readings of the novels yield an order within this variety that reflects as much the desires of the interpreter as it does any discovered or imposed progression between disparate texts.

The organization of the readings permits, as a matter of accretion, different kinds of discourse to be brought into the evolving discussion of hermeneutic activity in contemporary fiction. Thus, in the first two chapters on *Pale Fire* and *Travesty*, I discuss the conception of the "self" as a textual sign. The theory of the self or the subject of narrative is my concern throughout since, I argue, all interpretation springs from some form of self-conception. The nature of the self in contemporary fiction has been discussed at length within a number of theoretical concepts, including formalist, grammatical readings of the self as actant, deconstructions of the authorial self as the origin of the text, and performative conceptions of the self as a protean actor who brings under question the process of self-construction.[7] As my opening comments indicate, I take my departure from these approaches by emphasizing a *semiotic* theory which regards the self as a sign and as a reader of signs.[8] This discussion is enlarged in the third chapter, where *LETTERS* is viewed as a collusion of historical and fictional discourses within which the self, as an interpretation of history, is born. Chapter 4 comprises a further enlargement of the discussion in an analysis of *Gravity's Rainbow*. There, the trace elements of "self" and "history" are subsumed within a larger cultural discourse defined as the inscription of power relations engendered by Western fantasies. Chapters 5 and 6 on, respectively, *Wise Blood* and *The Franchiser* push to its limits the underlying concerns of the book thus far by observing the ends of interpretation in their movement between authorial domination and carnivalesque ambivalence, which produce versions of the self as mere referent or as disseminated voice. Taken together, these six readings suggest a progression from self-interpretation to a representation of singular and pluralistic worlds, though, crucially, each novel recapitulates this "progress" somehow within itself.

Along with this discursive organization, the choice of contemporary American fiction for the discussion of interpretation reveals some underlying assumptions. In the broadest sense, I consider problems of interpretation and reading to be at the heart of all narrative. However, this consideration can be seen in its historical and cultural specificities when we note the tendency of contemporary narrative to force issues of signification and interpretation to their limits, while conducting a discussion of limits. Much contemporary narrative strives to generate a disruptive, foregrounded relation with the reader which I have put in terms of passionate doubt. Specifically, contemporary narrative attempts to create in the reader a hyperbolic sense of doubt about the text's meaningfulness, the credences of its own language, the tautologies of its own sign system, even the existence of its own "subject." These qualities exist potentially in all narrative, but in contemporary fiction they are dramatically, structurally, and literally expressed, down to the most graphic manifestations of narrative inscription—the writing of alphabetic letters and the scattering of these across blank pages bound into a book. Such books, I think, are born within a culture riven by an ever-increasing realization of its self-critical abilities and discontents, paired alongside an obsession with legalistic and nationalistic certainties which threaten its very existence. That a contemporary American culture, so defined, also feels itself weighed down by a past which it may merely repeat, or only barely escape, speaks to the condition of "textuality" with which all the novels I discuss contend. Within this condition, contemporary novels struggle against the necessary burden of a literary tradition that questions the ideology of traditions, while relying upon earlier literary productions to form the grounds for response or revolt. When, as in so much contemporary fiction, questions regarding the conditions of textuality are compounded with questions regarding the conditions of meaning *inside* the text, we are exposed to the intense self-scrutiny and ironic alterity that paradoxically characterize many specific contemporary novels.[9]

Given this definition of "contemporaneity," the selection of individual texts can be defended only by the proposition that these novels both give rise to and are able to bear the interference of speculations about signs, the self, the reader, and the act of interpretation. The choice of texts is no more innocent than what I see in them: the hermeneutic circle is at work here and, as the ideology of my critical approach tends to the conservation of the text as self-conservation, so the texts I read reflect more readily than others this intention. Moreover, the novels I consider have in common a quality that Alan Wilde has termed "mid-fictional," one which "strenuously interrogates the world without foreclosing all knowledge of it and unsettles rather than topples our certainties and presuppositions by way of parody and other recyclings of fictional, cultural, even metaphysical givens."[10] Wilde's definition underscores one of the limits of my discussion, outside which other considerations that bear more upon the ideology and history of "postmodernism" must fall.[11] I begin the six readings with a dialogue that attempts to play off a series of critical concerns, and two voices, against each other, thus dialogically introducing those problems which the textual readings are intended not to neatly solve but to reproduce in varying contexts. I conclude more formally with a theoretical discussion of the reader's "consciousness," that semiotic self to be seen in the interpretation of these texts.

This book is designed not to promote a singular thesis but to work through a series of interrelated readings that reveal the lineaments and possibilities of interpretive acts in contemporary fiction. My readings are intended to be accessible both to generalists and specialists; hence, particularly here and in the introduction, I have tried to bring out those critical assumptions that inform my readings. The reader will find that the theoretical approach here is eclectic, an assemblage of openings or insights that are meant to reveal the power and work of the text at hand, unified by a focus upon the semiotic foundations of narrative discourse. Whatever has come to hand as illuminating a given text is used. Yet I do not wish to claim the privilege of an impossibly "innocent" reader: what has come to hand has been chosen, taken off the shelf and read, because it proleptically had something to do with the act of interpretation as a matter of textual strategy, self-construction, and the constitution of sign systems. In the rich variety offered by critics as diverse as Sartre, Derrida, Bakhtin, Binswanger, Said, Geertz, and Serres, working with or against them, my purpose has been to show the process of interpretation as the production of the self in the text within the context of other fictive, historical, and cultural discourses. I realize the arguable privileging of the subject that this approach maintains, but in the end interpretation, if it exists, is a matter of achieving identity. By this I mean that the reader forms a linguistic "relation" to the text which is her or his interpretation; this complex relation, in turn, parallels and supplements those others of "self" to "world" or "individual" to "society" that, together, constitute the self as a sign of social and linguistic relations.[12] Possibly the act of interpretation is a fantasy, or in the future it might disappear altogether; however, that suspicious prophecy is not the subject of my inquiry. The limited power of interpretation, I will argue, can be doubted and can embody doubt but, as long as we inscribe texts and signs, it cannot be thoroughly disowned.

INTRODUCTION
FICTION AND INTERPRETATION, A DIALOGUE

Hic and *Nunc*, meeting as arranged, in a private library.

Hic: When our paths last crossed, you were speaking of the "self" as a "mode of interpretation." Would you explain what you meant by that?

Nunc: I should have said that the self *is* an interpretation and not, abstractly, merely an interpreted form or configuration. The self is an interpretation of the world—at least this is the manner in which the self sees itself.

Hic: But this tells me nothing. In your point of departure you have made an equation between "self" and "world," both problematic terms which depend, for their separation, upon an empiricist conception of that relation as categorical. Then you throw in "interpretation" as a mediatory term, thus creating a tautology, for in fact you are insisting that while "self" and "world" are separate entities, the former depends upon the latter. For you, the self is a version of the world, as if there was some unquestioned reciprocity between the two.

Nunc: Agreed, my statement about interpretation is a tautology. Let me try to be more specific and interrogatory about what I see as the crucial relation between these two heuristic terms—"self" and "world." For the present, I will modify my proposition to say that "interpretation" is the definition of this relation or, even better, its framing, the understanding of its conceptualization. An example of what I mean by interpretation as framing can be seen in an overquoted (and overdetermined) passage from the preface to James' *Portrait of a Lady*, which contains the famous "house of fiction" metaphor. Admittedly, the image of the house speaks directly to the relation between an author and his or her "field of vision," but I think we may see that it more generally and more substantially discusses the relation between self and world. James describes the position of the artist as that of a watcher at one of many windows, "a figure with a pair of eyes" who has taken up residence in the multicameral "house of fiction." The watcher and neighboring artists

> are watching the same show, but one seeing more where the other sees less, one seeing black where the other sees white, one seeing big where the other sees small, one seeing coarse where the other sees fine. And so on, and so on; there is, fortunately, no saying on what, for the particular pair of eyes, the window may *not* open; "fortunately" by reason, precisely, of this incalculability of range. The spreading field, the human scene, is the "choice of subject"; the pierced aperture, either broad or balconied or slit-like and low-browed, is the "literary form"; but they are, singly or together, as nothing without the posted presence of the watcher—without, in other words, the consciousness of the artist.[1]

Hic: Yes, this is a very clever analogy, but doesn't it strike you as overstated? Isn't there a great deal of construction here to make a simple point about artistic choices and "consciousness"?

Nunc: Exactly—which is why I want to look closely at this passage. I want to see why James elaborates at such length on what appears to be a simple statement of the relation between the artist, the subject, and the generic or formal framing of the artistic production. There is much more here than meets the eye, especially when we regard what seems to be a certain anxiety present in the burdensome repetition of opposed qualities of vision: more and less, big and small, black and white, coarse and fine—a list whose inexhaustibility is implied by the doubled et ceteras following it.

Hic: But before we subject James' metaphor to this kind of transparent rhetorical scrutiny, perhaps we might frame the passage by viewing it within its historical and literary contexts. After all, James is clearly working with two crucial if, for us, familiar concerns in the preface. First, he wants to construct a proscenium for his novel, *Portrait of a Lady*, which largely recounts the heroine's passage through a series of rooms as metaphors for the expansions of her consciousness and her increasing power of choice. Second, he wants to establish here, as in so many other places, his aesthetic criteria for "point of view" and its importance as a technical development of modernism. Of course, his concern is more than just technical: thematically and technically, in *Portrait* as well as in *The Golden Bowl*, having the freedom to choose one's subject, field of play, or way of seeing confers upon the seer the responsibility of that choice which, in turn, places rather vague limitations on what can be seen. But really, isn't this all part of a larger epistemological development that we associate with the rise of modernism? Aren't we dealing with a historical configuration that, James' metaphor suggests, interweaves literary experimentation, a developing interest in human psychology, and a fascination with the visual arts which finds its technological analogue in the evolving art of photography?

Nunc: I agree that the passage exists within the framework of modernism. And I would want to argue that understanding this framework is crucial to any conception of interpretation entering fiction as a definition of the relation between self and world. But I think the fact that, in this prefatory statement, James elaborates at length upon the act of *seeing* encourages us to scrutinize the passage as it rhetorically conceives this visual activity, which must be represented linguistically. Let's return momentarily to what you, from the start, noted as the overstatement of the passage—a verbal residue that survives, I think, its incorporation into a historical or paradigmatic frame. You have already implied that what is at issue here in the quality of the relation between the watcher and what is seen is perception glossed as an act of interpretation. Clearly, the artist is no passive recorder of "the human scene" but one who *chooses* the subject (what is seen) and the vision's form (how it is seen). Ostensibly, interpretation enters the picture as the matter of choice that exists between viewer and viewed; more importantly, this choice seems open and indeterminate. For James, it almost appears as an instance of good luck that allows the viewer any number of perceptual options. Yet, there is more here or, perhaps, less: more, in terms of the rhetorical excess that is needed to convey this concept; less, in terms of a certain specularity that haunts the passage. The figure of the house is an extended metaphor that verges upon the embarrassment of being overdone, and contained within this figure we can spot examples of repeated metonymy (And so on, and so on), antithesis (black . . . white), double negative (no saying . . . not), and parataxis (one . . . one). This rhetorical ornamentation articulates what is, essentially, a *framing*, not just of James' novel, but also of the way significance is generated by the artist positioned in relation to "the spreading field." The metaphor suggests that the artist has no power over or immediate contact with "the human scene" but can, to some extent, view it through whatever kind of window or lens is desired. However, even this "incalculability of range," this indeterminate quality of the relation between viewer and viewed, has a certain "preformed" aspect to it. The viewers are *stationed* at their various windows. All are condemned to "the same show," and one assumes that if there are windows in the edifice—gashes or aporiae—then there are also blank walls beyond which one may not see. Even James' "figure with a pair of eyes" serves the doubly inclusive duty of standing as a synecdoche for the artist and for the figure itself or for the eyes of the preface-writing author gazing at us through the words of his construction. And let me add that the apertures through which the watchers look down upon "the spreading field" are themselves eyes: "slit-like and low-browed."

Hic: Indeed, as you suggest, the metaphor of "the house of fiction" is complicated from within, but I am not sure how these complications create the latency of expression that, you imply, somehow undermines or works against the obvious meaning of the figure.

Nunc: Perhaps it is wise to restate the obvious meaning of the passage in order to overturn it, as I think James' overdetermined rhetoric encourages us to do. His metaphor manifestly establishes an indeterminate relation between "art" and "life" wherein the artistic labor is caught up in an existential, even moral, choice of form and subject—a choice which allows artists to see as much as their abilities and wisdom, framed by these matters, will permit. The activities of construction and production rely wholly upon "the consciousness of the artist," which, in James' double-bound epistemology, forms and is formed by this experience of "seeing."

Hic: Let me stop you at this point to say that your summary of manifest content does not seem particularly objectionable, though it strikes me as repeating the tautology you began with. If we can accept, for the moment, the homology that you imply exists between artist/human scene and self/world, isn't your account, in fact, a restatement of how you view the act of interpretation? That is, as the construction of a relation between self and world or, to supplement the homology, between reader and text? I believe this is what you defined as "interpretation" at the outset, and we need add only that, for James, this relation is seen in terms of a perceptual phenomenology where, if I can cite a passage from a book I've been reading on the psychology of perception, "the life of consciousness . . . is subtended by an 'intentional arc' which projects round about us our past, our future, our human setting, our physical, ideological and moral situation, or rather which results in our being situated in all these respects."[2] The matter of "choice," then, is really a matter of intention—the artist's intention toward (or consciousness of) the human scene, the self toward the world, the reader toward the text, etc.

Nunc: But it is still unclear what such terms as "intention" and "consciousness" mean in these statements; moreover, the definition of this interpretive relation strikes me as too comfortable even if I, too, proposed that illusory comfort at the beginning of our discussion. Underlying your reading of James' obvious intentions in this figure is a logic of *identification*; Merleau-Ponty's synthesizing "intentional arc" implies a necessary temporal continuity and, ultimately, a merging between viewer and viewed, self and world. Yet within this logic, in James' figure, everything speaks of separation, rupture, and indeterminacy not as a matter of choice but as a kind of fatality that "subtends" the empty space that lies between those watchers in their separate rooms and the human scene unfolding on its own below, in the distance. Even the communal nature of the figure (they are all watching "the same show") begins to break down when we see that each watcher is isolated, both by the peculiarities of individual vision and by the framework which determines the artist's placement within the larger construction of "the house of fiction."

We might translate this image as a statement about the individual self's ensconcement within a certain historical configuration and the self-imposed limitations or excesses of vision that each individual generates as the framing elements of an interpretation of reality. Against what Paul de Man labels the conception of the "aesthetic self," who "strives for a mode of totalization that is reductive but, in Lukács' term, 'homogeneous,' with its original intent at self-immanence," the underside of James' figure presents an artistic self viewed as the double "not" of its relation to "the spreading field."[3] All the rhetorical figures within the passage refer, metaphorically, to frames and gaps as the constitutive qualities of the artist's relation to the "scene." Potentially, James' image is eternally regressive when we see that the framework of "the house of fiction" frames the viewers' windows which, themselves, frame each "pair of eyes" as an architecture ("pierced aperture," "slit-like," "low-browed") that beholds what is "out there" as the sign of "spreading," distance, and framing. In this schema, the observing self is a cipher, an "I" whose identification with the worldly scene is stated, paradoxically, as a self-mirrored separation from it; Jamesian "consciousness," in this regard, might be seen as an awareness of the frame within which this relation between self and world is conceived.

Hic: Your reading of the passage may be overcomplicating what is already, in your view, overdetermined. You leave me as much at a loss here as you did when you suggested, in the first place, that the act of interpretation is somehow the relation or bridge between self and world. We're still dealing with tautologies, whether this relation is defined as one of identity or as one of difference.

Nunc: Not quite. We have advanced to the point of being able to state, at least for James, who is in the unusual position of writing a preface that is actually a postface written years after the original framing of his *Portrait*, the nature of this relation: the terms of the homologies artist/scene, self/world, reader/text necessarily involve, as their substance, a focusing upon the framing and limits of their rhetorical positionings to each other. This attentiveness to frames and boundaries, which I see as the primary quality of the act of interpretation, is not so abysmal or infernally circular as it sounds, nor am I totally ignoring the questionable leaps that I have made from homology to homology. James' figure defines "the spreading field" as a scene or theatricalization which may be fairly compared to a text—so that the "out there" of the figure is not raw, unprocessed existence but something already staged. We might see a kind of interior homology at work here where, for example, the separate conceptions of self and world (a watcher in a window, a bounded field) are seen as framed constructions; thus, the relation between them is doubled as one recognizes, while remaining within, the liminalities of these constructions. This is a point Barbara Johnson makes when she states that the relation between readers and texts (to take another from the homological trivium I'm insisting upon) is "equivocal": "not an expression of symmetry in itself, but only an evocation of the interdependence of the two terms, of the *question* of symmetry as a *prob-*

lem in the transferential structure of all reading."[4] In this light, we might see the problematical relation between self and world (reader and text, viewer and viewed) as the vexed dyssymmetry that exists between them. Each term is, to some extent, as a knowable entity, the product of its framed relation to the other. Interpretation, then, is the understanding of this relation *as frame*. More precisely, as a relational activity, interpretation opens up the space between the terms of our homologies; paradoxically, it bridges the empty space, in James' figure, between watcher and field.

Hic: So that there *are* grounds for interpretation as the understanding of a reciprocity between differentiated but homologous entities—self/world, viewer/viewed, reader/text. I admire the dialectical qualities inherent in this theory, though I fear we are getting caught up in a rhetorical game where we are simply moving linguistic counters like "self" and "world" around on an epistemological chessboard. This seems to happen whenever we question what we do when we "mean" something or say that something "means," which conforms to a pet theory of mine. Especially when we are talking about the interpretation of written texts (which you suggest, for James, we are always doing no matter what the occasion), the act of interpretation inevitably involves the creation of a language supplemental to that of the work being analyzed—a language that mimes, mocks, and rhetorically dissembles that of the "original." Similarly, the interpretation of interpretation (what we are doing here) generates another such supplementary discourse, so that understanding what we do when we read or see necessitates a bifurcated fall into tautology and a form of linguistic self-reflexiveness. Which, I suppose, is a way of saying what many have already said, that we are always "in" language, and that all language is meta-linguistic: a signifying of this condition, a confrontation with the limits of this inwardness.

Nunc: It is difficult to avoid these linguistic leavenings and to deny the sense of the *mise en abîme*, or seeming groundlessness of our signifying activities, when we reflect on the nature of those activities. Geoffrey Hartman echoes your anxiety about endless inquiries on the order of "what do we mean when we mean" in suggesting that it is part of the modern condition, "our broadened historical perspective," that "there is now more helplessness about interpretation as it stretches toward an infinity of statements and contaminates art itself."[5] In a moment, I'll respond to this anxiety by asserting that interpretation has its limits, but first I insist on a bit more historical context which may tell us why we are subject to this hermeneutic helplessness. Indeed, we might point to such texts as James' preface to *Portrait of a Lady* as the culprits which have conferred upon us the large anxieties about the grounds, limits, and validities of our interpretive acts.

If we turn our discussion more specifically to a scrutiny of interpretation and fiction, it seems evident, as fiction moves through modernism to "postmodernism," that the activity of interpretation recurs upon itself. Increasingly, it is implicated as the subject matter of fiction, while becoming more deeply questioned, within these very fictions, as a framing of our desire for texts to mean something. For James, "the spreading field," however problematically, refers to some form of human existence. But for a contemporary writer such as Borges, whose work, in part, descends from the hermeneutic "contaminations" of works like James' "The Turn of the Screw" or *The Sacred Fount*, what takes place on the "field" is the activity of reading itself as the text devours the reader or the "scene" devours the artist. Here is a passage from Borges' "The Garden of Forking Paths," in which Stephen Albert, who is sought after by the story's protagonist, relates the qualities of a particularly labyrinthine form of fiction:

> In all fictional works, each time a man is confronted with several alternatives, he chooses one and eliminates the others; in the fictions of Ts'ui Pên, he chooses—simultaneously—all of them. *He creates*, in this way, diverse futures, diverse times which themselves also proliferate and fork. Here, then, is the explanation of the novel's contradictions. Fang, let us say, has a secret; a stranger calls at his door; Fang resolves to kill him. Naturally, there are several possible outcomes: Fang can kill the intruder, the intruder can kill Fang, they can both escape, they can both die, and so forth. In the works of Ts'ui Pên, all possible outcomes occur; each one is the point of departure for other forkings. Sometimes, the paths of this labyrinth converge: for example, you arrive at this house, but in one of the possible pasts, you are my enemy, in another, my friend. If you will resign yourself to my incurable pronunciation, we shall read a few pages.[6]

Hic: Notice, as in James, that even though Albert conceives of reading in the fictions of Ts'ui Pên as radically open and labyrinthine, the element of choice is still present.

Nunc: But only in the form of a paradox since, if one can theoretically choose all available alternatives simultaneously, then the activity of "choice" is erased. For James, choice and interpretation depend upon the opportunity to *eliminate* alternatives, to create distinctions; another way of putting this is to say that taking a point of view upon existence corresponds with the framing activity that sets off that view from others. Borges' narrator, impossibly, suspends this activity in the attempt to articulate a form of inscription (a penning of the *suis*, or self) which allows for the kind of interpretive infinitude that Hartman sees as our historical inheritance. Incidentally, Borges' conception tries to eliminate not only frames but also temporality. The adventurer within the labyrinth of this fiction, or the reader of it, follows Albert's "incurable pronunciation" or the proliferations of a narrative line that forks in all directions *at once*. Impossibly, reading this text would demand that the reader generate as many reading selves as there are paths—a hermeneutic fantasy worth considering, but one hardly subject to fulfillment.

Beyond these textual illusions, what I want you to see in this example is the hidden agenda of Borges' garden, which exfoliates texts rather than plants. Frames and temporality are the necessary conditions of reading, perhaps, again, its very substance. James' "spreading field," I suspect, incorporates the temporal element of perceptual processes by seeing them as unfolding in time, which we experience in reading fiction as a progression or a route by which we trace the linear development of the story. The fictions of Ts'ui Pên attempt to negate these conditions but succeed only in ironically reaffirming their shadowy presence as the liminal factors determined by and determining the act of interpretation. The imagined proliferation of paths and futures is preceded by a determinative causality: "Fang, let us say, has a secret; a stranger calls at his door; Fang resolves to kill him." For the reader of this passage, Fang's unrevealed secret is the origin of the story, its initial limit, what Edward Said refers to as its "beginning intention"—the inscribed desire of a work to produce meaning, to make something happen, or to signify its difference from other texts.[7] Fang's story conceals its beginning as a secret, but from this original cause arises the labyrinth of possible results which

Albert can describe only metonymically, in succession as we read them, despite the proclaimed simultaneity of their occurrence. It may be that with his "incurable pronunciation" Albert will be able to articulate the convergences and synchronies of the story labyrinth's exfoliations, but this possibility is the end limit of his story, beyond which we may not comprehend the "incurability" or incompletion of his diction. In some sense, Albert's recitation is a parable of the self-inscribed, interpretive limits of fiction, which requires from the reader an awareness of its borders and beginnings, no matter how marginalized or hidden they might be. We are additionally required to confirm its diachronic, linear processes (as they are situated within beginnings and ends, promoted by the reader who pursues the lines of plot and intention), no matter how much these may convey the illusion of simultaneity.

Hic: But in all of this, you seem to be more concerned with establishing the boundaries of fiction and interpretation, rather than—as I thought you would—indulging in the possibilities of free play and indeterminacy that a writer like Borges (even James, if we critique his preface in a certain light) seems to encourage. I'm still not sure how understanding in what ways stories frame themselves and enforce their enslavement to time is a problem of interpretation. These seem more like the complications of authorial conception.

Nunc: I suppose my point is that, even with the projected fictions of Ts'ui Pên, or with Robbe-Grillet's *The Erasers*, or with Calvino's *The Castle of Crossed Destinies*—even with fictions that attempt to create the illusion of interpretive infinity, everything happening at once, endless plots, interconnections, and possibilities—the limits we have been discussing as origin, frame, and temporality keep appearing, if only as shadows or secrets. Understanding these limiting factors is, in my opinion, what constitutes "interpretation." To put the matter in Jamesian terms, novels, as "houses" or metaphorical containers of significance, are founded upon their own architectural designs. These designs are the matter of fictions, a point that only *seems* to contradict James' characterization of the subject as "the spreading field" of "the human scene." As we have pointed out, the scene itself is a performance, a designed entity, so that the act of interpretation is improperly seen as some form of "free play" within the self-proclaimed limitations of fiction. Rather, to interpret is to recognize and repeat these limits (which are the technical as well as the self-questioned teleological ends of fiction) in the language of the critic.

Hic: But what is the purpose of knowing these limits, whether they be imposed on the interpreter by the text or by the text upon itself? If I may employ your own scriptable metaphors, you seem to be focusing upon the margins of the pages rather than upon the words of the text. What about the ideas or themes a novel conveys? Aren't your notions about fiction and interpretation limited to the kind of metafictional situations one might well find in contemporary critical narratives or the preface to a novel, rather than being applicable to all fiction?

Nunc: Not really. We have only to look at *Don Quixote* or *The Arabian Nights* (or biblical parables or ancient charms and riddles) to see examples of "older" fictions that refer, sometimes as matters of life and death, to their own conceptions. Even so-called "realistic" fiction, which affects the illusion of a "slice of life," of having no self-referential fictional qualities or boundaries, actually incorporates these in such a way that they become crucial to the story's meaning. Can one read Balzac without an essential consciousness of the place of each novel within the larger theatrical and genealogical arrangements of *La comédie humaine*? And isn't each novel's placement within these liminal frames somehow its primary "subject"? Of course, novels contain ideas or themes, but these, drawn out and summarized by critics as a given novel's meaning, usually appear in the form of propositions about human life that might be more economically conveyed in sermons and pedagogic essays. The old explanation that stories are, rhetorically, a more convincing or appealing way of purveying such propositions simply does not hold up—no more for *Don Quixote* and *Père Goriot* than for the *nouveau roman*. The same stories are told over and over again, in different guises; almost compulsively, they create repetitions, frames, and modes of rhetorical self-consciousness as linguistic residue or excess that bury, distort, and confute the would-be transcendent significances ("themes") which form the propositional dimension of a given story.

Perhaps contemporary narratives highlight what I have been calling the boundaries of fiction by neutralizing the protective coloration assumed by some "older" fictions as an attempt to erase these boundaries through the creation of certain mimetic illusions. But the boundaries have always been there. The act of interpretation, then, is an attempt to recognize the assumed conditions under which a given fiction generates significance—whether this comes in the form of heroic action, a reified theme, a totalizing world view, or a complication of these. It is the *desire* to produce such significances, and the language which produces them, that we must interpret. I think, by the way, that this allows us to go beyond the concept of interpretive free play, which is just a way of saying that we can introduce a form of erotic subjectivity into the act of reading fictions, whereby (within the allowances conferred by a given narrative) we can "make it mean anything we want to."

Hic: I still have difficulty seeing how "meaning" comes from a critical awareness of the limits, frames, or architecture employed by a given novel.

Nunc: Perhaps, in order to accept its ramifications, you have to accept what appears to be an *a priori* statement on my part: significance is, exactly, the observed conditions of meaning permitted within the world of a fiction. What, for example, does the narrator of *Tom Jones* concern himself with? He questions what it means to be a narrator; he continually attempts to redefine the population of his audience; he seems most taken not with what he will tell in the story (for it is, as he all too often observes, an old story) but with *how* he will tell it. In short, despite his comic posture, he agonizes over the means of communication he uses to relate his history. For Fielding's narrator, this anxiety is authorial, as it is for James and for Borges' Stephen Albert. But more to my purposes, this seeming obsession with the signifying conditions of the narrative concerns the reader, too: it forms the basis for a hermeneutic activity in reading the story. For at least one version of the reader is that she or he is but another author or narrator, whose interpretation of the story is another rendering of how the story came to be and under what conditions it is received.

Hic: Well, at least your selective examples reveal another aspect of your preconceptions about the act of interpretation, one that says that authors and readers are conceivably identical entities.

Nunc: Not identical, but similar to the extent that they both worry about the problem of the source of meaning (and, too, authority) in a fictive world.

Hic: Perhaps I can get at the bothersome sense I have of interpretation becoming a form of solipsism if we accept your conception of "hermeneutic activity" by going back to what I perceived as the dialectical element that surfaced in your critique of James' preface. Having discussed what you see as the limits of the interpretive act by suggesting that it is a perception *of* textual limits, can you specify more clearly what you referred to as the relational quality of this activity?

Nunc: The question is an important one since it returns us to the discussion of "groundlessness" that we suspended earlier, though I regret your using the word "dialectical" in the attempt to talk about the relation between selves and worlds, readers and texts. "Dialectical" implies that there are two somewhat stable entities (say, in some versions of Marxist terminology, "base" and "superstructure") that exchange, as a form of mutuality, qualities or affects. But the homologous conceptions we were talking about are far from stable; rather, they are relational, which means they are incompletely defined in their relation to each other—incompletely, because they are always shifting within the terms of that relation. But this is too abstract, so let me work with a specific set among those we discussed in order to see the connection between understanding "relation" and understanding fictions. Does the relation between readers and texts resemble enough the perceptual, authorial, and psychological constructions we have brought up (self/world, viewer/viewed, reader/text) so that one can stand for all? Sufficiently so, I think, for this reason: in fiction, the relation between the protagonist and the fictional universe is analogous to (as well as, in some ways, different from) the ones *conceived within the text* between readers and texts, authorial self-conceptions and authored creations, identity and "social reality."

We could extend our speculation on any of these pairs, but since the relation between the reader and the text speaks most directly to our question about the act of interpretation, I'll use it, briefly, as a point of departure. This relation is complicated, but we can summarize some of its elements. It is, clearly, not one of simple identification, especially since we have asserted that the text forces upon the reader some awareness of its frames, thus creating a separation between the text and the reader's "self"—this is one of the most dramatic effects of James' figure. Neither is this relation a self-discovery in any reductive sense, as if the ego of an individual reader could somehow be successfully projected or found within the text, save through an unworthy self-imposition. Rather, I would like to see this relation as a form of elision between two mutable discourses that, in this relation, signify each other. If I had to give a label to this defined connection between reader and text, it would be "semiotic," though only in a loose sense of the word. As readers read and, thus, understand the framing devices and strategies of the text, so they are framed by their reading, *as readers*. Moreover, this process is dynamic, always unfolding, as long as the book is read, which means that we can't freeze it at any given point and say that *this*, in this instance, defines the relation between the reader and the text. I can state the process only through an illusory metonymy: readers become conscious of, say, a certain metaphorical quality of each book read which signifies metaphor's desire to make meaningful connections between disparate rhetorical elements. They become conscious, thereby, of their own desire to generate significance in literary texts by the forging of metaphorical links; with this new "self-conception" as readers, they go back to the text and read differently, now viewing textual metaphors as structural rather than semantic complexes. And so on; the work of interpretation is endless.

Hic: We're back to the fictions of Ts'ui Pên.

Nunc: In a way, at least in that they recognize the act of interpretation as a continuous process, but certainly not a "timeless" one.

Hic: But where is the ground here? Aren't you creating a kind of hermeneutic monster by suggesting that this relation between reader and text never ends and is always, in a sense, changing the rules of the game whereby things "mean"? I question, too, your view of "text" and "reader" as similar discourses, rather than utterly different entities—one, black print on white paper; the other, a human being.

Nunc: I agree that my formulation has a certain provisional quality to it that fits its statement of a very provisional relation. It is true that readers and texts may be far more different than they are alike, but they do share this essential quality: as human beings, readers are part of a larger social discourse or "text" in which they are signifiers to each other and elements in that heterogeneous social array of intentions and acts that make up a discursive world. This is to argue, I know, that as self is to world so reader is to text, a symmetry that will take us only so far but one which allows us to see, among other things, what the grounds of interpretation might be. I'll have to define these grounds by introducing a crude analogy. It is probably as useless to question the presence of "reality" as it is to question the fact of a word's inscription on the page. Certain things "really" happen in the world, just as in a text, no matter how open to interpretation, we will find certain words arranged in a certain order—certainty here being a matter of position and appearance rather than knowledge. There is a literal quality to reading and to existence that, whatever we may say about perception or interpretation, we can't deny, but neither can we know this quality except as it is already perceived, interpreted, made metaphorical. (Incidentally, this analogy breaks down rather rapidly when we compare events to words—but let it stand for as long as it may remain useful.) Interpretation has already entered the scene before we question the meaning of texts or events, though our *desire* to do so is part of the act.

More crucially, interpretation becomes self-reflexive and is *always there* when we question the sources of texts and events, their ends, their arrival and departure in whatever larger fields, world views, or epistemologies that, themselves, if we pursue the issue, are elements in still larger interpretive designs. The literal or the "what happened" and our creation of a relation to it are the grounds of interpretation, but, of course, they don't mean anything by themselves. Another way of saying this is that every text or event is already interpreted before we get to it: it has already entered into a language which is historical, which exists within certain ideological frames. And it is read by an individual who is already, as "consciousness" or "self" or "sign," part of a biological, personal, and social history that frames this reading. These complicated interactions, then, do not take place in a vacuum, nor are they subject to the charge of being indeterminate. They take place *in language* which, if it may be seen as the confinement or dispersal of our being, may also be seen as the arena of its problematic articulation in an unfolding story, a history, not as an evolutionary but as a relational process.

Hic: I think this is to announce a conception of the "self" which, time drawing short, we cannot go into now and which we may be able to uncover only when we read actual texts. But we have covered some ground on this occasion, though I must say it strikes me that your formulation of "relationality" as defining the process of interpretation, while useful, is uncomfortable.

Nunc: Why uncomfortable?

Hic: Because it suggests that whenever we try to make an interpretive statement we are acting in bad faith by putting down what you describe as a mutable, dynamic movement.

Nunc: That's quite true, and this discomfort or bad faith might be called the curse of writing, which always falsifies the process of interpretation. But, to rest in paradox, that falsification also creates another manifestation of the "literal," providing grounds for further interpretation.

Hic: It makes one long for an impossible silence and simplicity.

Nunc: That, too, is a desire which founds writing and interpretation as monuments to death, while they are still among the noisy upsurgings or adumbrations of human existence. However, these matters, as well as the question of what the specific nature of this hermeneutic anxiety might be, must be saved for some other occasion. Meanwhile, I'd like to suggest as a parting thought that the discomfort you speak of is a form of the interpreter's self-alienation—a quality that coexists with the act of interpretation as its primary affect. By that internal resistance, interpreters know that they are "really" interpreting or at least moving toward interpretation. We may have to experience our reading as a displacement of our selves and of textual signs which, to state a final tautology, are the signifying movements that open up the world *to* significance. A compilation of ultimacies: "meaning," for us, is that relation to objects, selves, events, and texts in which we know not "things themselves" but only what is there by dint of our reading the signs of these things.

PASSIONATE DOUBTS

CHAPTER ONE NABOKOV'S WATERMARK

WRITING THE SELF IN *PALE FIRE*

The words of a dead man
Are modified in the guts of the living.
W. H. Auden, "In Memory of W. B. Yeats"

According to Mikhail Bakhtin, one of the novel's primary generic traits incorporates a commentary upon the semantic conditions that prevail when a given text is produced. Bakhtin writes that "the novel . . . emerges consciously and unambiguously as a genre that is both critical and self-critical, one fated to revise the fundamental concepts of literariness and poeticalness dominant at the time."[1] It is in the nature of the novel he argues, to recognize and criticize the complex of discourses (philosophical, social, literary) in which it is born, as well as to be critical of itself, thus self-reflexive. In the present era of intensive self-scrutiny and the novel's dominance, it seems fitting that one of the reigning hallmarks of contemporary fiction is its complication of "reflexivity." The notion of reflexivity in fiction is certainly more problematic than a term often associated with it, "self-consciousness," and its existence, Bakhtin suggests, is hardly coterminous with the advent of contemporary literature. As Robert Alter has shown, reflexivity has manifested itself as a quality of fictions since (at least) *Don Quixote*.[2] The understanding of reflexivity as a determining element of those contemporary novels which concern me here must be tied to a contemporaneous concept of the "self-critical" which goes beyond Bakhtin's understanding of the traditional, generic critique of established literary modes and discourses. This concept differs from mere self-consciousness in a notable way. "Self-conscious" fiction is aware of itself *as* fiction and thus indulges in speculations about the relations between narrative and "reality"; it is, above all, concerned about its own fictive status or the rhetorical successes and failures of its own narrative operations. As Alter demonstrates, *Don Quixote* is unquestionably self-conscious in this regard, as are *Vanity Fair* and *Herzog*. "Self-critical" fiction, I suggest, is more interrogative and not only in its intense self-awareness as it directly questions the principles of its own composition or reflects ironically upon relations to the discourse of "reality" which it, by turns, mirrors, transmutes, fragments, and distorts. Doubly reflexive, self-critical fiction ponders the very conditions of its reflexivity as it, more specifically, raises questions about its *own* language, the substance and vehicle of its expression. Moreover, these questions are asked from within the texts where they appear, as if the text was an echo chamber that reproduced in endless variation the soundings of its own title or table of contents—those expressions which name what it is and define what it contains.

The rhetoric of my definition of the self-critical text exhibits the kind of hyperinteriority characteristic of reflexive fictions, which many readers find merely precious or annoyingly solipsistic. And, too, this self-critical fiction is not only a contemporary phenomenon: *Tristram Shandy, Gargantua and Pantagruel*, or *Moby-Dick* could, conceivably, render examples of my definition as easily as the particular instance of a contemporary self-critical novel to be considered shortly, Vladimir Nabokov's *Pale Fire*. Regarding the question about the validity of these reflexive forms, it may be said that the interior scrutiny they perform is a crucial alternative and corrective to a culture (any, not just ours) that assumes the merely instrumental, functional aspects of language and builds world views upon these. The contemporary nature and attitude of self-critical fiction are not so much historically unique as they are compounded by the novel's place *in* history. Contemporary narrative is written in a culture obsessed with the origins and ends of history, with the reflexive nature of its own "contemporaneity," and with its own confinement in the languages through which it makes itself known. Given this context, the ironic, questioning, disruptive function of self-critical fiction must be balanced against its opposite. While these fictions play language games and deconstruct the philosophical assumptions that lie behind enabling stories about the world, they also *construct* their own semiologies. They are engaged, thematically, structurally, and stylistically, in generating fictive sign systems that designate their status as self-questioned discourses. They stand as linguistic topographies that proclaim their emergence from a realm of silence into a noisy, contradictory, sign-filled world which is that of the text.

In this broad definition, self-critical fiction can be seen to dwell more narrowly on the first term of my hyphenated label—the nature of the "self," as that entity which writes itself into existence through the complex, interwoven language of a given fictional text.[3] The narrating "I" of *Tristram Shandy*, "HCE" of *Finnegans Wake*, and the Barth-like, letter-writing "Author" of John Barth's *LETTERS* can all be seen as verbal, even alphabetic inscriptions who doubtfully construct a "self" in narrative through the reflexive manipulation of narrative signs. These constructions reflect a concern with the identity of texts paralleled with an anxiety about the origins and identities of selves in texts. As one of these self-critical fictions, *Pale Fire*, which most surely is a parody of the critical act and a compendious examination of paranoia, is also a presentation of the autobiographical self as a sign within a textual system of signs: the mad commentator, Charles Kinbote, finds "himself" within the seemingly irrelevant markings of John Shade's poem, "Pale Fire." In so doing, Kinbote creates a language—his interpretation of the poem—that in its structuring of linguistic relations, samenesses and differences, defines the writing, interpreting self. The subject of the novel may be seen as a process rather than a theme; indeed, the subject of *Pale Fire* is the dethroned "subject," Kinbote, seen watermarking the text with the sign of his own identity.[4] That this identity is a fiction which reflects upon the operations of language and the creation of linguistic kingdoms suggests the larger purposes of Nabokov's hermeneutic parody and of self-critical fiction in general: to discover the limits of the self conceived in language, as well as its constructive possibilities.

Ostensibly, *Pale Fire* is the annotated text of an autobiographical poem. Perhaps an exercise in self-irony, it was published only two years before the appearance of Nabokov's own lengthy translation and annotation of Pushkin's *Eugene Onegin*. The reader does not have to venture far into Kinbote's annotations of Shade's "Pale Fire" to discover that the novel is more Kinbote's autobiography than a scholarly edition of Shade's confessional poem. *Pale Fire* is actually comprised of four separate texts, the central two being Shade's poem and Kinbote's "commentary" on the poem. Kinbote's function as editor is made suspect immediately when we discover that the incomplete poem has come into his hands as a bundle of index cards, which he removed from the dead poet's body and hid in his own house. These texts are flanked by two others, Kinbote's foreword and index. Nabokov thus creates in *Pale Fire* the visible effect of "intertextuality": the four texts mirror each other and reverberate against one another so that our attention is diverted from assessing the truth or informational value of the poem or the commentary. Instead, as one reader states, we are compelled to note "correspondences and coincidences, not only from note to note but from notes to poem," resulting in the revelation of "the correspondences the mind can perceive or invent between them."[5] The whole novel reflects Shade's discovery in his search for empirical evidence of an afterlife: it is not the proof of divinity itself which is important but the associations one can see between life and afterlife, or the real and the imaginary, or (later, for Kinbote) poem and commentary. As Shade writes:

> But all at once it dawned on me that *this*
> Was the real point, the contrapuntal theme;
> Just this: not text, but texture; not the dream
> But topsy-turvical coincidence,
> Not flimsy nonsense, but a web of sense.
> Yes! It sufficed that I in life could find
> Some kind of link-and-bobolink, some kind
> Of correlated pattern in the game,
> Plexed artistry, and something of the same
> Pleasure in it as they who played it found.
> (C. III, ll. 806–15)[6]

This much-cited passage imitates through its verbalizations Shade's discovery that life is a matter of pattern and relation. The phonic interplays between "text" and "texture," "sense" and "nonsense," "link-and-bobolink," "plexed" and "pleasure" immediately suggest what Kinbote, in his commentary, will confirm as the primary concern of *Pale Fire*: to enact a scene of writing, where significance is achieved through the creation of sonorous pleasure and alphabetical correspondences.

In his poem, Shade recounts his search, after a near-fatal stroke during which he has had an eschatological vision of a luminous fountain, for a corresponding validation of his having "crossed the border" (C. III, ll. 699–700). He thinks he finds it when he reads a newspaper account of a woman who has also "died" for several seconds and who has seen a vision with a fountain in it. His conception of life as an aesthetic game, a "web of sense," where not the linear exposition of "text" but the spatial correspondences of "texture" are the objects of the search for truth, arrives after his now infamous discovery that what he thought was proof of the afterlife is based on a misprint, evidence of a misreading: the woman has seen a mountain, not a fountain. Shade concludes that whatever truths are to be found about the ultimacies of existence rest upon coincidences and imposed patterns of perception; the truth becomes for him a matter of cross-reference, correspondence, and analogy rather than a statement of fact or a proposition.

To go no further in this analysis of Shade's discovery would be to reiterate the standard critical positions regarding Nabokov's mannerist vision of artful intricacies and verbal prisons. But a closer reading with an eye to phonic, alphabetic "texture" reveals that Shade's discovery is based upon a correspondence that is, essentially, a linguistic pattern of sameness and difference. "Mountain" and "fountain" are nearly identical, save for the difference in their initial letters. Both words designate elemental phenomena that rise into the air, but one is constituted of earth, the other of water; one is natural, the other usually artificial. Both are backlighted in Shade's vision by the pale fires of life's fading so that, together, they establish a tableau of the primary elements of the universe (air, earth, fire, water); yet, in the difference of initials, they designate the sexual distinctions, male and female, that regenerate the "life" of this elemental world. The effort may seem Kinbotian, but the text of *Pale Fire* encourages us to make such construals. Out of the misread and misprinted relations between events, a wholly constituted, structured universe of elemental and sexual identities can be detected, within which Shade proclaims that the pattern of his own life can be traced.

Earlier in the poem, Shade parodically evokes Wallace Stevens in lines on the remembered pleasures of mortal life:

> And I'll turn down eternity unless
> The melancholy and the tenderness
> Of mortal life; the passion and the pain;
> The claret taillight of that dwindling plane
> Off Hesperus; your gesture of dismay

On running out of cigarettes; the way
You smile at dogs; the trail of silver slime
Snails leave on flagstones; this good ink, this rhyme,
This index card, this slender rubber band
Which always forms, when dropped, an ampersand,
Are found in Heaven by the newlydead,
Stored in its strongholds through the years.
(C. III, ll. 525–36)

Much of this is hilariously bad poetry, but it is notable that Shade translates experience into sign as he recalls the ephemera of domestic life. A disquisition on the ineffability of human passion turns to more concrete notions—reflections of light, gestures, mollusk trails—and ends with a reference to the very cards upon which the poem is presently being written. Even the rubber band that binds these fragments inevitably forms, when dropped, a symbol that looks suspiciously like the mirrored, cursive letter of Shade's initial; as an ampersand, it represents the unfinished, metonymical etceteras of his incomplete poem and quest for certainty. The passage suggests that the perceptions and desires of the autobiographical self are transcribed into letters on the page; thus, it often seems, as in the first lines of "Pale Fire," that it is not the "I" of Shade who speaks but the poem itself, giving voice to its own tenuous existence:

I was the shadow of the waxwing slain
By the false azure in the windowpane;
I was the smudge of ashen fluff—and I
Lived on, flew on, in the reflected sky.
(C. I, ll. 1–4)

Similar to the floating, butterflylike ashes of the variants to the poem which Kinbote describes Shade burning, "Pale Fire" is the self's remnant and supplement, Shade's shadow, the inscribed mark of the fingerprint that survives as the writing, reflected self. Shade's poem is an enactment of self-inscription, down to the letter, as it generates a universe of signs bound together by the emerging trace element, the "S" that designates the poet's name and self. From the "text" of experience or the misprintings of existence, the poet traces the design of the self and reinscribes it in the text of his poem.

If "Pale Fire" enacts a process of self-inscription, Kinbote's commentary does so doubly. For Kinbote, Shade's rambling poem about his life, his daughter's suicide, and his acceptance of uncertainty concerning the nature of eternity is a secondary text into which are woven the "wavelets of fire" and the "pale phosphorescent hints" of Kinbote's former life as the king (now exiled) of Zembla, land of shadows and mirrors (297). Kinbote's remembered or fantasized life in Zembla is transcribed by him into the commentary which, on first reading, bears only marginal resemblance to the poem. He hopes that Shade will "recreate in a poem the dazzling Zembla burning in my brain" (80). But when he first scans the text after his prodigious, obsessive efforts to provide the poet with information about Zembla during the writing of the poem, he is distraught: "Instead of the wild glorious romance—what did I have? An autobiographical, eminently Appalachian, rather old-fashioned narrative in a neo-Popian prosodic style . . . void of my magic, of that special rich streak of magical madness which I was sure would run through it and make it transcend its time" (296–97). However, a second reading convinces Kinbote that the poem's "dim distant music," "vestiges of color," and "invaluable variants" reflect the "echoes and spangles of my mind" (297). The poem, rather than being a perfect mirror reflecting his Zemblan past, becomes for him a *deflection*, a scattering of signs and clues to be regathered in the commentary's autobiography. The poem is the novel's pale fire or lamp, which "in its pale and diaphanous final phase" (81) dimly illuminates the commentator's past.[7] We are thus exposed to the comically vertiginous spectacle of Shade creating a text, "Pale Fire," inspired by another text (the misprinted newspaper), which delineates the hieroglyphic signature of the poet's "self." This is used by Kinbote as a cipher or Rosetta stone that translates, if obscurely, Appalachian into Zemblan, wherein he detects the sign of a personal past that mixes memory and desire.

Accordingly, in much of his commentary, Kinbote is anxious about matters of translation and concerned about the authenticity of several specious variants to the poem which he claims he has discovered. These, he argues, can be construed as a "refuge" for the story of Charles Xavier, king of Zembla, which has almost disappeared from the poem, "drained of every trace" of the king's presence, bearing now only as a "minute but genuine star ghost" the "specific imprint of my theme" (81–82). The unrevised or discarded variants which survive to tell Charles' story emerge as shadows, traces, or ghostly imprints, which are also descriptions of the relation of the commentary to the poem. Kinbote often mentions Conmal, the Zemblan translator of Shakespeare, whose rendition of *Timon of Athens* the misanthropic Kinbote awkwardly retranslates into English as he comments upon an obscure variant in lines 39–40 of Shade's poem. Kinbote's notable mistranslated translation reads:

> The sun is a thief: she lures the sea
> and robs it. The moon is a thief:
> he steals his silvery light from the sun.
> The sea is a thief: it dissolves the moon.
> (80)

The original from *Timon of Athens* reads:

> The sun's a thief, and with his great attraction
> Robs the vast sea; the moon's an arrant thief,
> And her pale fire she snatches from the sun;
> The sea's a thief, whose liquid surge resolves
> The moon into salt tears;
> (IV, iii, ll. 432–36)

What Kinbote obviously misses in these crucial lines is the title of Shade's poem, which he fails to translate and upon which he offers no comment—this certainly undercuts his reliability as an editor. But of more importance is the texture of similarities and differences which a comparison of the original to its doubly rendered translation offers: Kinbote, via Conmal, has made the sun female, the moon male, an "m/f" transliteration that parallels Shade's own "mountain/fountain" skewing. As the suspicious variants are to the canonical text of Shade's poem, so this translation is a reversal and a shadow of the original, Shakespeare's "pale fire" transformed into Kinbote's "silvery light," a linguistic alchemy which transmutes gold into base silver, fire into diffuse moonlight. Through this translation, Kinbote writes himself into the text, though only as a seemingly irrelevant supplement to "Pale Fire." His sun becomes "she," the homophonous "son" becomes female, inscribing the inversions of his flagrant, comic homosexuality; the "silvery light" inscribes the shadowland of Kinbote's

Zembla and the refracted, illuminating element by which he detects the mark of the self in Shade's text.

Moreover, like sun, moon, and sea, Kinbote's retranslated translation robs the "original" of its poetic power: the fluid and verbal richness of Shakespeare's poetry becomes, in Kinbote's hands, monotonous repetition. However, both texts share a vision of elemental thievery that undermines the very notion of "origin," since for both even the sun's power is entropic and derivative. The Shakespearean metaphor, applied to Kinbote's commentary and Shade's poem, suggests that there is no "authoritative" text in *Pale Fire*, no ultimate fount or source of significance, just as in nature there is no beginning to the cycle that transfers power from sun to moon to sea and back again. Instead, we have Kinbote's annotations, which scan a poem in order to refract the pale fire of its title. The poem itself is incomplete, a stack of index cards which, arranged in some varied manner, may tell the story of an exiled king or the poet's attempt to find mirrored in the "text" of his life the pale fires of life's supplement, the reflected glow of the afterlife.

As his name implies, the "Shade" caught in the poem is the self's shadow, an "otherness" translated into language and defined by the poem's dull illumination; at a further remove, Kinbote exists as a thieflike Hermes, a commentator and interpreter who, in the act of comic transference, generates the image of the self in a process that both violates and recreates the "original."[8] So as Shade and Kinbote are sun and moon to each other, every text in *Pale Fire*—foreword, poem, commentary, and index—is supplementary to the others, a corruption and thieflike translation. The novel enacts what Jacques Derrida, in an analysis of the difference between writing and speech, cites as a mythical instance of "supplementarity" evidenced by the story of the Egyptian god of writing, Thoth:

> As the god of language second and of linguistic difference, Thoth can become the god of the creative word only by metonymic substitution, by historical displacement, and sometimes by violent subversion. . . . This type of substitution thus puts Thoth *in Ra's place* as the moon takes the place of the sun. The god of writing thus supplies the place of Ra, supplementing him and supplanting him in his absence and essential disappearance. Such is the origin of the moon as supplement to

the sun, of night light as supplement to daylight. And of writing as the supplement of speech.[9]

Derrida's translation of the Thoth story into an allegory of the scene of writing infers a mythological "origin" in the sun, Ra, or speech, from which writing is a falling away, a second-rate substitution for the full presence of the spoken word or the blinding light of the sun. All of *Pale Fire* speaks its own supplementarity in this regard: it is an inscription of the yearning for lost kingdoms and the manifestations of divinity, a realization of their absence, and a translation of this loss into a system of signs which marks the history of the self's desire.

The novel is concerned with matters of translation in the less usual sense of the word: to transfer, to cross or carry over. *Pale Fire* is replete with physical analogues of this sense, from the underground passages and overland passes which Charles must traverse in order to escape from Zembla, to the fatal, frozen lake that Hazel Shade unsuccessfully walks upon "at Lochan Neck where zesty skaters crossed / From Exe to Wye" (C. II, ll. 489–90). In the novel-long metaphor which equates the writing of texts with the creation of worlds, topography comes to represent textual and metaphysical anxieties. While Shade in his poem worries about "crossing the border" to preexistence or afterlife, Kinbote is paranoiacally anxious about his ability to show the "crossings"—the web of not-so-coincidental similarities—between poem and commentary. Crossings and borders, the "lemniscate" pattern of a bicycle tire or the footprints of a pheasant left on "the blank page of the road" in a winter landscape (C. I, l. 21), all resonate with significance as the locations where the act of writing is seen as a "translation," or where the marks of the self's transference appear within the text. In Kinbote's commentary, the seemingly insignificant lane that runs between his and Shade's houses acts as the space that separates the critic's vision from the poet's, as well as the sign of the common thread that runs between their lives via their interconnected texts. Like all of the transverse, intersecting streets of the novel, the lane can be seen as a line (to be fatally crossed for the last time by Shade seconds before his death) that marks the distance between and the reciprocity of "Pale Fire" and its annotations.

The significance of this demarcation of sameness and difference is dramatized by another "lane" in the novel. Late in his commentary,

Kinbote makes an obscure reference to the letters of Franklin Lane, particularly to one fragment from those written by Lane on the eve of his death, which reads: "And if I had passed into that other land, whom would I have sought? . . . Aristotle! —Ah, there would be a man to talk with! What satisfaction to see him take, like reins from between his fingers, the long ribbon of a man's life and trace it through the mystifying maze of all the wonderful adventure. . . . The crooked made straight. The Dedalian plan simplified by a look from above—smeared out as it were by the splotch of some master thumb that made the whole involuted, boggling thing one beautiful straight line" (185; Kinbote's ellipses). As June Perry Levine has noted, Franklin Lane is not an invention of Kinbote's or Nabokov's but a real historical personage, as authentic as the passage that Kinbote quotes. When combined with the obsessive concern for reading the patterns of nature and divinity promoted in Shade's poem, Levine suggests, Lane's vision of "crossing the border" connotes the possibility of viewing the self in the novel as "a moebius strip ribbon whose Shade side and Kinbote side are revealed as one."[10] In this sense, the whole of *Pale Fire* is a "lane," line, or "inky maze" (C. IV, l. 852), a tracing of "the long ribbon of a man's life," but hardly the "crooked made straight" or the "Dedalian plan simplified," as Kinbote hopes his commentary will make Shade's poem. Instead, as variant, translation, and labyrinth, the novel mixes the interweaving voices of Kinbote and Shade; it skews the "one beautiful straight line" and reveals the fictionalized, textual self as a collation of incongruities and specious similarities. Thus, the "lane" that exists between Kinbote and Shade is the text: the sign of their botched relation and the language that inculcates it.

In another sense, the amount of attention that Kinbote gives in his commentary to his escape from Zembla (as King Charles the Good) signifies the novel's concern with a "translation" whereby a language, which serves as a discrete articulation of the self, emerges out of a realm of perfect resemblances. At one point during the escape, Kinbote describes Charles looking back on the northern mountains of Zembla as he traverses a westward pass:

> Great fallen crags diversified the wayside. The *nippern* (domed rocks or "reeks") to the south were broken by a rock and glass slope into light and shadow. Northward melted the green, gray,

> bluish mountains—Falkberg with its hood of snow, Mutraberg with the fan of its avalanche, Paberg (Mt. Peacock), and others,—separated by narrow dim valleys with intercalated cotton-wool bits of cloud that seemed placed between the receding sets of ridges to prevent their flanks from scraping against one another. Beyond them, in the final blue, loomed Mt. Glitterntin, a serrated edge of bright foil; and southward, a tender haze enveloped more distant ridges which led to one another in an endless array, through every grade of soft evanescence. (143–44)

Like many of the descriptive passages in Kinbote's commentary—the portrayal of Charles' castle, the secret tunnel that runs from the king's bedroom closet to a dressing room in the state theater, the landscape of Wordsmith College—this celebration of Zembla's topography is a replication of Kinbote's self, emerging from the linguistic prison by which the commentator/king is defined and from which he unsuccessfully flees. The view of the mountains reveals a panorama of samenesses and differences that reenact the repetitions and variations of Kinbote's language throughout his commentary. The "reeks" to the south are broken into "light and shadow," the primary "colors" of Kinbote's world which form a pure opposition that creates a meaningful correspondence between its elements in terms of their placement against each other. There would be no understanding of light without the shadow cast by the reflected pale fire of objects, and there would be only undifferentiated darkness without the light that breaks it into sun and shadow.

The description of the mountains is analogous to the symbiotic relationship that exists between poem and commentary, original and translation. The latter is the shadow of Shade's poem; the former is the illuminating light (which, paradoxically, maintains its status as the phantom of Shade's self) that casts this shadow over the commentary as its rays are intercepted by the opaque markings of Kinbote's self-inscriptions. The ridges of the mountains in the distance seem to fade into one another as the vista of an "endless array" unfolds, yet they remain distinct, passing through "every grade of soft evanescence." Arising from this geographical grid of repetitions and gradations are Zembla's great peaks, including Mutraberg and Paberg, whose names are guttural and vernacular echoes of the familial past

Charles is leaving behind, as well as repetitions of the primary sexual and typographical oppositions—father/mother, m/f, sun/moon, mountain/fountain—that elsewhere mark the text. Essentially, Charles' (or Kinbote's) flight from Zembla and his passage through the mountains are illusory, since the peaks mark the linguistic boundaries of his past and self, never to be traversed but always reinscribed at every turn in his autobiographical commentary.

Charles' view of the peaks is also a linguistic revelation of the adversary who chases him out of Zembla and who pursues him into exile. Paberg is, Englished by Kinbote, Mt. Peacock, a name that recalls Argus, the Greek monster of self-reflection who was transformed into the many-eyed peacock. Hence the mountain also recalls the name of Jack D'Argus, a pseudonym of Gradus', the hired assassin who hunts down the exiled king within the commentary as "Pale Fire" is written:

> We shall accompany Gradus . . . through the entire length of the poem, following the road of its rhythm, riding past in a rhyme, skidding around the corner of a run-on . . . reappearing on the horizon of a new canto, steadily marching nearer in iambic motion, crossing streets, moving up with his valise on the escalator of the pentameter, stepping off, boarding a new train of thought, entering the hall of a hotel, putting out the bedlight, while Shade blots out a word, and falling asleep as the poet lays down his pen for the night. (78)

Gradus is a member of an antiroyalist cadre, the Shadows, and here he is the elusive shadow of Kinbote's poetic double, his second self, who, like Conrad's secret sharer, is a manifestation of self-destructiveness as well as the uncanny "other" whom the writing of the commentary seeks to circumscribe and pin down.[11] Gradus is also associated with Mt. Glitterntin, as he is a glazier and mirror maker who corresponds, in Kinbote's mind, to a tin clockwork toy of a man pushing a wheelbarrow which belongs to Shade. To complete the circle of relations, the last lines of "Pale Fire" read: "And through the flowing shade and ebbing light / A man, unheedful of the butterfly— / Some neighbor's gardener, I guess—goes by / Trundling an empty barrow up the lane" (C. IV, ll. 996–99). The gardener is closely connected by events with Gradus, who finally tracks down the exiled king but kills Shade by mistake, instead of Kinbote, and who is felled in the act by Kinbote's wheelbarrow-trundling gardener; it is equally possible, of course, that "Gradus" is really Jack Grey, a vengeful madman of this world rather than a Zemblan assassin.

For the reader, Gradus' ambivalent status (escaped lunatic or assassin?) reduplicates the interpretive difficulties faced throughout the novel, for how can "Gradus" be Gradus and Grey at the same time? Forced to choose between Shade's version of "reality" (in which Grey would be a madman who mistakenly kills the poet, thinking he's a hanging judge) and Kinbote's (in which Gradus is a Zemblan conspirator), we may feel compelled to focus our attention on the novel's accidents, rather than noting its phonic overdeterminations. The game Nabokov constructs here is one in which he plays off our readerly expectation and desire for noncontradictory meanings against our ability to "hear" the phonetic, graphic differentiations of the novel, from which these readings arise. The verbal movement between Mt. Peacock, Argus, Mt. Glitterntin, a tin toy, the Shadows, Gradus, and the gardener (who is black) creates an area of linguistic "gradation" that encourages us to indulge in the forging of linguistic chains and punning relations, while revealing the nondeterminative nature of these. We could as easily perceive the shadowy aspects of this description, as well as notice its reflective tendencies. The scene of traversing the mountains formulates a partial language, a complex interweaving of verbal associations wherein discrete words—"shadow," "haze," "tin," "glitter," "light," "grade"—become coordinated into a narrated world that inscribes the storytelling self, Kinbote. His past and his future, his hope for an eternal life (even if it is the "afterlife" of an exiled king living in the shadow of his former brilliance), and his anxiety about the "serrated edge" of the assassin's blade are erected into the topographies of text and the system of signs from which the self emerges, as the intercalation of that system.

Appropriately, it is from Zembla, the realm of resemblance, "a land of reflections" (265), that Charles attempts to escape. More specifically, he runs from Gradus, to whom "generality was godly, the specific diabolical," for whom "difference itself was unfair" (152). Kinbote's story arises as a flight from the landscape of perfect similitude, narrated in a language that annotates the self through the relations of difference and paradox; these are especially notable when he tells us that "resemblances are the shadows of differences" (265) and that the name of the hater of differences, Gradus, connotes the gradations of variation. Significantly, Gradus, who has participated in the construction of an elaborate, unworkable code system for the revolutionary party, is often associated with noise and mistranslation. In one scene, Kinbote imagines him in a Nice hotel on "a transverse street, between two thoroughfares parallel to the quay, and the ceaseless roar of crisscross traffic mingling with the grinding and banging of construction work proceeding under the auspices of a crane opposite the hotel (which had been surrounded by a stagnant calm two decades earlier) was a delightful surprise for Gradus, who always liked a little noise to keep his mind off things" (251). The noise of construction and crisscrossing traffic on a transverse street is matched by the noises and crossings of the passage itself, with its harsh assonances and meandering descriptiveness.

Later, aboard a plane going to America, suffering from acute indigestion, Gradus is exposed to another kind of noise: "he found himself wedged among several belated delegates to the New Wye Linguistic Conference, all of them lapel-labeled, and representing the same foreign language, but none being able to speak it, so that conversation was conducted (across our hunched-up killer and on all sides of his immobile face) in rather ordinary Anglo-American" (279–80). No doubt Nabokov the translator and master of many languages is mocking at the linguistic competence of academicians in this passage, but its real importance is to present Gradus, maker of reflective surfaces, as a contradiction: a foe of difference and a lover of order, yet liking noisy surroundings and acting, here, as a kind of "translator" across which the language of these polyglot monolinguists is spoken. As such, Gradus represents Kinbote's contradictory anxieties and desires as he constructs his verbal topography—for what Kinbote wishes to see in Shade's poem is his own perfect, mirrored image, his Zembla/emblem; what he fears is the utter difference between poem and commentary. What he manages to create is a textual self related as a network of words that sonorously echo each other yet reveal their alphabetic, imagistic differences in the play of the novel's sun and shadow. Gradus, who parasitically pursues the parasitical Kinbote through the text, acts as the site or occasion for this construction, which is known by its noisy rumblings and crossed connections.

Gradus serves as a textual catalyst in a most elaborate scene that reveals the disguised seams of Kinbote's linguistic tapestry. This occurs during the assassin's visit to Libitina, a Swiss villa owned by a "Karlist" where King Charles is thought to be hiding in exile. Gradus does not find Charles there, but Kinbote, who is reconstructing this visit to the province of Lex, marks the text with the words of his being. Comically, he invokes the vision of an adolescent boy, Gordon, who conducts Gradus about the villa while undergoing a series of miraculous costume changes, and who doubtless reflects Kinbote's own sexuality. A close look at the patina of the villa's description reveals the verbal dimensions of the world of Lex. Kinbote writes that the sun over Libitina "found a weak spot among the rain clouds and next moment a ragged blue hole in them grew a radiant rim" (198); that the owner of the villa collects pornographic scenes painted on lampshades, called *ombrioles*; that Gradus and Gordon walk "through light and shade" (200); that Gradus, driving away from the villa, comes to a promontory where Charles once stood, observing "on a misty and luminous September day, with the diagonal of the first silver filament crossing the space between two balusters . . . the twinkling ripples of Lake Geneva and . . . their antiphonal response, the flashing of tinfoil scares in the hillside vineyards" (201–02). Kinbote notes that at Libitina, which is the name for the Roman goddess of corpses and tombs, Gradus is barely able to communicate with a footman even though he speaks in three different languages.

This is to cite only a few examples from the baroque patternings of the world of Lex, which effect, for us, an elaborate series of verbal correspondences. Sun and shade intersect, the diagonal filaments of the sunlight appear as the markings of a pen, the reflections of the lake serve as responses to the reflections of the tin scarecrows in the vineyards, all observed by a "tin man" whose alias is, among others, Vinogradus. The multiple reverberations and mirrorings of the description are set against a background of noisy miscommunications, presided over by the reflective name of a goddess (Libi*tin*a) who commemorates the inscriptions of the self-entombed. Kinbote thus makes a world of words at Lex which doubly reflects the sign of his own self and that of the text out of which the self arises. As he sees the desired relation between poem and commentary represented by an intricate play of teasing reflexivity, so the textual language of this passage is a play of similarities and differences, descriptions of black engravings on white spaces, chance echoes, and punning relations. At the poles of this scene of inscription are, on the one hand, the scriptural commemoration of death and silence and, on the other, meaningless noise. Kinbote's description infers that in between noise and silence, utter dissemination and utter similitude, language and self, departing from these extremes, are generated.

Ultimately, everything in the world of *Pale Fire* is made to correspond to the exigencies of Kinbote's personal destiny and to bear his autobiographical stamp as commentator. The irony and reflexivity inherent in a series of annotations turned to self-revelation are illuminated by Nabokov's comments on self-knowledge in his own autobiography, *Speak, Memory*. There, he equates the function of art as self-discovery to a mechanical process of inscription: "Neither in environment nor in heredity can I find the exact instrument that fashioned me, the anonymous roller that pressed upon my life a certain watermark whose unique design becomes visible when the lamp of art is made to shine through life's foolscap."[12] At first glance, Nabokov seems to indulge in a pseudoreligious metaphor for inspiration and individuality, grounded in Plato with overtones of Augustine and Pope. The "anonymous roller" appears as a godlike aesthetic authority who impresses upon the artist the watermark of selfhood, to be discovered in a process of self-divination. The image appears to agree with the crucial watermark analogy of Kinbote's commentary, which proclaims that the self of the believer, detecting the signs of "our Lord," knows infinity: "When the soul adores Him Who guides it through mortal life, when it distinguishes His sign at every turn of the trail, painted on the boulder and notched in the fir trunk, when every page in the book of one's personal fate bears His watermark, how can one doubt that He will also preserve us through all eternity?" (221–22). Kinbote's watermark is one more expression of his desire as a reader of texts to find in the book of his own past the markings of eternal life, the divinity of his kinghood, and his accession (as "Xavier" or "savior") to godhead. It is an inscription, he realizes elsewhere, never to be found in human life or worldly books.

A closer look at the artistic metaphor of *Speak, Memory* shows that it is a complex analogy for the connection to be made between the act of writing and the inscription of the self, annotated, into the world's text. For this anonymous authority who authenticates and forges the mark of selfhood, this "roller" or "instrument," is but another version of the artistic self implicated in the quest for self-knowledge that is charted by the "graph" of autobiography. We can imagine Nabokov, inscribing the words of *Speak, Memory* upon the blank page, conceiving of the creation of personality as another inscription upon another unmarked page. This inscribed self (the watermark) is revealed only through an act of interpretation (the shining of art's lamp upon the page) which mediates between the self writing and the self as written. In Nabokov's metaphor, these separate movements become unified into the act of writing as such, which is at once self-creation, interpretation, and demarcation, all of which designate their coming into being *as* writing. To return to the problem of originality discussed earlier, the watermark analogy of *Speak, Memory* illuminates the act of writing as a quest for the "original" self, pregiven in nature—an unimaginable "self" that exists prior to life, writing, and consciousness, whose shadow is all that writing is able to embody.

In *Pale Fire*, this "original" self is King Charles, last monarch of Zembla, not as he exists via the annotations of Shade's poem or the imposed anxieties of Kinbote's transliterations but as he inconceivably *was* in the timelessness of his youth and the power of his kinghood. In this sense, Charles is Kinbote's "original," but one who never existed in time or space and whose continued existence comes about only through the glimmerings of a faulty memory or the misinterpretations of an obsessed imagination. There is also the "original" text of "Pale Fire," but by the time we read it, its originality has been translated into the secondariness of commentary by Kinbote. Moreover, the poem subverts its own origin and authority (God, the self) in portraying Shade interrogating the marks of divinity he vainly searches for, finding only the incomplete, accidental correlations and patterns of his partially inscribed existence. The discoveries of Shade's autobiography and the translation of Kinbote's commentary can be seen as "the process of indirect reconstruction" which Claude Lévi-Strauss defines as the mark of writing and culture or which Jonathan Culler calls "the 'reactivation' of modes of intelligibility: that which is natural is brought to consciousness and revealed as a process, a construct."[13] In this view, writing becomes a deformation of the "original" self as it passes into the time of narrative, exiled from the land of perfect identifications and exact mirror resemblances, into the realm of the sign, where the text is the texture of misreadings, translations, and noise that work to define the "self."

The process of inscription in *Pale Fire* thus marks the articulation of a writing/interpreting/written self into a system of signs and a "history" that does not exist before this process but is realized by it. As the Nabokovian metaphor suggests, this textual self is the sign of its own creation.

Many commentators have remarked that *Pale Fire* is a game wherein reader and author are engaged in a complex, frustrating, but ultimately pleasurable battle of wits that relates the playing of language games to the construction of fictions.[14] More precisely, *Pale Fire* indulges the "game" of self-creation—that of our readerly selves as well as of Kinbote's comic mirrored image arising within the crosshatchings of the text. As we have seen, this game is one of imprecise rules. The novel's roads, paths, branches, labyrinths, barriers, passages, bridges, crossings, tunnels, maps, and topographies, with their twistings and inversions, are analogous to the "noise" of Kinbote's commentary: its "interferences" with the text and its obscurations of the imagined encoded message of "Pale Fire." Moreover, it is through such unruliness that the outline of a world and the king who is imprisoned within it appears. Misprision, superimposition of legend upon poem, red herrings, detected designs and frames of reference form the intertwined paths of communication braided into a language world founded upon the disasters of a personal history.[15]

Pale Fire both performs and judges this translation of the dim past into the present. Its "subject" is the blazoning of the self into time and narrative, but the judgment that falls upon Kinbote's self-inscribed world is the knowledge that it is mutable and entropic. At one point, Kinbote describes this wordy, textual kingdom as a "miracle" of readability, a product of "blue magic," an artistic opportunity to "pounce upon the forgotten butterfly of revelation, wean himself abruptly from the habit of things, see the web of the world, and the warp and the weft of that web" (289). Miraculous as this world may be, it comes about only through "warp," defamiliarization, and the pain of exile: "I found myself enriched with an indescribable amazement as if informed that fireflies were making decodable signals on behalf of stranded spirits, or that a bat was writing a legible tale of torture in the bruised and branded sky" (289). So the world reflects Kinbote and his self-tortured translation of being into writing—an inscription that inevitably commemorates the mortality of words and worlds.

Pale Fire is an elegy in this sense: it marks a highly mutable world in which the premise for its writing, Shade's poem, remains unfinished, now a bundle of index cards in the dead poet's hands, subject to Kinbote's mishandlings. The legendary Zembla erodes before our eyes as it drifts back into the haze of Kinbote's memory, its glass towers destroyed by revolutionaries, its palaces gutted, its magical tunnel collapsing under the weight of the earth. And even though the commentator is, finally, a self-confessed failure as he awaits a "bigger, more respectable, more competent Gradus" (301)—a true repressor of differences—Kinbote does write himself into existence, if not immortally, then fully implicated in a temporary and temporal design now given over to our only partially competent hands. There, Nabokov demands, in the annotated pages of the book, we must engage in the construction and watermarking of our own interpreting selves as we pull together the fragments of a broken, time-bound world. There, as David Packman argues, we are compelled to fulfill our readerly desire to resolve "the tension between progression and simultaneity" as we observe the workings of a text that hedges against, while fully realizing, its own mortality.[16] For Nabokov, in *Pale Fire*, the self is textual and mortal: an entity who comes into being by establishing its relation to the elements of the language in which it is born, through which it is identified, to which it dies. His novel is ultimately a celebration of our legibility, our being readable within the confinements of language—that "currency" of the human world.

CHAPTER TWO SELF-ALIGNMENT
JOHN HAWKES' *TRAVESTY*

While *Pale Fire* erects a linguistic self through mistranslation and verbal disruption, John Hawkes' *Travesty* portrays the paradoxical suppression of this self in death and silence. The self-abandoned narrator who appears in Hawkes' burlesque of the confessional novel and the existentialist récit projects his own decease, and that of his narrative, while speeding in his car at "one hundred and forty-nine kilometers per hour on a country road in the darkest quarter of the night."[1] "Papa," the doubled, Freudian name he assumes for himself, explains to the passengers in the car—his daughter, Chantal, and her lover, the poet Henri—that he will run the car into a brick wall near an isolated village approximately one hour's drive distant, thereby obliterating its occupants in a fiery crash. *Travesty* is a transcription of this explanation; it comprises Papa's monologue on the design of his existence and the imagined death he has planned which, inexplicably, will negate not only his being but also the logic of his attraction to nonbeing.

Hawkes creates in this absurdist self-justification the imagined possibility of a "self-consuming artifact." Papa's last words, spoken, supposedly, seconds before the crash—"there shall be no survivors. None" (128)—imply that his plan, projected into the unwritten future, will be successful. Yet that eventuality, if fulfilled, makes impossible his monologue, since (recorded and transcribed by whom? Certainly not by his protesting, terrified passengers) it would have also vanished in what he terms "my private apocalypse" (47). It is as if *Travesty* was written with disappearing ink; the reader, at the end, looks back over the narrative and regards its impossible drive to self-destruction as a weightless absurdity or a well-crafted practical joke. The novel's title tells us that, indeed, we are dealing with a "travesty" of the narrative act. Yet, along with the essential parodic element of

Travesty, there emerges a substantial concern with the presentation of the self as an act of interpretation, where the world's signs are arranged into a tableau known by its fading or as an absence conveyed through the voice of a narrator who is already a phantom.

In many ways, the narrator of *Travesty* is as concerned as the "editor" of "Pale Fire" to authorize and inscribe the correct impression of his personality. One sense of the word "travesty" which parallels that of a parody or burlesque is the wearing of another's clothes, a disguise. The whole novel can be viewed as an attempt at disguise, a verbal stitching of the self into the cloth of narrative, or, to change the terms, a prodigious effort at self-management in order to create a desired dramatic effect. Erving Goffman has written of "self-theatricalization" in these terms, as a forced, nearly obsessive imprinting by which an observed entity can construct for its observers the "proper" impression:

> But there is another way, a shorter and more efficient way, in which the observed can influence the observer. Instead of allowing an impression of their activity to arise as an incidental by-product of their activity, they can re-orient their frame of reference and devote their efforts to the creation of desired impressions. Instead of attempting ends by acceptable means, they can attempt to achieve the impression that they are achieving certain ends by acceptable means. It is always possible to manipulate the impression the observers use as a substitute for reality because a sign for the presence of a thing, not being that thing, can be employed in the absence of it.[2]

The language of this seemingly straightforward commentary on role playing is revelatory, for it suggests a view of the self as both performer and theater manager, who disguises the hollowness within through the created signs that generate the illusion of a presence they conceal. To use one of Hawkes' favorite images for narrative surface, *Travesty* is a disguise, a verbal covering or "skin." It maintains an assemblage of signs that vocalize the nonexistence of their origin and the mad, assimilatory desires of their author. For the narrator, Papa, the mask is constructed as an interpretation of existence that will "explain" to Henri and Chantal the reason for their murders; interestingly, Papa parallels the death of the self and the death of interpretation by insisting that the planned apocalypse will be a "clear 'accident,' so to speak, in which invention quite defies interpretation" (23). But for the reader of a document that claims its nonexistence progressively as each sentence unfolds, *Travesty* is a different kind of disguise: voice itself covering over absence, language and interpretation staving off the "purity" and "clarity" of silence. If *Pale Fire* confronts the reader with the problem of invalid alternative interpretations only to undermine the notion of validity, *Travesty* argues, in its absurdist, either/or fashion, that the excessive noise of Papa's voice is a screen behind which lurks the "non-sense" of the abyss.

Near the beginning of his journey, Papa proclaims to Henri that understanding the shock of this predicament is "a mere question of adjustment" (19), an alignment of expectation, desire, and fear with the facts of the situation. By extension, all that he says may be termed matters of adjustment, the narrator tinkering with the imposed design and disguise of the self projected by means of the planned "accident" so that his listeners—Henri, ourselves—will accept entrapment, death, and the ultimate uninterpretability of these events.[3] For this compulsive narrator, the world is a chaos of signs and incongruities to be welded into the aligned extremities that define the parameters of his estranged, painful life. Papa confesses to Henri that, as a youth, if "the world did not respond to me totally, immediately, in leaf, street sign, the expression of strangers, then I did not exist—or existed only in the misery of youthful loneliness" (85). Though he claims he has transcended his youthful anxieties and that state of being where the world exists as a collection of profane signs that must needs reflect the visage and fate of the perceiver, Papa's mature narrative attempts to recapture the response sought in youth.

In telling his story, Papa effectively reduces the world to the shape of the car destined for obliteration. The time of the narrative becomes the measure of its existence when he tells Henri that "we are traveling as if inside a clock the shape of a bullet, seated as if stationary among tight springs and brilliant gems" (16). Car and narrative are thus depicted as the speeding objects within which the ceaseless voice of the narrator creates the "stationary," frozen presence of his self-image, sealed within the glass and metal casing which is both cocoon and time bomb. Papa constructs a world of absolute immediacy over which he has complete control—a world as responsive to him as the wheel of his car. In this realm of precise measurements and subtle, nearly unobservable gradations, he proclaims to Henri that "you cannot be as aware of [the dashboard settings] as I am, yet for me the mere climbing or falling of needles, the sometimes monstrous metamorphosis of tiny, precise numbers behind faintly illuminated glass . . . these for me are the essential signs, the true language, always precious and treacherous at the same time" (33). Seen in this light, Papa's monologue appears, in Rodolphe Gasché's figure, as a scene of writing that "sets with its letters the time marks which open up the dimensions of temporality in the tissue of its textuality. A time machine, a dial on which the shadow often goes back, writing engenders time only to put it to death."[4] Papa's "time machine" of narrative presents us with the paradox of a temporal opening—the hour-long drive to the wall—wholly given over to the accelerated intonations of his voice enunciating the desire for timelessness and silence. Here, road, car, and self merge into a single intention: "these yellow headlights are my eyes; my mind is bound inside my memory of this curving road like a fist in glass" (15). Unlike the inconsistent world of his youth, the suicide car represents a precise alignment of Papa's being with the "facts" of his constricted existence, as roads, trees, villages, and the final wall—signs of the progression toward death—serve as the responsorial elements of his emotional landscape.

In idealizing for Henri the scene of annihilation, Papa voices the tortured conceit that underlies the motivation for his incomprehensible act:

> I would prefer that the remains of our crash go undiscovered, at least initially. I would prefer that these remains be left unknown to anyone and hence unexplained, untouched. In this case we have at the outset the shattering that occurs in utter darkness, then the first sunrise in which the chaos, the physical disarray, has not yet settled—bits of metal expanding, contracting, tufts of upholstery exposed to the air, an unsocketed dial impossibly squeaking in a clump of thorns—though this same baffling tangle of springs, jagged edges of steel, curves of aluminum, has already received its first coating of white frost. In the course of the first day the gasoline evaporates, the engine oil begins to fade into the earth, the broken lens of a far-flung headlight reflects the progress of the sun from a furrow in what was once a field of corn . . . And then darkness, a cold

> wind, a shred of clothing fluttering where it is snagged on one of the doors which, quite unscathed, lies flat in the grass. And then daylight . . . And despite all this chemistry of time, nothing has disturbed the essential integrity of our tableau of chaos, the point being that if design inevitably surrenders to debris, debris inevitably reveals its innate design. Until one day two boys stumble upon the incongruity of a once beautiful automobile smashed in the barnyard of an abandoned farm. (58–59)

While Papa emphasizes the secrecy and potential meaninglessness of the projected crash in this prophecy, taking place in darkness, hidden until discovered by two boys who will find "only delight" in the incongruous spectacle, he admits the impossibility of this entropic revelation: "Nothing will prevent our sudden incandescence in the night sky. And then we shall have blue lights, motorcycles, radio communications, the arrival of several of our little white ambulances" (60).

Papa expresses pleasure in this moment as he imagines what the world's response to the accident will be. But, unaccountably, he also expresses relief in the fact that there is an alternative to the spectacle envisioned as a romanticized, slow return to nature, where the debris of the accident becomes the incremental design of a mutable world, its only remnants fragments of clothing and the wrecked door which would serve as the detached portal to the car's mystery. Though he protests that the "incandescence" of the crash more realistically conceived will be "sad," "a brutal sport" (60), he implies that heat and light will happily combine to weld and reveal instantaneously the paradox of design as debris, debris as design. For Papa's self-imposed heroic task, like that of any dominating father, is to impose order upon an unruly world and, like that of any paranoid artist, to certify an impression. But this Papa, attracted to death as he is to the accidents and losses of existence, celebrant of the lung he claims to have lost in "the war," patron of a one-legged physician, also wishes to detect the "innate design" of his own scattered, annihilated being. The incandescence of the crash will be a sign; it will embody his desire to "explain" himself by creating a self-revelation that is destroyed at the moment of its epiphany. As Papa puts it, he wishes to confer upon himself "the power to invent the very world we are quitting. It is as if the bird could die in flight" (57). The narcissism of youth has been transformed into the image of Narcissus, gazing at his own reflection in the pool at the instant of utmost clarity, which is also the instant when he drowns.[5] So Papa, through the crash, projects the incongruity of the apocalyptic illumination of the accident and the negation of the self as the revelation of the self's design.

Yet the accident never occurs, at least not anywhere within the pages of *Travesty*: it is completely "imaginary." Just as Papa wishes, the event is unseen; the monologue is thus both preface to and aftermath of a narrative "hole," like that conceived by Michel Leiris in an epigraph to *Travesty* from *Manhood*: "the poetic structure—like the canon [*sic*], which is only a hole surrounded by steel—can be based only on what one does not have . . . ultimately one can write only to fill a void or at least to situate, in relation to the most lucid part of ourselves, the place where this incommensurable abyss yawns within us."[6] Papa's car, as bullet, is like Leiris' "canon," an analogy for the structure of his narrative and the placement of his death-driven being. The words of *Travesty*—Papa's memories, philosophical arguments justifying his actions, ludicrous expressions of concern for his daughter's carsickness and Henri's asthma—create so much "noise" that they hide the lack of event, motivation, and self which are the real but absent subjects of the novel. These are known only by negation, as they are superseded by the seeming irrelevancies and "spontaneous" confessions of Papa's monologue. What he voices to Henri as the focal point of his digression is "this idea precisely that lies at the dead center of our night together: that nothing is more important than the existence of what does not exist; that I would rather see two shadows flickering inside the head than all your flaming sunrises set end to end. There you have it, the theory to which I hold as does a wasp to his dart" (57). Like the shape of the car that surrounds the darkness within, Papa's narrative, fancifully, a device which can only "sting" its hearers, is a projection of being turned inside out, the confessional self portrayed as a shell or veneer. His monologue, as a travesty, is constituted by the layering of language coerced into the shape of a narrative of wrenched consistency which rushes forward to its own annihilation while containing it, as surely as does the car, a more literal vehicle for *Travesty*'s narrative drive.

Quite expectedly, Papa's narrative forcing bed reveals certain significant patterns and obsessions which, if they point to his essential nonbeing, also represent his desire to create an ironic monument to himself through explanation and accident. One of these imaginative constraints is his attraction to human and geometrical triangles, which are structures predicated upon a number often thought to represent perfection and completion. In this regard, Papa's own perfectionist tendencies contrast sharply with the enormous holes in his narrative and gaps in his logic, just as his obsession with the ritualistic completion of his suicide/murder is at odds with the impossibility of finishing his monologue. When Papa speaks of his design, triangulated upon the novel's women, he reveals its center as an absence. As he proclaims his love to Chantal, who is hidden, nearly forgotten in the backseat of the car, he assures her that she is an integral part of his vision: "You are no mere forgotten audience to the final ardent exchange between the two men in your mother's life, men whose faces you cannot even see. Not at all, Chantal. No, I have thought of you with utter faithfulness from the beginning. In my mind there were always three of us, never two, and in all the accruing elements of this now inevitable route . . . there you were in the very center of my concern" (39). Typically, that which is unseen or absent is viewed at the "very center" of Papa's construction. Similarly, Papa says his wife, Honorine, supposedly lying asleep in the château he will drive past minutes before the accident, is "the source of my private apocalypse" (125).[7] In an earlier vision, Papa imagines Chantal lying within the unearthly chateau, which is called Tara, a name that mimes both the "Terra" made of solid ground and that paradisiacal, racist mansion of the popular imagination which imprisoned fairytale women within its chivalric confines. Papa sees Chantal in "a glimpse of a large modern car standing empty inside the iron gates of the very castle where the sleeping princess lies in all her pallor" (54). Both Honorine and Chantal, identified at different times as the source and center of Papa's design, are portrayed as "sleeping beauties," in their "pallor" representing the living dead, the Poesque, enchanted corpses who are the mediators of Papa's vision.[8]

The women of *Travesty* are the hinges in the symmetrically triangular relationships upon which Papa suspends the geometry of his imagination. One reason that Chantal is along for the ride might be "paternal": Papa feels at times that he is a father to Henri, and so it is appropriate that his daughter accompany them to an event which will annihilate father and offspring, leaving behind the suffering, sleeping Honorine as the only witness to the generational collapse of her family. The textual analogue is clear: Papa, as author, wishes to kill off his imaginary children in an act that will simultaneously establish his paternal authority while obviating its issue and necessity. The possible interpretation that emerges from this triangulation is distinctly Oedipal, the jealous, titanic father destroying his children or, to alter the variables, the incensed father/lover murdering his rival/son and the object of their rivalry, who is both daughter and lover to Papa. Papa encourages an Oedipal reading of this triangle when he speaks of Chantal as a "porno brat" and recalls for Henri a strange, adolescent ritual which involves blindfolded and bound girls groping for and eating carrots that dangle before them; for her proficiency in this ludicrous contest, Chantal earns the title of "Queen of the Carrots." Papa also recalls the memory of his son, Pascal, who died at the age of three. He depicts Pascal as "an infant Caesar" (85), "fatly and gently erotic" (86), and imagines him coming quietly into his parents' bedroom, then sitting astride his mother's lap while Papa looks on. The father/daughter/son triangle is thus repeated, with slight variation, in the father/mother/son relationship.

In a further complication, Honorine is at the apex of another series of triangular relationships that interlock with these. As Henri's mistress, she is in a position of rivalry with her daughter that recalls the Papa/Henri/Chantal relationship; as Papa's wife, she is the focus of a rivalry between husband and lover or putative "father" and "son." Depending on the view one takes (and all are encouraged by Papa's insinuatory monologue), Papa may be Oedipus or Agamemnon; indeed, as one critic suggests, he may simply be insane, alone in the car, projecting the personages and triangles which will allow him to justify suicide.[9] The effect of these complicated triangulations is geometric: everybody involved, at one time or another, seems to occupy all the positions available within a threefold system of syllogistic relationships. In a given context, Papa is father, husband, jealous lover; Chantal is daughter, lover, and (when Papa sees her as a repetition of Honorine) wife. All the novel's triangles, if overlaid, would thus appear to be identical, revealing a structure of inescapable rivalry. At the dead center of each relation of threes, there is an absence—deceased son, sleeping wife, hidden daughter—who seems to exist as the force generating the energy by which these constructions are sustained.

Yet the carefully erected constructions of Papa's geometry are imminently collapsible; they are imagined structures of desire which arise from, and threaten a return to, perfect similitude. On the one hand, *Travesty* portrays, parodically, what René Girard refers to as the "triangular" desire that structures the relation between self and other which is at the foundation of narrative. Girard argues that the novel, seen as a mediation of "reality," depicts the relation between subject and object, self and other, thus representing a dialectical relation that becomes triangular when a mediatory device—a model of reality, a rival in a relationship, an object of desire—is brought into play. For him, the erection of this structure is the motive and end of fiction, which is always referring to itself in this labor as its own mediation.[10] In this view, the triangulations of *Travesty* may exist as a manifestation of Papa's narrative impulse, represented by his ability, no matter how suspect, to arrange the world according to mutable, tangible, and therefore "living" structures of desire.[11]

On the other hand, Papa's collapsible world contains a possibility described by Jeffrey Mehlman, discussing Leiris' *Manhood*, of an "absolute" dream where "differential opposition itself is obliterated: neither subject nor object, neither male nor female. The crime merges with its expiation, the dreamer with the dreamt. The subject invades the world; every verb aspires to reflexive form."[12] Papa's world seems erected in order to disappear, its function to speak the sameness whence it came. He tells Henri, for example, of his "most dangerous quality," his "propensity toward total coherence" (75). One result of this propensity is the "formative event" of his "early manhood," a hit-and-run "accident" (or a near miss; even Papa is not sure which) where he attempted to run down a young girl walking in the street with an old poet. In memory or imagination, Papa constructs another triangle that, with minor variations, foreshadows and repeats that formed in the death car: the young girl, "a poor and sacred child" (126), is a back projection of Chantal—mere transposition of the letters in the second adjective would describe Chantal's present state. The old poet is an aged Henri reflecting, perhaps, the elderly Papa's jealousy or self-hatred. The first accident clearly prefigures the second and underscores Papa's lifelong attraction to the "sacred sites" of car accidents, "the symmetry of the two or even more machines whose crashing results in nothing more than an aftermath of blood and sand" (20). Both triangles appear to be constructed so they necessarily fall back into pure "symmetry."

The symmetrical aspects of Papa's design are such that everything he gives voice to arises from and points toward an unadulterated "reflexive form." The car, so closely identified with Papa's "self," becomes the trap from which he, assembling symmetry, repetition, identification, and recurrence into a mirrored, labyrinthine verbal world, cannot escape. As Mehlman suggests of Leiris, in Papa's world the distinction between self and other, and the mediacy of that relation, is dissolved. Chantal and Honorine are equally "sleeping beauties" and "porno brats"; both are variously identified with Monique, Papa's former mistress, whose diminutive proportions "mimed the small size of Chantal and Chantal's grandmother" (140). Monique is twenty when Papa first meets her, as is Chantal when she first meets Henri. Mother, daughter, and mistress merge into one figure for Papa, as they do for Henri (who takes both Honorine and Chantal as mistresses), thereby completing the identification among the novel's women. Equally, Papa and his antagonist are the same. At first they appear to be perfect opposites: "I" and "you," self and other, murderer and poet, father and son, husband and lover. Henri is a poet who theatricalizes death and advertises in his poetry the "*persona* of the man who has emerged alive from the end of the tunnel" (42); he imagines himself to be the resurrected man who has undergone the nothingness of death and anxiety. Papa protests that he is different from this ersatz Hemingway (whose own paternal nickname is surely not accidentally identical to that of the narrator's) and that he despises "the pomp and frivolity of organized expiation" (43). Yet his entire monologue is given over to establishing the validity of his theatrically planned, ritualistic "accident." He is also a poet of organized death. His celebration of the "aftermath of blood and sand"—the result of the accidents whose symmetry delights him—is a telling expression identical to the title of the most famous bullfight movie, thus implicating him in Henri's Hemingwayesque fantasies.

Since Papa is involved, if only figuratively, with both Honorine and Chantal as lovers, the identification with Henri is complete. In that sense, Papa might as well be talking to himself. He achieves in his monologue the perfect, sought-after alignment of the "world" with the self projections of his erotic, dreaming consciousness—he *is* the speeding car, the anxiety-ridden poet, the voluptuous wife. The relations he manufactures are interchangeable and reversible to such an extent that in the visionary accident they disappear into simultaneity and similitude, debris (difference) becoming design (sameness). At times, Papa's hyperbolic sensitivities, especially to cold, echo those of Poe's Usher (a story often obliquely referred to in *Travesty*). Like the triangle of Poe's story which exists between the narrator, Roderick, and Madelaine, Papa's triangles disintegrate, as the fragmented architecture of the Usher mansion collapses, into the tarn of sameness and perfect resemblance. Along with the projected disappearance of relationality in his narrative there is the loss of its significance or, more precisely, its interpretability. For, as he seems to know perfectly well, meaning arises as a construal of differences or the comparison of variegated similarities. More radically than Kinbote, Papa desires his construction to recede into a "meaningless" realm, beyond language, where those opposites, design and debris, become absurdly one.

It seems appropriate, then, that Papa is obsessed with the "purity" and "clarity" of his vision. As if a clear windshield, figuratively, implied both the clearest expression of the self, its trans-parent status as mediator of the world's signs and, simultaneously, its disappearance, Papa tries to assure Henri of the translucent qualities of his projections. While Kinbote's world is filled with distorting mirrors that reflect different perspectives of the self, Papa's construction seems determined to be a series of transparencies or crystalline images gathered from the past and recollected in a single projection toward the "clear 'accident'" (23). Perhaps this explains the structure of *Travesty*, which is broken up not into chapters but into fifty-five untitled, unnumbered sections of lengths varying from one sentence to several pages and separated by white spaces. Papa's monologue appears as a series of snapshots in a family album which he hopes will "clearly" or "purely" represent the absolute, inexplicable design of the self not as a reflection but as a manifest construction, a "perfect formation which is lofty and the only one possible" (15).

Papa maintains that this design "underlies all my rambling and . . . like a giant snow crystal, permeates all the tissues of existence" (27). He recalls for Henri a visit to a local church where he discovers what is, according to a local legend, "the Fountain of Clarity." There, he gazes at his own face and sees the end of a lifelong quest: "The creators of that ancient legend could not have known that I never expected anything at all from my life except clarity. I have pursued clarity as relentlessly as the worshippers pursue their Christ" (103). For Papa, "clarity" can be seen as the primary element of a vision that, like the snow crystal, becomes the sign of its own delicate, dissolving state of being. It might also be seen as a quality of Papa's narcissism, except that at the Fountain of Clarity his reflection in the water is immediately transformed into a vision of the "essential" Honorine: "But my own face . . . was nothing, nothing at all compared with the intensity with which I was then contemplating the existence of our own Honorine. Your Muse, my clarity, I cannot convey to you my satisfaction as the thought of Honorine filled the silence of an earthly spot which, except for the fountain, was otherwise perhaps a little too picturesque" (104). Here, the crucial desire around which Papa's design is formed reveals itself: gazing at the self, Papa sees the Other, the silent, absent Honorine, his onerous, oneiric counterpart. As with the other imaginative constraints of his vision, clarity, if achieved, implies the collapse of distinctions into pure simultaneity. When Papa looks at himself, he appears to be as much anti-Narcissus as Narcissus; he sees that "clarity" which is the negation of the difference between subject and object, self and other.

The imagined incident is the most dramatic example of the possibilities effected by the collapse of *Travesty*'s triangles. The recollection of the fountain portrays Papa construing what is actually a monomaniacal incorporation of everything into his own self-conception as a form of transcendent self-negation: he becomes Honorine's contemplated existence, which is the embodiment of clarity, the absolute translucence of "otherness."[13] Of course here, as always, the complexity of Papa's vision and delusion is undermined by the self-conscious fussiness of his anxiety about the proper reconstruction of the scene, which is "too picturesque." Nevertheless, his desire is clear: by enacting the planned accident, he declares that driver and passengers "are simply traveling in purity and extremity down that road the rest of the world attempts to hide from us by heaping up whole forests of the most confusing road signs, detours, barricades" (14). The completion of his design depends upon his clearing away the debris of existence and forging its multiplicity into the one pure, clear sign of the self that is its own end and meaning. Ultimately, Papa's design portends more than the planned annihilation of the self, which is merely the physical analogue of a larger, antihermeneutic purpose. Along with the self, he desires that the world be subsumed into the final manifestation of a "clarity" where the troubled relation between things and the signs that stand for them simply disappears.

Papa's contradictory claim that he is a lover of incongruity is thoroughly betrayed by the forced "total coherence" of all differences which this paradoxical disappearing proposes. At several points, the dichotomy that exists between "design" and "debris" is translated into the fundamental difference his vision seeks to erase, that between eros and death.[14] Papa sees the wasted "landscape of spent passion" that passes before his gaze as thoroughly eroticized. "The little paper sacks of poison placed side by side with bowls of flowers on the window ledges of each village street" (62) in the vaguely European country where he dwells elicit "a pessimism indistinguishable from the most obvious state of sexual excitation" (63). Growth and poison, sexual excitation and philosophical negation are thus joined in this realm of opposites, where Papa defines himself as one among the "gourmets and amateur excavators of our cultural heritage . . . [who] have only to pause an instant in order to unearth the plump bird seasoning on the end of its slender cord tied to a rafter, or a fat white regal chamber pot glazed with the pastel images of decorous lovers, or a cracked and dusty leather boot into which some young lewd and brawny peasant once vomited" (63). As the constructor and psychic historian of this landscape, Papa brings to coalescence the images of the plump but dead fowl, an erotic scene painted upon a receptacle of waste, and the boot of the "lewd" peasant filled with disincorporated human detritus.

This is only one in a series of startling instances where "debris," or waste, is converted into the "design" of Papa's eroticism. Logically enough, Papa is disturbed whenever he perceives a lack of such connection between waste and lust, life and death. Though he has never seen it, he imagines for Henri his vision of the village, La Roche, which lies near the scene of the projected accident. He is especially concerned about La Roche's inadequate hospital, to which, proleptically, their shattered corpses will be brought via the hospital kitchen: "Do you see the humor of it? The outrage? But everywhere it is the same: rooms without doors, sinks without drains, conduits that will never be connected to any water supply, corpses or bleeding victims forever passing through the kitchens of our nation's hospitals" (98). Though he is appalled by the physical disconnectedness of this vision, it is interesting that Papa imagines that the corpses' route to the hospital morgue passes through its nutritive center, a grisly, cannibalistic cohesion forced upon an entropic world by which sustenance and waste are joined. The merging of opposites occurs on a more personal level for Papa in his sadomasochistic relationship with Monique, particularly in one scene where she flogs the "dead bird" of his sexuality, an experience that makes him "a specialist on the subject of dead passion" (74). Taken a step further, this mania for the reconciliation of opposites can be seen in the fragmented structure of *Travesty*. Its fifty-five disconnected parts are welded into the total coherence envisioned by Papa's version of the accident; its life continually anticipates the desired containment of its death; in its repetitions and symmetries, it seeks (through Papa) to silence the noise of his illogical explanations and unreliable protestations. In this way, Papa's narrative attains the status that Hélène Cixous confers on all fiction: "a secretion of death, an anticipation of nonrepresentation, a doll, a hybrid body composed of language and silence that, in the movement by which it turns, invents doubles, and death."[15] So Papa's "hybrid" of "dead passion" turns its incongruities and repetitions to symmetry, an invention whereby the death of its maker is aligned with the fiction of death which everywhere haunts the life of *Travesty*.

Cixous' definition of fiction, applied to *Travesty*, points toward another crucial aspect of Papa's design, as well as implying an explanation for Hawkes' portrayal of an artist who destroys his own artifact. We see Papa making, and prospectively unmaking, his own world; we hope for some understanding of the significance of this act, but we are told by the narrator that we cannot hope to interpret the "aftermath of blood and sand"; we observe the absurd spectacle of performed self-interpretation made over into the world's body, only to see its purpose imagined as disembodiment, disappearance, return to similitude. All this takes place within the confines of a book we know to be a fiction, and we thus experience a sense of the uncanny in reading this "travesty," where the self-conscious weaving of a narrative tapestry labors to unravel itself, as if the emperor struggled to remove his own new clothes.

The verbal underside of *Travesty* reveals Papa often referring to himself as a tailor who clothes the "doll" of his self-image as a matter of disguise and protection. When he describes Monique, he reflects on her remarkably white skin: "Tight, painfully and wonderfully tight over the entirety of her little face and limbs and torso, so thin and tight that actually I used to fear the consequences of a slip of the threaded needle" (65–66). By itself, Papa's image presents a simple metaphor for the erotic delicacy of Monique's skin. But later in his narrative, accused by Henri of madness, Papa proclaims to him, "so you think that my brain is sewn with the sutures of your psychosis." Papa elaborates on his conception of what was done to Henri while at a mental hospital: "I am well aware that in that short time they so sutured the lobes of your brain with designs of fear and hopelessness that the threads themselves emerged from within the skull to travel in terrible variety down the very flesh of your face, pinching, pulling, and scoring your hardened skin as if they, your attendants, had been engaged not in psychological but surgical disfigurement" (120).

Taken together, these images reflect more upon Papa than upon the "stitched" skins to which they refer. When seen in light of his obsession with maps and roads, his fascination with car accidents and mutilated bodies, Papa's propensity for the images of sewing may be viewed as the repressed manifestation of his specious self-creation. The writing of this self-generated fiction is conceived as a travesty, a making over, a marking up, a disfigurement disguised by a rage for "clarity" and perfection.[16] Papa's figural conception of Monique reveals his fear that his creation may be too fragile, its "skin" too thin for his threading needle. The manufacture of Henri is even more problematic: not only is there the possibility of identification between maker and monster ("my brain is sewn with the sutures of your psychosis"), but there is also the fear of revelation. The "design" of Henri's face manifests his mental suturing, as a book its badly-sewn binding. This is a projection of Papa's anxiety about the success of his artistic desire to conceal an inner, flawed construction or to present what is really a palimpsest as a harmonious, self-generating whole. At a remove from the narrator, Hawkes' novel is a travesty of Papa's travesty, a fiction that parodies the parallels between self-creation and the making of fictions. This creation takes place within a framework that shows up self-theatricalization and fiction making for what they are: disguises, constructions that contain an ironic desire to disable themselves, flawed perfections, patchwork portrayals of similitude, re-membered dismemberments.

If *Travesty* is placed in the larger context of Hawkes' *oeuvre*, it becomes clear that the interior metafictional movements of the novel take on larger proportions.[17] *Travesty* is the third of a proclaimed "triad" of novels that includes *The Blood Oranges* (1971) and *Death, Sleep & the Traveler* (1974). The first-person narrators of these novels are also attracted to certain numbers and geometries. Cyril, of *The Blood Oranges*, constructs a "quaternion" of two married couples that resolves itself into two conflicted love triangles which ruin his created paradise. Allert, of *Death, Sleep & the Traveler*, is obsessed with the symmetrical trios of husband/wife/lover and husband/mistress/rival as well as with the "triangulations"—from the sailboat patterns on his window blinds to the outlines of female genitalia—that possess his imagination and define the shape of his world. The narrators of *Travesty*'s predecessors are also compulsive about matters of pattern and clarity. Cyril refers to his terrestrial paradise as "the silken weave of Love's pink panorama," and Allert proclaims that his recollections are hesitant attempts to "confront [my] own psychic sores in the clear glass."[18]

As the third in a triad of novels proliferate with human triangles, *Travesty* takes to the third power Hawkes' triangulations, thereby burlesquing, in a novel about paternal control, his own authorial power. For example, Hawkes has made detachment the hallmark of his work. He has often commented upon the aesthetic distancing that permits the artist to view the extremities of human existence with candor and, once seen, compassion. In an early interview, he noted that one of the artistic habits to be seen in his work is a "quality of coldness, detachment, ruthless determination to face up to the enormities of ugliness and potential failure within ourselves and in the world around us."[19] When Papa declares to Henri that "in my youth I also had my taste or two of that 'cruel detachment' which was to make you famous" (47–48), when he mocks the writer's relation to his audience—"telling those eager and hostile women that the poet is always a betrayer, a murderer, and that the writing of poetry is like a descent into death" (80)—in a novel by an author known for his statement about the artist's affinity to the "criminal mentality," we are presented with a dizzying perspective. *Travesty* appears to travesty Papa's self-authorized vision, the aesthetics of the "real" author who wrote it, the progression of novels which it concludes, and the encompassing act of writing, and reading, fictions.

All these various, constructive acts seem to collapse in the apocalyptic destruction, the "design of debris" that *Travesty* figures as its end.

The effect of *Travesty*'s inner and contextual travesties is to create an infinite regress or black hole into which the fictive constructions of the novel vanish. Like the novel's "self," Papa, who metaphorically performs various skin grafts to cover or make over a self-conception founded on nothingness, *Travesty* survives as a fictional patchwork which defies interpretation by means of a hyperbolic reference to its own unfounded making. There is no "world" outside Papa's car, no sound but his voice, no substance but the language with which he surrounds the negation that is himself. He succeeds in molding the world to the romantic vision of his own being which, impossibly, imagining the accident, he desires to be a transcendental sign without content, an instantaneous presence that portends its immediate vanishing. Compared with Kinbote's self-translation, Papa's desired expression of the self may be seen to move beyond reflection, even beyond skewed communication, into an iconic realm where the relational boundaries between the self and others, or author and text, are erased. *Travesty* makes it clear that this realm signifies the death of narrative; it is an imagined state which, according to Peter Brooks, is the end of textual "desire": "The desire of the text is ultimately the desire for the end, for that recognition which is the moment of the death of the reader in the text."[20]

The "you" addressed in *Travesty* is not only Henri but ourselves, as we both dread and rush to the end of the story we read, and as we seek the meaning of this self-presentation which compels us to accept its impossible nonsignificance. *Travesty* can then be seen as an inscription upon a tombstone forming the concrete sign of the nonexistence lying within. It forces us to behold, through "clear glass," what is at the bottom of the narrative impulse and the act of reading—the desire to signify the end of signification. Yet this inscription is also an alphabetic dance upon the tomb, a "goose on the grave," to use the figure Hawkes chose as the title for an early novella. *Travesty* performs a series of (self) constructions that undermine themselves but that, in the play of their incongruities, create a "living" verbal world, while the book is read, while the road is traveled. Since we come in at the middle of Papa's journey and never see its end, the life of this narrative seems eternally prolonged in a mockery of narrative and readerly impulses, and in a celebration of what confounds them. Finally, *Travesty* does attempt the impossible—a reduction of the "self" to its essential nature through a destruction of its relation to the world. This denial, romanticized in *Travesty*, is questioned and revised in John Barth's *LETTERS*, where the inscriptions of selfhood are situated within the reconstructions of human history.

CHAPTER THREE SELF, NARRATIVE, HISTORY
THE SYSTEM OF JOHN BARTH'S *LETTERS*

I cannot grasp the act of existing
except in signs scattered in the world.
Paul Ricoeur, *Freud and Philosophy*

A system, whether mathematical, biological, philosophical, or linguistic, can be seen as a narrative organizing structure within which the elements of the system—whether integers, organs, selves, or phonemes—exist in relation to each other. The network of relations between elements can be defined as the story of the system, which "narrates" the correspondences between elements, and the identity, within the system, of each element. The essential relation of part to whole and of whole to part is dialectical, as each acts to define the other in some way. The letters of the alphabet provide a fortuitous example of this relation since, John Barth tells us, the novel *LETTERS* is in part about alphabetic inscription and its discontents. As he speaks about one of Italo Calvino's stories (from *Cosmicomics*), Barth notes that "in the last lines of the story the narrator imagines pursuing [his] rival around the curls of the letters, hiding in the bend of the C or around the loop of the R—[it] raises my hair to hear that, because that's the kind of preoccupation I am involved with, the recognition that everything we do, everything we express comes around to those empty spaces between the letters."[1] Written language is made up of words, which are constituted by individual letters; thus the whole system of a given language, according to Barth's analogy, derives its significances from the relationships between alphabetic parts. These "relationships," dialectically construed by and contributing to the larger system, exist as the white spaces between black letters, a field of play where, Barth's reading of Calvino suggests, the narrative quest for meaning and finality takes place. It is admittedly fanciful to attribute motivations to alphabetic letters, but Calvino's story implies that a narrative conflict resolves itself in the configurations of strokes into letters, letters into words, words into story, each element along the way striving to find its telos within the larger system to which it pertains and from which it gains meaning.

This sense of relationality is clearly more than alphabetic—it is the essential quality of all systems. These include the structures of society and its narrative, history, made of individuals as languages are made of letters and words. According to Raymond Williams, we are all part of a "social process, into which individuals are born and within which they are shaped, but to which they then also actively contribute, in a continuing process. This is at once their socialization and their individuation."[2] The analogy that can be drawn between written sentences and alphabetic letters and between society and individuals, while limited, is again fortuitous. Barth's *LETTERS* is an enactment of the scene where writing, as a gathering of letters into meaningful words, takes place. Derrida's notion that writing is "the constitution of structurality" and, like the repressed psyche, "a topography of traces, a map of breaches," accords with Barth's "preoccupation" to inscribe a series of letters into a narrated system which is also the structuring of spaces between letters.[3] Analogously, *LETTERS* is also a documentation of the "place" where selves are born into history. History, capitalized, is for Barth the intersection of personal histories, those self-signifying narratives of how individuals perceive their historical roles, their place in familial declensions, and their position in History's larger story. In *LETTERS*, this act of positioning defines a process of interpretation, which is a "reading" of the self into time and history, as if the self was a sign—a word on the page or a letter of that word. As we shall see, Barth's novel portrays a sense of "self" and "system" as a network of alphabetical, numerical, epistolary, and historical correspondences which foreground a collation of gaps and interstices that define the novel's subject: how the act of narration structures a world, how the self is an interpretation of that narrative.[4]

Barth has always been fascinated by systems of all kinds, from the mythic to the biological, and by how identity is achieved within the patterns of a given narrative structure. His protagonists are usually either avid systematizers or innocents caught up in a cosmic design that defines their destiny and herohood. From the beginning, in *The Floating Opera*, where Todd Andrews hilariously sketches out the mathematical permutations of a three-way relationship with Jane and Harrison Mack, to the intricate metafictions of *Chimera*, where that second-rate imitation of Perseus, Bellerophon, vainly attempts to escape the pattern of his life's first half in its mirrored, Perseus-like second half, Barth's stories have compounded narrative systems within systems that both imprison and certify the heroic self. Just as frequently, Barth is interested in antisystems, contradiction, and chaos. The same Todd Andrews who flow-charts the progress of passion also presents himself as a model of inconsistency, a breaker of habits who does not break all habits in order to assure himself that he is not consistently a habit breaker. In *Giles Goat-Boy*, the hero who seeks to crack the code of a universe run by a computer discovers that this gigantic binary system arises from a paradox positively Zen-like in its arcing contradictions: "Pass All / Fail All." Inevitably, in Barth's capacious universe, all things are pulled into the gravitational fields of order and synthesis, even if individual elements resist these as antimatter, thereby ever renewing the system in the dualistic struggle between incorporation and expulsion.[5]

The paradoxical nature of Barth's systematic narratives is complained of most vocally by Ebenezer Cooke, the hero of *The Sot-Weed Factor*, who cries to his mentor, Henry Burlingame III, that this worthy's fantastic deceits regarding his part in Cooke's history are unbearable: "La, methinks expedience, and not truth, is the tale's warp, and subterfuge its woof, and you've weaved it with the shuttle of intrigue upon the loom of my past credulity! In short, 'tis creatured from the whole cloth, that even I can see doth not hang all in a piece. 'Tis a fabric of contradictories."[6] Cooke's hyperbolic, catechretic figure contains the essential terms of Barth's fictional project: fiction is a weaving of contradictories, a systematic network of unsystematic relationships that speak their discontinuity; fiction concerns itself not primarily with truth but with its own scandalous self-verification through the ironic motions of expedience, subterfuge, and intrigue; fiction is a patchwork creation that refers more to its own clumsy making than to an abiding presence ("the whole cloth") standing behind it or perfectly mirrored as the symmetrical relation of part to whole. These examples suggest that Barth's fictions are essentially concerned with patterns and systems, indeed with their own narrative order. But like his favorite mythical figure, Proteus, Barth's narratives—whether they be heroic quests or metafictional discussions of narrative structure—continually transform, contradict, and reduplicate themselves, revealing the double threat of their falsity and disorderliness contained.

For Barth, this logically impossible narrative act, which he labels the effect of the "formalist novel," is what "replenishes" art and creates within the worn-out forms of language and fiction the possibility of renewal.[7] The author's stated purpose in *LETTERS* is to demonstrate this concept of narrative as protean system: "the book's true subject [is] Reenactment, or Recycling, or Revolution—the last in a metaphorical sense rather than in a political sense. . . . if one looks about to see, as I do, how many readings or aspects of a story can be made to reflect the main concerns of the story—if one endeavors to see that everything reflects everything else—then one of the things you might think of recycling along the way is recurrences in history: repetitions, echoes, reverberations, second cycles of human lives."[8] Barth's statement is suggestive in several ways. First, it indicates that the matter of *LETTERS* is the observance of "echoes" and "reverberations" of everything that exists within the novel, including symmetries between characters' lives, disparate historical events, numerological correspondences, and the evolutionary "plot" of nature. Second, Barth's prospectus projects the making of a (r)evolutionary narrative system that tells the story of these echoes and, in so doing, regenerates itself by reconstituting itself. Furthermore, he infers that *LETTERS* is "about" the process of this recycling, the gathering up of formal narrative elements and their recombination into new shapes. These may appear, randomly, as beautifully innovative emergent forms, as mismatched monstrosities, or as mere repetitions of what came before, though for Barth no repetition is "mere" since the system in which it appears is constantly mutating. Even more, *LETTERS* recycles the entire tradition from which it is born: it is an intertextual compendium of the history of the novel, the novel as history, and the larger movement of "letters" to which the particular species of the epistolary novel makes its own formal contribution. Barth suggests here that the "metasystem" of *LETTERS* creates both a labyrinth of mirrors—everything reflecting everything else as a repetition of its own history—and a recirculatory force that drives a kind of narrative economy wherein exchanges are made and equivalencies charted.

The illusions of the novel suggest that, between reflection and renewal, the vast system of exchange which is *LETTERS* generates itself.

Appropriately, then, *LETTERS* recycles all of Barth's previous fiction, presents a fictional recreation of American and European history since the Revolution and the Napoleonic Wars, and recapitulates the history of the novel in the modern age. An "old-fashioned epistolary novel," *LETTERS* is comprised of the correspondences of seven writers, including three who have appeared in former fictions by Barth, two whose progenitors have appeared in earlier novels, one "new" character who is a composite of several predecessors as well as an incarnation of "the Great Tradition," and "the Author," who is contemplating an old-fashioned epistolary novel and thus corresponds with these six friends and creations. Out of this complex, often disorderly exchange of personal correspondences, Barth creates a novel that contains interrelated "histories" and that mimes, in its integration of historical fact with the events of fictional lives, the larger processes of History. As a realization of a vast network of scattered letters, genealogical strains, and historical coincidences, *LETTERS* is the culmination of Ebenezer Cooke's fabric of contradictories. It is a monstrous palimpsest comprised of letters found, reprinted, and forged, brief notes and protracted histories, family trees, unfinished novels, movie scripts, alphabets, graphs, etymologies, and inscriptions of all kinds. These are structured into a series of competing yet synthesized narrative orders.

Each author of *LETTERS*, including the Author, either creates or is implicated within a narrative pattern where personal history and History converge. Seventy-year-old Todd Andrews, born in 1900 and thus Barth's "man of the century," still corresponds with his dead father about his present life's recycling, wherein the thirteen crucial events of his youth, recorded in *The Floating Opera*, are to be repeated in old age; the two halves of his life thus mirror each other and confirm his "tragic view of history" as pure repetition. Jacob Horner, still on the Remobilization Farm fifteen years after the death of Rennie Morgan, spends his time committing to memory great and minor historical anniversaries while compiling his "Hornbook"—not an alphabet but a list of the world's most famous cuckolds. He is forced by a deranged Joe Morgan, now an administrator at the Farm, to redramatize the events of *The End of the Road* in order to "change the past" and resurrect Rennie—a recycling that ends as tragically as the first installment of Horner's story. A. B. Cook VI presents the letters of his ancestor, A. B. Cook IV, and his own recountings of the Cook-Burlingame history, largely concerned with the "real" events of Napoleon's exile and the travails of the American Indians during the 1789 and 1812 wars. Cook directs his correspondence to his son, Henry Burlingame Cook VII, to warn him of the family curse, a telling summary of the novel's recyclings and reversals: "how each [son] has honor'd his grandsire as a fail'd visionary whilst dishonoring his sire as a successful hypocrite."[9] In the Cook history as related by A. B. Cook VI, the mirrored polarities of passage and failure seen in *Giles Goat-Boy* are doubled by the repetitions of vision and hypocrisy recapitulated in each generation.

Perhaps in a more literal manner, Barth doubles himself in the portrait of Ambrose Mensch. Mensch, an author who constantly despairs of his authority, writes an autobiography which fills in the blanks of the "water-message" he first received from the Choptank River in *Lost in the Funhouse*; at the same time, he formulates a paradigmatic narrative about narrative structures, the "Perseus fiction." In his juggling of parallel "projects," Mensch also writes a script for the avant-garde film director, Reg Prinz, which recapitulates and translates for film the Author's (that is, Barth's) previous fiction—all this while carrying on an obsessively patterned love affair with Lady Germaine Amherst. She, historian, administrator, direct descendant of Mme. de Staël, and mistress to nearly every major literary figure of the modern era, is the novel's richest voice. Germaine metaphorizes herself as the book upon which the literary tradition is inscribed, renewed by the progress of *LETTERS*, as her advancing pregnancy at the novel's end suggests. Jerome Bray's letters recount his madness as he tries to program his gigantic computer, LILYVAC (descendant of *Giles Goat-Boy*'s WESCAC, as Jerome is of that novel's Harold Bray), to create a revolutionary novel that will both reincorporate the history of the novel and instigate a historical revolution. Finally, there is the Author, John Barth's twin, who cajoles and offends each invented author as he searches for the "key to the treasure," the founding pattern that will define and renew the frame of his own fictional project as it evolves from *The Floating Opera* to *LETTERS*.

The effect of our exposure to *LETTERS*' competing authors is defined by the Author at the outset as the historical motive for writing his "own" epistolary novel: "Rereading the early English novelists, I was impressed with their characteristic awareness that they're *writing*—that their fictions exist in the form, not of sounds in the ear, but of signs on the page, imitative not of life 'directly,' but of its documents—and I considered marrying one venerable tradition to another: the frame-tale and the 'documentary' novel" (52–53). Each author of *LETTERS* presents to the reader a collection of documents by which he or she is "framed" within the larger narrative. Each manages self-definition by assembling, often in patchwork fashion, a series of correspondences that are related, in their writing, to the letters of the novel's other writers by means of crossed genealogical lines, the chance joining of mutual political purposes, the coincidental meeting of distant and forgotten ancestors, or the significance to be found in the relation between corresponding anniversaries. Each, finally, realizes an authorial crisis, where the attempt to design the autobiographical self potentially founders on the crossed destinies of history and personality.

As the novel unfolds, letters change hands and seven voices emerge through the cacophonous exchanges of life histories; therein, we see a narrative system being born as the separated elements of conflicting stories betray their symmetries and correspondences, from the alphabetical to the astral. Reading the novel, we are compelled to seek the isomorphic resemblances between, for example, everything referring to the number 7, which is the number of books in *LETTERS*, the number of correspondents in each book, even the number of alphabetical letters in the novel's title. (The total number of letters in the novel's full title—*LETTERS: An Old-Fashioned Epistolary Novel Told by Seven Drolls and Dreamers*—as well as the total number of epistles recorded therein is 88, a suggestive, doubled number, considering the many "keys" that appear in the register of Barth's literary piano.) The number 7 stands as well for the number of stages in the Germaine-Ambrose affair, those in Bray's ultimate project, a collation of all number systems into the computerized *NUMBERS*, and, as he breathtakingly notes, the magic number that grounds a far-flung series of biblical correspondences:

> We remarked upon the reckoning of the climacteric years in the Hebrew calendar . . . also its designation of sabbatical and jubilee years, the 7 days of Levitical purifications and of 2 of the 3 major Jewish feasts, the 7 weeks between the 1st and 2nd of

> the latter, and the 7 years of Nebuchadnezzar's beasthood and of Jacob's service with each of his wives; we were reminded of the Hebrew tradition that the 7th son of a 7th son has a special destiny; that God is called by 7 names and created Creation in 7 days; that Solomon had 700 wives and 7 seals, and his temple 7 pillars; that Balaam would have 7 bullocks and 7 rams sacrificed upon his 7 altars; that Naaman was commanded to dip 7 times into the Jordan; that 7 priests with 7 trumpets marched daily for 7 days around the walls of Jericho, and 7 times on the 7th day; that Pharaoh dreamed of 7 kine and 7 ears of corn; that Samson's wedding feast lasted 7 days, on the 7th of which he told Delilah the secret of his strength, whereupon she bound him with 7 withes and shore him of 7 locks of hair; that Salome danced with 7 veils. (326)

This list is exhausting but hardly exhaustive, for the novel forces a symmetry between orders of 7's—mythological, biblical, historical—which echo the sevenfold interlardings of its structure. The "meaning" of these sevenish symmetries seems to lie exactly in their collation upon the page, down to their striking, repetitious typography, or our gleaning them from their scattered manifestations throughout the novel. They contain no more—and no less—significance as the numbers identified with the rituals of creation, marriage, sacrifice, and purification than do the aleph and beta whose roman equivalents, doubled and mirrored, are framed in a word that describes the year of ritual relaxation—"sabbatical"—which is Barth's next novel after *LETTERS*, and, arguably, his seventh. The effect of these perspicacious biblical correspondences is to generate an intricate narrative that appears to be an infinitely reflexive system of symmetrical orders layered upon one another. Playing what she calls "the Game of Portentous Coincidences, or Arresting but Meaningless Patterns" (384), Germaine lists the correspondences between the myth of Bellerophon (the last tale in the novel preceding *LETTERS*, *Chimera*) and Napoleon's exile (the ship that brought him to England for trial was named *Bellerophon*), the burning of Washington during the War of 1812 (the same British admiral conducts Napoleon to St. Helena and presides over the destruction of the capital), Byron's poetic production in 1815 and 1816 (his *Ode to Napoleon Buonaparte* and *Ode to St. Helena*, inspired by his new friendship with Germaine's ancestress, Mme. de Staël), Marx's *Eighteenth Brumaire* (written in response to Louis-Napoleon's "replay" of his ancestor's career), and her own relation to each of these events as they are recycled, over one hundred and fifty years later, in *LETTERS*. Germaine concludes that these correspondences mean nothing, only "that the world is richer in associations than in meanings, and that it is the part of wisdom to distinguish between the two" (385).

Yet *LETTERS* convinces us that what Germaine perceives as the coincidental intersection of myth, history, autobiography, and Barth's literary career *is* what is meaningful in this fiction, that the perception of the correspondences between Bray's biblical 7's is an act of interpretation pertinent to the writing, narrating self which discovers such significant patterns. Association, in *LETTERS*, is meaning. This is an example of what Fredric Jameson, reading Althusser, defines as "expressive causality": the search for "a vast interpretive allegory in which a sequence of historical events or texts and artifacts is rewritten in terms of some deeper, underlying, and more 'fundamental' hidden master narrative."[10] With its many hidden keys and references to some master plot that underlies the divagations of its eighty-eight letters, *LETTERS* both encourages and, in the end, frustrates this readerly quest for expressive causality. Surveying the presentation of Bray's sevenish correspondences or the historical coincidences that link a "second-rate" mythic hero (as Barth describes Bellerophon in *Chimera*) with a military mastermind, an epistolary genius, and a radical reviser of history, we are inevitably caught in the familiar hermeneutic game that causes us to question whether the revealed patterns are only arrestingly playful or are indicative of something more significant about the narratives we make of ourselves, which seem to be so frequently organized upon base numbers and random repetitions. How these correspondences are achieved and what concerns about the self, narration, and signification they represent comprise the central issues of Barth's novel.[11]

Through an encyclopedic accumulation of metaphors that represent the processes of its own creation and narration, *LETTERS* generates a literary system which, in Northrop Frye's terminology, is an "anatomy": a heterogeneous collation of facts, catalogs, styles, and stories assembled for the purpose of ironically speculating upon narrative discourse.[12] Most of these metaphors for the work of narrative in *LETTERS* have to do with matters of exchange, accumulation, fluidity, and generation, which act as analogies for how stories are produced and reproduced. Among the most pervasive of these are the images of circulation associated with the novel's many waterways—marshes, lakes, bays, rivers—that suggest the flow of narrative in *LETTERS* and the fluid force of its fictive energy. Barth echoes the "Ithaca" chapter in Joyce's *Ulysses* and the "commodious vicus of recirculation" in *Finnegans Wake* by metaphorizing the narrative process as a route of circulation that eternally recycles itself.[13] The novel as a whole, driven by the narrative force that courses through it, may be seen as a vast circulatory drift of letters, alphabetical and epistolary, as the marsh wherein they float, or as the tide in which they are awash. Ambrose Mensch suggests this concept of narrative to "Yours Truly," the addressee of his several letters who is the anonymous sender of the "water-message" he retrieved from the Choptank River as an adolescent. In the prologue to his own narrative within the narrative of *LETTERS*—*The Amateur, or, a Cure for Cancer*—Mensch writes: "A curse upon tides, Yours Truly, that run, and, turning, return like misdirected letters what they were to carry off! Thought well drowned, our past floats back like Danaë with infant Perseus, to take eventual revenge. Would that the Choptank were that trusty sewer the Rhine, flowing always out, past the Loreleis and castles of our history; mercifully fetching off our dreck to some Nordzee dumping-ground of time—whence nothing returns unless recycled, distilled, laundered as Alpine snow" (152–53).

Ambrose's complaint reveals a twofold conception of the circulation of his "letters" to the world. On the one hand, he demonstrates an anxiety regarding the narratives of self and history as a mere return of what has been cast upon the waters. On the other hand, he expresses a desire for a rite of purification (but put in terms of a counterfeit, "laundered" recirculation) where the narrative process is a true recycling, inculcating a renewal of self and history and suggestive of the immortal, infinite narratives Barth so fondly sees represented by such predecessors to *LETTERS* as *The Ocean of Story* and *The Arabian Nights*.[14] Even so, the "purified" or infinite narrative is tainted by its suspicious origins, and its recycling comes about only by means of its passage (or "laundering") through several hands.

The tension Mensch's prologue creates between narrative as repetition and as renewal is present in every aspect of *LETTERS*. In a letter to the Author (and "To Whom It May Concern"), Mensch suggests, in a definition of "dramaturgy," the novel's plot: "the incremental perturbation of an unstable homeostatic system and its catastrophic restoration to a complexified equilibrium" (767). This Aristotelian concept of plot married to the jargon of systems information theory forms an analogy for the "dramaturgy" of the novel's whole and parts, as a more homely comparison by which Barth distinguishes its plot would suggest: "If you think about it you might see there's a kind of metaphor for the plot [of *LETTERS*]—a metaphor of waves crashing ashore on a tidal beach. The plot surges up to a given point, then seems to recede a little, then crashes back upon the beach."[15] Whether the "incremental perturbation" or the surge of tide leads to a Hegelian qualitative change in the cosmos or serves merely to repeat what has come before is the moot point wrought by the novel's circulatory metaphors. The narrative of *LETTERS* is seen as a disturbance, a noise in a system of communication that will eventually return to equilibrium and silence, or an incrementally corrosive tidal surge that questions by this analogy its own epistemology and purpose. Whether through these processes *LETTERS* can somehow "renew" itself or only mirror its own self-conscious, tradition-bound repetitions of past histories and narrative devices, the processes themselves are entropic, leading to waste and silence. This rather fatalistic view concerning the ends of circulatory, communicative, and narrative systems defines Barth's tragic view of fiction, parallel to Todd Andrews' tragic view of life as an endless repetition leading to death. Barth's tragic narratology is alleviated only by the idea that if entropy is at the end of narrative, it is only by the processes which lead to this end that narrative is generated at all.

The tension between the possibility of narrative as repetition or renewal is sounded again in Ambrose's proposal, at mid-life, to change himself by repeating, with variations, the stages of his life's first half and "the story thus far." On a larger historical scale, this pattern is recapitulated by the tendency of each heir in the Cook-Burlingame line to repeat the past, at second remove, by renouncing his father as a fraud and accepting his grandfather as a political martyr. This discovery inspires one member of the line, A. B. Cook IV, to write in a letter to his son about "the double edge of Heraclitus's famous dictum" that he "cannot step into the same stream twice because not only the stream flows, but also the man" (614). Cook's image of the self as ever-changing flux is largely undermined by what happens to each son in the family history: by denying his father, he ends up repeating his father's denial of his grandfather; hence, revolution becomes repetition. The dizzying prospects of this paradox are dramatized most clearly in the tale of the insane kingpin of an Eastern Shore commercial empire, Mack Enterprises. This is Harrison Mack II, who at one stage of his madness imagines himself to be George III driven mad, existing under the insane delusion that he is one Harrison Mack II living in twentieth-century America.

The circular double reversal of Mack's madness is a comic version of Burlingame's tragic family history, where every revision of a previous avatar of the self becomes, simply, a reduplication. And, in *LETTERS*, what applies to conceptions of plot, history, and self also applies to "the American psyche," as Germaine notes in a letter to the Author concerning a ferryboat converted into a restaurant, where she has recently dined: "I remarked upon the American passion for conversion, wondering whether it stemmed from the missionary energies of the early Puritans and later revivalists or the settlers' need, born of poverty and dearth of goods, to find new uses for things worn out or obsolete—a need become mere paradoxical reflex in a people notorious for waste" (232). The comment is made to Ambrose aboard a converted boat, an echo of Barth's own "floating opera"; it glosses Mensch's desire to purify the "dreck" of narrative, converting waste into story; it dwells finally on the "paradoxical reflex" of American society, whose "missionary energies" and pragmatic genius for reinvention are compiled against its enormous wastefulness—a paradox, in its very statement, that "converts" religious zeal into industriousness and repeats, again, the reflections of *LETTERS* as a whole. These examples suggest that in the novel the narrative act is, analogously, a circulation of letters, a system in flux where self-discovery or the interpretation of history takes place. This "system" is, itself, the expression of a desire for the story's continued, unending renewal, as well as an admission that all possible stories spring from a narrative "past" that is "a holding tank from which time's wastes recirculate" (427; Ambrose Mensch to "Yours Truly"). Repetition and rebirth thus exist as the poles of a narrative system that exposes a process in which, magically, we shall see, these two ends meet.

The conception of narrative process as circulation is complicated by another narrative metaphor in the novel, represented by its many bridges and conduits. These links across or routings of water can be seen, analogically, as the "message" of the narrative—the alphabetic, linguistic, or historical connections which, interwoven, form a network of correspondences that "crosses over" the narrative flow of the novel's circulatory systems. In his essay on literary space, Michel Serres discusses the image of the bridge as a metaphor for what is communicated in a narrative system: "The bridge is a path that connects two banks, or that makes a discontinuity continuous, or that crosses a fracture, or that patches a crack. . . . Communication [is] interrupted; the bridge re-establishes it vertiginously."[16] Serres' conception of the communicative bridge applies to Barth's novel to the extent that the literal bridges in *LETTERS*, which are manifestations of "connectedness" or the relations constructed between its scattered letters, are graphs for the continuities that ground the novel's eternally recurrent flux within the crosshatchings of time and history. Welland Canal, saved by counterinsurgency during one of the Burlingame clan's complicated political schemes; the Chesapeake Bay Bridge, saved from destruction by Todd Andrews when he helps abort a bridge-blowing plot hatched by underground revolutionaries; the Peace Bridge; the bridge over the Chappaquiddick to which the Author refers in a discussion of etymological correspondences, the making of fictions, and the overwhelming presence of tragic fact; Niagara Falls, about to be "turned off" by American engineers observing structural damages—all serve as fragile, threatened analogies for the network of communication in *LETTERS* and the crossings that structure its meaning.

In a "P.S." from a letter to the Author recounting his ancestors' attempt to destroy the Welland Canal, A. B. Cook VI digresses on the seemingly insignificant correspondence between the road on which he lives (Chautaugua), the lake by which the Author dwells (Chautauqua), and the bridges or ferries that cross their proximities:

> As to the orthographical proximity of your *Chautauqua* and my *Chautaugua*: the Algonkin language was spoken in its sundry dialects by Indians from Nova Scotia to the Mississippi and as far south as Tennessee and Cape Hatteras, and like all the Indian languages it was very approximately spelled by our forefathers. The word in question is said to mean "bag (or pack) tied in the middle." Chautauqua Lake was so named ob-

> viously from its division into upper and lower moieties at the narrows now traversed by the Bemus Point-Stow Ferry, which I hope it will be your good fortune never to see replaced by a bridge. Chautau*g*ua Road, where this will be typed for immediate posting to you at Chautau*q*ua Lake, is near the similar narrows of Chesapeake Bay (now regrettably spanned at the old ferry-crossing, as you know, and about to be second-spanned, alas), which divides this noble water into an Upper and a Lower Chesapeake. The scale is larger, but the geographical state of affairs is similar enough for the metaphor-loving Algonquins, wouldn't you say? (424)

Literally, the passage is a meandering digression on some suspicious alphabetic correspondences and etymological sources; figuratively, it can be seen as a paradigm for all the connective aspects of *LETTERS* which traverse its inverse recyclings. Cook's etymology is, first of all, about metaphors, the crossings and transferences of language, as well as a topographical, typographical description of "crossings." The simple system of correspondences it creates, between road and lake, Chautau*g*ua and Chautau*q*ua, reveals a structure of similarities and differences—the nearly identical names, the "moieties" or divisions of lake and bay they describe, the resonating consonants of Al*g*on*q*uin—that, for Barth, is the work of narrative and the product of its circulation. A. B. Cook VI's conservatism regarding the bridges of the passage identifies the creaky traditionalism he upholds as "poet laureate" of Maryland in response to the modern, sped-up, excessive "traffic" of communication that characterizes contemporary life. Within the complex system of *LETTERS*, linguistic identities and oppositions bridged over by the correspondences to be found between them weave a fabric of alphabetical and historical relations which cross (organize, give texture to) the novel's wandering, excessive, wasteful flow of letters.[17] As the figure of the "bag tied in the middle" suggests—a figure 8 which, doubled, is the number of letters in the novel's title and, projected into three dimensions, one of Barth's favorite topological paradoxes, the Möbius strip—the narrative discourse of *LETTERS* inscribes the sign of its own double-looped infinity. Yet this discourse is inextricably temporal: it is located within, as *LETTERS'* abundant documentation testifies, an intricate exchange of linguistic and historical relations.

What occurs in the alphabetic example of Cook's supplementary postscript is, once again, echoed throughout every dimension of *LETTERS*. Part of the reader's function is to discover that what may appear to be seven fairly unrelated histories of the novel's letter writers infiltrate each other to the extent that they may share a common ancestral relation (Napoleon Bonaparte) as well as participate, most of them unknowingly, in the mastermind scheme of A. B. Cook VI to initiate the "Second American Revolution."[18] Then, we see that this projected event (which begins as political but ends, if Jerome Bray has his way, as hermeneutical, numbers to replace letters as the bytes of signification) has parallels to the War of 1812, the French and Indian Wars, the first American Revolution, and the history of the Napoleonic Wars. We circle back to alphabetic correspondences when we notice that "the metaphor-loving Algonquins" and their linguistic relatives are implicated in all these conflicts and have family ties to several of the novel's principles. Indeed, to return to the lake and the name which the Algonquins gave it, we can observe Germaine's recounting of an ill-fated cruise around the Chautauqua, taken by the cast and crew of Reg Prinz' film company after shooting a recreated event from the War of 1812. The cruise is captained by Jerome Bray, who insists on airing a travelogue over the ship's loudspeaker:

> And so we steam down past the state fish hatchery towards the narrows where *Chautauqua*—French *voyageur* spelling of an Indian word supposed to mean "bag tied in the middle"—is tied in the middle by an old car-ferry. Regardless of us merrymakers, our captain is delivering the routine tourist spiel on the ship's P.A., with what sounds like embellishments of his own, in a voice that seems itself pieced together by computer in the days when such artifices were still recognisable. The boat, we are informed, is named after his Iroquois father. *All* this was Iroquois country, he declares, and by rights ought still to be, unpolluted by the white man's DDT and marijuana and purple martins and bats (!) . . . The Baratarians whistle and turn up the rock music. Bray escalates his own amplifier to full volume: Our elevation is 2,000 feet above sea level, 700 feet higher than Lake Erie. A raindrop falling into Lake Erie, 8 miles to the northwest of us, will make its way over Niagara Falls, through Lake Ontario, and up the St. Lawrence Seaway

> to the North Atlantic; one falling into Chautauqua Lake will exit via Chadakoin Creek (a variant spelling of the same noble Indian word) into the Conewango, the Allegheny, the Ohio, and the Mississippi, then into the Gulf of Mexico and the Atlantic, itself a great Bag Tied in the Middle by its "narrows" at the latitude of the equator, where South America once fit into Africa . . . (369)

After a series of farcical events, Bray manages to pile the boat up on the rocks, but Germaine's account depicts much more than just the setting of the episode. Here, narrative circulation and crossing come together to suggest the complete and paradoxical system of the novel. There is, first, the drift and noise of narrative, the sound of loud music drowning out Bray's travelogue, and the routing of imagined parallel drops of water making their way into the Atlantic. The circulation of the world's water is of some concern to Germaine's companion, Ambrose, who is ever posting his messages to "Yours Truly" and casting them into proximate bodies of water, as he does on this occasion. But against the meandering drift bearing Ambrose's (and Barth's) narrative, one notes the echoes and connections: the shape of the Atlantic is the shape of Chautauqua Lake writ large; Germaine writes that the routes of the two spurious raindrops "between them traced the boundary of New France, or Upper and Lower Canada, the latter following the route marked in 1749 by Céldron de Blainville, or Bienville, 'discoverer' of Chautauqua Lake, with lead plates bearing the coat of arms of the house of Bourbon, that dynasty deposed by the Revolution in order to make way for the Emperor Bonaparte" (369–70). Thus, "circulation" is bound over to a series of historical relations between the lake on which Germaine cruises, its discoverer, Napoleon, the division of Canada into Chautauqua-like moieties, the 1812 War (repeated for Prinz' film), and the country for whose formation it was largely responsible.

This is surely an instance where everything reflects everything else, from a drop of water to the history of modern Europe, all seen as intersecting tracings or parallel routes. How far does such hyperreflexivity go? Can we make anything of the fact that Bray speaks about his absent father over a device which anagrammatizes a paternal nickname, thereby aligning genealogical relations with the repetitions of geography and history? Should we notice the symbolic numbers, the 7's and 8's of the passage? Clearly, Barth is the manipulator of these echoes and parallels as he comments on the circulatory and connective elements of his own narrative, but his novel also acts as its own interpretation in this regard. It is the assemblage of a massive series of relations that is the "matter" of *LETTERS* as its historical dimension is laid over the energetic currents of its unfolding. That many of these connections are contrived or puckish is a comment more on Barth's understanding of narrative processes than on the flaws of his craft: for him, the "wastes" of narrative coincide with its circulatory purifications; its significances are engendered as a *process* that amasses its own quantities to the point where a significant, qualitative change occurs. The hope of this process for its own recycled infinity is crossed by its desire to signify, its will to make connections and "bridge" the flux in order to see the emerging pattern of similarities and differences. This movement, clearly forced and yet uncannily fortuitous in Barth's novel, implies a further, crucial dimension to be explored: how, out of the confluence of narrative circulation and historical coincidence, the self of the writer of letters, who is the reader of his own scribblings, is born.

The aspect of *LETTERS*' narrative work that reflects Barth's concern with the identity which arises at the intersection of narrative and history is aptly represented by the accumulative and generational concerns of the novel. One of the first and most critical metaphors for the narrative process in *LETTERS* occurs when Bray writes of his scurrilous narrative, *Backwater Ballads*, that it is a cycle of 360 tales "told from the viewpoint of celestial Aedes Sollicitans [a breed of mosquito], a freshmarsh native with total recall of all her earlier hatches, who each year bites 1 visitor in the [Backwater National Wildlife] Refuge and acquires, with her victim's blood, an awareness of his/her history"; she then "infects" Bray with "her narrative accumulations" (29). The implications of this metaphor for narrative production are as elaborate as the situation itself is absurd. The "writing" of *Backwater Ballads* portrays the act of narration as a recollection of past lives reincarnated and as an accumulation, or synthesis, of those scattered historical events associated with the 360 victims randomly bitten by this miraculous insect/muse. The author, in this case, is viewed as the compilation of these past lives, which are stories of stories, paradigms of how stories are told. These "infections" take place in the marshes of Dorchester County, which in *LETTERS*, as in all of Barth's fiction, are scenes of creation. They stand for the primal effluvium or gene pool from which the generation of Barthian heroes and their stories emerge and to which they return. As my analogy suggests, the marsh may be seen, narratively or genetically, as the collection of all stories told thus far, a full 360-degree "cycle" of gathered narratives of a cosmic or personal past, which accumulate to "infect" the author with a new narrative created from stories recombined.

"Narrative accumulation" is an appropriate name for that aspect of the novel's narrative work that assembles all of Barth's former fictions into the framework of *LETTERS*, almost literally arising from the Maryland marsh where fell Bellerophon, last hero of *Chimera*. Bellerophon himself is an accumulated recycling of all mythical narrative paradigms as well as of his own life's story. So the Author of *LETTERS*, describing how he was inspired by "three concentric dreams of waking" to write an epistolary novel, recalls waking in a marsh "half-tranced" at the midpoint of his life. He scratches the bite of an *Aedes sollicitans* and sees a former avatar of his sleeping self wearing a vest with an initial stitched upon it, "bee-beta-beth, the Kabbalist's letter of Creation, whence derived, like life itself, from the marsh primordial, both the alphabet and the universe it described by its recombinations" (47). The Author's scarlet letter is both the initial of Creation—the alphabetic origin of the universe as it is reflected in the myriad combinations of written language—and the mark of "Barth," the infected, Maryland-born author who is the accumulation of these past stories. The "primordial marsh" is later defined as "associated with both decay and fertility," as "sacred to Toth, inventor of writing" (48); thus, it is the imagined, dreamed source of creation, the narrator's writing self, and the narrative which tells the story of creation and self. Taken together, the scenes of creation in Bray's *Backwater Ballads* and the Author's concentric dreams of waking suggest that "narrative accumulation," as a designation for narrative processes in *LETTERS*, is circular yet historical and archaeological. The act of narration described therein always speaks of its unknown source, and returns to it, while standing as an accumulation in time where the various layers of the history of its telling are piled on each other, like geological strata. The marsh in which the Author is "infected" is the image, too, of the inspired accumulations of a given narrative consciousness. It is as if the authors were born, with stories in hand, witnessing this miracle sprung from what each already is—a collection of inherited sensibilities, ancestral habits, and regenerated memories assembled in the present historical moment. In many respects, every author of *LETTERS* enacts a similar discovery about the act of writing and narrating as they tell the tales of their own self-creations within the novel's larger, evolving universe.

Creation and self-creation, certainly implied by these conceptions of circulatory, connective, and accumulative narrative processes, are ultimately represented by the novel's overwhelming assemblage of paternal and generational metaphors. During the half year in which the letters of the novel are dated and posted (March 3 to September 26, 1969), its "heroine," Germaine Amherst, is impregnated either by Ambrose Mensch, André Castine/A. B. Cook VI, or Jerome Bray. It is clear that the "who" of the child's father (a crucial identification to be made in "generational" novels from *Tom Jones* to *One Hundred Years of Solitude*) is less important than the fact that a child has been begotten. Much of *LETTERS* is given over to birth pangs, literal and literary, ranging from Ambrose's anxieties about his ability to inseminate Germaine to his analogous concern about his capacity to write a new novel: "last-ditch provincial Modernist wishes neither to repeat nor to repudiate career thus far; wants the century under his belt but not on his back. *Complication*: he becomes infatuated with, enamored of, obsessed by a fancied embodiment (among her other, more human, qualities and characteristics) of the Great Tradition and puts her—and himself—through sundry more or less degrading trials, which she suffers with imperfect love and patience, she being a far from passive lady, until he loses his cynicism and his heart to her spirited dignity and, at the *climax*, endeavors desperately, hopefully, perhaps vainly to get her one final time with child: his, hers, theirs. (cc: Author)" (767). For Ambrose, a "carbon copy" of the Author, the creational anxiety is both biological and literary, the latter concern expressed as a fear that the burden of the past will render the struggling author impotent, along with the hope that carnal and bookish knowledge of "the Great Tradition" will lead to production and renewal.

Authorial insemination, in this sense, can be placed opposite the "infection" of an author by the accumulations of narrative portrayed in Bray's ballads; together, these metaphors of narrative activity suggest that the "father" of the story is the intersection of past and future, both a repository of old narratives and a genetic producer of new ones. They also underscore the self-conscious anxiety of Barth's novel concerning its own begetting, from its beginnings in the swamp to its final hope, reflected in Mensch's statement, for "offspring." In a performance that must be viewed as a vulgar parody of the fallacy of imitative form and epistolary hastiness, Germaine writes (near the novel's beginning) a postscript in a letter to the Author while indulging in sodomy with Ambrose atop her writing desk: her message re-cites the beginnings of great modern novels, including *Magister Ludi*, *Finnegans Wake*, and *Brave New World*, authored by men who might well be Germaine's past lovers and critical inheritors of "the tradition." The problematic nature of literary beginnings, reflected by the inverse sexuality of this scene, is compounded by the simultaneous writing of the supplementary postscript, which contains only repetitions of past beginnings.

As with the other narrative metaphors of the novel, those of sexuality and human beginnings suggest Barth's self-conscious concern with begetting a new work, *in medias res*, weighted down by tradition, echoing only what has come before. Edward Said has noted that this anxiety is common for modern texts which have, as do all texts, a "beginning intention";[19] but the modern text, whose beginning contemplates even the plausibility of beginning anew, questions the possibility of its own "beginning intention." Modernity in this sense is an attitude rather than a matter of chronology; it is a self-conscious fear of beginning, as well as a hope that one can begin, and though this problem is seen increasingly in the reflexive texts of twentieth-century literature, it can be seen equally in *Don Quixote* and *Tristram Shandy*. But additionally, *LETTERS* necessarily bears the weight of its predecessors' beginning anxieties. Here, abortion and miscarriage occur as frequently as the delivery of children; the narrative questions its own novelistic, genetic status as an authentic work, a new production, or a stillborn child of the tradition.

This suggests that *LETTERS* parallels two activities in its generational metaphors as the production of human selves is equated with the production of literary texts.[20] As I have been inferring up to this point, these are the twin subjects the novel puts into question by problematizing the conception of texts and selves as part of a paternal or hierarchical tradition. As letters go astray or appear, ghostwritten by fathers already dead, received by sons already orphaned, so too heirs revolt against their benefactors and daughters commit incest with their fathers, thus undermining accepted notions of communication, family, and community. Said, again, notes that this movement is characteristic of modern texts; it is doubly so of *LETTERS*, which questions, while enacting, its own "modernity": "one of the chief characteristics that [modern writers] share in common has been a necessity *at the beginning* for them to see their work making reference, first, to other works, but also to reality and to the reader, by adjacency, not sequentially or dynastically. The true relationship is by adjacency, while the dynastic relationship is almost always the one treated ironically, the one scoffed at, toyed with, or rejected. Therefore, the production of meaning within a work has had to proceed in entirely different ways from before, if only because the text itself stands to the side of, next to, or between the bulk of other works—not in a line with them, nor in a line of descent from them."[21]

Thus, working against the traditional "births" of *LETTERS* are such relations as those recorded by A. B. Cook IV, writing to his "unborn child" of a painful case in eighteenth-century America. Cook, a revolutionary, tells the story of Elizabeth Whitman, who had died in childbirth and whose stillborn infant may be, without certainty, the child of Cook's father, Henry Burlingame IV. Cook relates the fate of Betsy Whitman's last letter, found in her deathbed, addressed only to "B": "Inspired by that fateful letter (and by the success in America of Richardson's *Pamela* and *Clarissa*), a relative of Betsy Whitman's named Hannah Foster turn'd her story into a romance on the wages of sin called *The Coquette* (1797): the 1st American epistolary novel. Inspired by that later epistle from Bell Tavern, your father stay'd in Paris to join in the Terror & to applaud the guillotining of the whole paternal class" (144). In this series of incidents, life and death lead to art, but what is made is a text fostered by a birth that is illegitimate and unproductive (though the inspiring letter bears as its address the initial of Creation), announced within the context of the French Revolution and the death of "the whole paternal class." There is a rejection in this incident, as in the whole of *LETTERS*, of textual "generation" and tradition, as well as a suggestion that stories are born out of chance, adjacency, or collusion between historical events, as Hannah Foster, vaguely a relative of Betsy Whitman's, succeeds in undynastically transmitting her story or "herstory." *LETTERS* manages these antidynastic relations in such a way as to question its own textual strategies as a system of exchanged letters that can produce new meaning or merely repeat the past. The story of Betsy Whitman—in name, at least, ancestress of *the* American celebrant of self-creation—implies that the hope for the production of narrative can come about only through disruption and discontinuity, as the earlier metaphors of circulation suggested it can come about only as waste or noise.

Perhaps the issue of the novel's self-questioned success in bringing about its own creation arises most emphatically in the collective history of the Cook-Burlingame line, which parallels the misalliances of an entire family with the making of texts. For the reader of *LETTERS*, this parallel is effected in a significant way, since this eccentric family views the "text" as history and the "self" as its interpretation. This alignment reflects and repeats our own readerly activities as we work through the novel's circular, accumulative, disruptive narrative to acquire its meaning, which may be a pattern of correspondences or an emergent system of signs, rather than an articulated theme. The Burlingame-Cook history is conveyed through a series of letters from fathers to progeny (many to sons unborn, from fathers thought dead) in which each patriarch encourages his offspring to revolt from the family pattern, the design of conspiracy that has cursed the line from its beginnings. In each generation of Cooks and Burlingames (interrelated by marriage in a parodically elaborate kinship system to themselves and their Canadian cousins, the Castines), fathers have committed themselves to revolutionary or reactionary causes that their sons reject, taking their place in the family line as counterrevolutionaries or counterreactionaries. The rebellion of each son is complicated by his doubt that, in a long succession of forgers, triple agents, and imposters, his father is who he claims to be. In looking for his "true" father, each son searches through the past for the authentic origin and author of the questioning, history-writing self. But in every case the past is cancelled out as sons reject their fathers and start over again, becoming the self-fathered conspirators who cause *their* sons to reject them. Thus every other generation in the line repeats itself in history, even to the extent that grandfathers and grandsons bear the same surname. This self-cancellation is despairingly complained of by A. B. Cook IV in a letter to his unborn child, dated May 14, 1812: "We have misspent, misspent our powers,

Cookes & Burlingames cancelling each other out. May we live, Andrée & I, to be the 1st of our line to cancel out *ourselves*, to the end that you (guided by these letters, which must be your scripture if aught should take us from you) may be the 1st to be spared the necessity" (323). The irony of Cook's plea is evidenced in the idea that self-cancellation can lead to new generation. These letters from father to son are themselves sent and "cancelled" as each antinomian son, reading them, searches for the coded message that would identify the author as his authentic father and rejects them as the forged markings of a counterfeiter.

The star-crossed history of this tragic family affects the possibility of individual sons becoming the erased hieroglyphs of a recurring history.[22] In one episode, A. B. Cook IV records his mistress' response to his imposture of Napoleon, escaped from Elba: "*she fear'd I was become the counterfeit, not of Napoleon, but of Andrew Cook. And that the cypher whose key I had yet to hit upon, was my own self*" (634). The possibility of the self as cipher, or key, is literally realized in A. B. Cook VI's account of his grandfather's (A. B. Cook V) anarchist attempt to blow up the twenty-five locks of the Welland Canal, and his father's (H. C. Burlingame VI) treachery in foiling the plot. A charge of dynamite is to be placed at each lock, the latter keyed to its own letter of the alphabet which, when telegraphed in Morse code, will set off the charge. One letter of the alphabet's twenty-six, "S," is reserved for a common signal that will detonate the charges simultaneously in an emergency: "the one hallowed by Marconi seventeen years before and by James Joyce as the first in a scandalous novel he'd just begun serializing in *The Little Review*" (418). As three truckloads of twenty-five conspirators, each with his own charge and radio receiver, rush to the canal, the "S" is telegraphed, killing all of them, including A. B. Cook V and his uncle, Gadfly Junior, but sparing H. C. Burlingame VI, who is stationed at the master transmitter some distance away. A. B. Cook VI, who suspects that his father transmitted the master code to kill *his* father or his Great-uncle Gadfly, an innocent amongst the duplicitous Cooks and Burlingames, reflects upon the resulting explosions and their pattern of dispersal:

> Alone or between them, my father and grandfather monogrammed the Niagara Frontier visually with the apocalyptic

> Morse-code S: an aerial photograph would have shown the two larger craters and the central smaller one as three dots, or suspension points . . . And acoustically they shook the heavens with the initial . . . the big *G*, not for God almighty (with whom no Cook or Burlingame, whatever his other illusions, has ever troubled his head), but for the man who was to my father what Tecumseh and Pontiac were to my remote ancestors: well-named Tuscarora, boom boom bang, Great-uncle Gadfly! (421–22)

The landscape and accidents of history combine in this unlikely incident to create a system of signs which encodes the initials of reaction and betrayal, communicating the family curse by which Cooks and Burlingames have always identified their roles in history. The accident metaphorically portrays a scene of misdirected communication, where the "keys" or ciphers of alphabetic letters are meant to "unlock" history and enable the presence of a historical, revolutionary self (A. B. Cook V). Instead, event and landscape conspire to represent, visually, one initial which we are told is that of a scandalous literary beginning as well as the first letter of telegraphic communication—but it is also the sign of the conspirators' annihilation. Acoustically, the scene gives rise to another letter that anagrammatizes the repeated betrayals of the past, Gadfly becoming the avatar of those Indian leaders, Tecumseh and Pontiac, whom Cooks and Burlingames have purposefully or unwittingly destroyed by means of their complicated, double-reversed conspiracies. The historical events associated with the conspiracy, and their results, become the inscriptions of these selves into the larger movements of a History that continually, repetitiously writes its name across the landscape as a form of self-representation.

Through these cabals of sight and sound, *LETTERS*' history, like its narrative processes, turns revolution to repetition. The "self" that emerges from scenes like the Welland Canal incident is viewed not as a wholly original, self-created entity but as, in Antonio Gramsci's phrase, "the synthesis not only of existing relations, but of the history of these relations."[23] Self as key, as cipher, as the repeated embodiment of the past in the Cook-Burlingame history, suggests a semiotic conception of the self as sign or as the mark of its relation to the past and present world. For A. B. Cook VI, this conception is uncomfortably deterministic; for every writer of *LETTERS*, the self is born of an assemblage of letters which inscribes the interpretation of its history. Hence, the literary problem of the novel is paralleled to the personal one: is it possible to give birth to an original work out of "the Great Tradition"? Is the "self," like an unoriginal text, merely a product of generic and historical repetitions? Knowing that texts and selves, in the novel's definitions, exist as the intersections of literary or social relations, what, if anything, signifies their revolutionary aspects—or are they wholly determined?

In a different context, Ambrose Mensch writes that "History is a code which, laboriously and at ruinous cost, deciphers into *HISTORY*. She is a scattered sibyl whose oak-leaf oracles we toil to recollect, only to spell out something less than nothing, *e.g.*, *WHOL TRUTH*, or *ULTIMATE MEANIN*" (332). That is, in a universe where "the world is richer in associations than in meanings," it is the inscription of these associations or relations themselves that gives rise to selves and texts. "History" only, repeatedly, spells out its own initials. Our interpretations of history—our gatherings of its scattered leaves into the Book of Life—yield the incomplete meanings that are the anagrams of our reading and history-writing selves. The significance that is born of such a textual, historical world comes about through the relations *between* its events and letters, which may be as accidental as they are necessary. We shall see a similar conception of the self as a relation to history and the constructions of culture in *Gravity's Rainbow* and *The Franchiser* in different—archaeological and linguistic—contexts. What Ambrose suggests in his oracular statement here is that "meaning" is not intrinsic but alphabetical, relational; interpretation a gap filling or supplement; self and text a partially accidental, partially determined gathering of similarities and differences.

The self defined in *LETTERS*, whether it is a Cook or a Mensch or a Bray, becomes a reader who scans the text of history for the ghostly ciphers that contextualize, repeat, and resonate with the inscribed lineaments of that self's own being. Each writer becomes a sign in a system that is the narration of a being in history, which is, precisely, the collection of documents and narratives that record the genealogy of the self. The heroic function in the novel becomes, for its letter writers as well as its readers, the establishment of signifying chains that connect documents and narratives which constitute the patterns of selfhood; these weave with other patterns to create a world that is both intertextual and intersubjective. As a writer in the process of authoring a fictional autobiography while contemplating the theoretical complexities of a self-reflexive fiction, Ambrose Mensch is most conscious of the parallels to be made between textual production, interpretation, and self-discovery. In *A Cure for Cancer*, his partially completed autobiography, Mensch recalls the infant Ambrose, reposing in a porch swing: "For a time, though centered in a baby lying on the front-porch glider, A. was also what he compassed. How describe this. If for instance I declare that through a breathless August forenoon a cottonwood poplar whispered from the dooryard, dandled its leaves on squozen petioles when not a maple stirred, you'll see past that syntax? Tree and baby were not then two unless in the manner of mouth and ear: he in the poplar addressed to him in the glider not truths but signs. Coded reassurances. Recognitions" (163–64). What Mensch describes is, in some sense, preconscious and prerelational. The child and the tree speak in signs, are signs, but of their total mutual identification rather than their differences. Later, when A. comes to recognize his name as his own, Mensch writes of this distinction as the hero's painful emergence into the world of language and consciousness: "Thus was altered Ambrose's initial view of things, and thus he came to call by the name Ambrose not his brother, his mother, or his nanny-goat, nor yet (in time) his foot, his voice, or his port-wine mark: only his self, which was held to be none of these, indeed to be nothing Ambrose's, but solely Ambrose. [Paragraph break in text.] What the infant learns in tears, adult suffering must unteach. Did it hurt you, reader, to be born? Dying will be no picnic either" (165). Bearing his name, the autobiographical self is immersed in a series of linguistic relationships that resonate with the sound of difference, a world of signs that indicates what the self is by what is not the self, framed by the context of birth and death.

Still later, eleven-year-old Ambrose discovers the crucial message in the bottle with a "head and tail," salutation and compliment, but no body, a blank letter he spends his life filling in. Mensch writes of this incident:

> *Lying in the seaweed where the tide has left it: a bottle with a note inside. "Past the river and the Bay, from continents beyond . . . borne by currents as yet uncharted, nosed by fishes as yet unnamed*

> *. . . the word had wandered willy-nilly to his threshhold." By all the gods, Germaine: I still believe that* here *is where Ambrose M. drops out of life's game and begins his career as Professional Amateur, one who lives but does not know: with the bursting, by brickbat, of that bottle; with the receipt of that damning, damnèd blank message, which confirms both his dearest hope—that there are Signs—and his deepest fear—they are not for him. Cruel Yours Truly, falsely mine! Take* that, *and* this, *and* the next, *and never reach the end, you who cut me off from my beginnings.* (167–68)

In this passage, the "self" of Mensch's autobiography enters fully into the world of textual signs and relations. After he receives the wandering, blank text, Ambrose's lifework becomes an act of self-interpretation, where the world is organized as a matrix of responsive echoes and irrelevant noises, repetitions and divagations, out of which the reading and writing self is born. For Ambrose, the authored self is indeed the history of its relations and its relation to history, conceived as a fall into time and language, the latter made of the alphabetic signs that mark these relations. This process, as Roland Barthes suggests and as the endless straying of Ambrose's named self from its alienated beginnings indicates, is "the labor of language": "to find meanings [which] is to name them; but these named meanings are swept toward other names; names call to each other, reassemble, and their grouping calls for further naming: I name, I unname, I rename: so the text passes: it is a nomination in the course of becoming, a tireless approximation, a metonymic labor."[24] Here, too, the narrative metaphors discussed earlier can be brought to bear on the notion of the self as text: the self is both the interceptor of the straying, circulating letters of narrative and history and their supplement; it is the point of intersection of linguistic and historical relations; it is the accumulation of these relations, as well as their manifestation. Thus, the self repeats its own genealogy, while enacting through the responsorial process of self-interpretation its alienation from the primal world of its beginnings and its orphanage from the authorized text of the father.

Mensch engages in what Mikhail Bakhtin refers to as a "process of introspection," where "we engage our experience into a context made up of other signs we understand"; yet this process also reveals the alterity of language and the irrelevancy or "noise" of much that the autobiographical hero examines.[25] The polarity of relations that gives rise to narratives, as well as condemning them to their own repetitive, textual nature, forms the system within which, for Barth, the self in language and history is born, lives, and dies. To address the questions raised early about originality and repetition, textual or human, Mensch's autobiography reveals that selves, and texts, are both the same as yet different from what came before them. They emerge from a literary or historical matrix which is itself an interpretive language woven of similarities and differences. They exist as the production of the historical or textual tradition that bears them, so they bear the weight of the past and, to some extent, repeat it. Still, selves and texts are born into time, which dictates the erosion of traditions and the elements within them. Human selves age and die; texts, in an "age of mechanical reproduction," may be infinitely copied but, to use a metaphor from the theory of communications, their fall into time is represented by the "jamming" or noise generated by the accumulated interpretations and annotations that accommodate their significance to passing generations. This, clearly, is Barth's version of entropy, stated as a form of erosion and exhaustion that leads to renewal since texts and selves do not *merely* repeat the past by means of their entropic change over time. Put another way, Mensch's process of introspection suggests that the world is made of signs and that individual selves or texts are unique recombinations of these. Yet, as writing is condemned to the combinations of twenty-six letters, so selves are condemned to a limited "pool" of historical and genealogical codes. As a narrative system that embodies these possibilities, LETTERS is both a repetition and a renewal. Indeed, if we follow the logic of Barth's narrative, it is only through the intersection of sameness and difference, thus through repetition, that stories and selves are born. Similarly, this birth into time, language, and history is a falling out of perfect similitude—the difference by which we are known.

As an ill-fated revolt of the romantic or originary self against the social, written conception of the self in LETTERS, many of its writers try to break out of the historical, linguistic systems in which they define themselves. In one sense, the failure of these rebellions indicates Barth's rejection of a self that could exist outside of or before the history of its own narrative. But in another sense, the antisystematic impulses of the novel are as essential as its overwhelming presentation of "relationality." *LETTERS* suggests that it is through a resistance to the repetitions of the past, or by the creation of "noise" within a system of communication, that self and narrative reorganize themselves. Because of "noise" or "drift," new networks of correspondence are generated in order to join together fragments and irrelevancies, stray frequencies or newly found letters that must be contexted.[26] It is from this relation between a system and its antinomies that all the oppositional relations of *LETTERS*—father/son, conformity/revolution, repetition/renewal—derive and from which the narrative gains its struggling life. Thus, *LETTERS* contains its loose ends, broken genealogical lines, and historical irrelevancies, as well as several protagonists who attempt to transcend the patterns of their experience by de-signing themselves.

The most obsessed pattern maker in *LETTERS* is the self-conscious Ambrose Mensch, who sees his marriage to Germaine Amherst as the sixth and final stage of his affair in progress which has, in its first five stages, recapitulated the five stages of his sexual maturation and his five former love affairs. He expresses this hope in marrying Germaine on the sixth day of the sixth week of the sixth stage of their affair: "If we're to have Series Six, let it be the stage of our day's sixth sex together, that initial legal lovemaking, and *its* 6th point of our first connubial climax. Betcha we can, Milady—and be *damned* if I can think of any fitter way to peak, vindicate, purge, and be done with this obsession for reenactment" (764). So, Ambrose and Germaine enter a new, seventh stage of marriage which both incorporates and surpasses "the story thus far." Their marriage can be seen as the classic resolution of fiction—to use Ambrose's definition of "dramaturgy"—as the equilibrium that validates and finalizes the "system" of life and narrative. Similarly, we last see Todd Andrews about to commit suicide by leaping from a university tower as he attempts to transcend what he sees as the reenactment of his life's first half by its second; he chooses that other classic solution, the equalizing act of death. However, these revolts against the system's metonymies either extend or repeat it. Ambrose and Germaine's seventh stage is another in the chain defined by the previous six. They are, literally, at sixes and sevens with the cycles of their lives, as is H. B. Burlingame VII, the last of the line, when he mentally cancels out his father, the sixth A. B. Cook.

The reader of *LETTERS*, who observes six characters in search of a "father" (an author or history), who in turn becomes the seventh, is placed equally at odds with the novel's unclosed, unfounded "system." Todd Andrews' fatal jump, if taken, will simply repeat the attempted suicide of *The Floating Opera*, just as his affair with Bea Golden in *LETTERS* (who is quite possibly his daughter) recapitulates his earlier fictional affair with Jane Mack, her mother. If his attempt succeeds, he will be inscribed into the text of history and transformed into the response to that question with endless answers, "Why?" If he fails, he will simply repeat the failed suicide of his youth. In any case, we never know from the novel if Andrews takes the leap; we are left only with his will, one more remnant of the self that must be interpreted and inscribed into the pattern of history.[27] Beyond language, history, and system, Barth suggests, are silence and self-cancellation; what lies beyond culture, no matter how imprisoning its systems and discourses may be, is self-annihilation, a fact attested to by the deaths of several writers in *LETTERS* who attempt to escape narrative and history. In this sense, the work of language and history, like the formation of the self, is an unending, metonymical process, as Barthes earlier suggested of the reading of texts. And as such a historical, textual world is bereft of its beginnings, so it is robbed of its ends. Death is not, as A. B. Cook VI proclaims in some lines from his verse, "the key / Of keys, the cure of cures" (671), any more than it is a satisfying "cure for cancer" in Mensch's autobiography. Rather, it is an event, like any other, subject to interpretation and redefinition—a conception to which the inconclusive events surrounding Andrews' and Cook's deaths in the novel bear witness.

Appropriately, *LETTERS* ends with a letter from the Author to the reader, written from Chautauqua Lake, in which he compares the several stages of revision and production that *LETTERS* has undergone to the clearing of grounds and the restoration of an old house: "testing the wiring and plumbing, hanging doors and windows and pictures, waxing floors, polishing mirrors and windowpanes—and glancing from time to time, even gazing, from an upper storey, down the road, where he [the Author] makes out in the hazy distance what appear to be familiar loblolly pines, a certain point of dry ground between two creeklets, a steaming tidewater noon, someone waking half-tranced, knowing where he is but not at first who, or why he's there. He yawns and shivers, blinks and looks about. He reaches to check and wind his pocketwatch" (771). The metaphor, moving between the familiar Edenic marsh of creation in the Maryland tidelands to the resurrected house of fiction in upstate New York, suggests that the discovery and inscription of the self find their culmination in the reconnections, conduits, mirrorings, and transferences of language. This self in language is part invention, part repetition, ever given over to the erosion and downwindings of history, but always renovated by its placement in a chronic system of relations. Barth's final metaphor in *LETTERS* moves backward from nature to culture, from rebirth to reconstruction, from nonawareness to self-conscious renewal, and from slumberous silence to the noise of production. This is the direction in which language, hedged by time and circumstance, always carries us and to which our "being" corresponds.

Ultimately, if it is to be seen as successful, *LETTERS* realizes Ambrose's expressed hope to the Author that he transform the notes of Mensch's self-conscious "Perseus fiction" into a living story:

> Enclosed is my ground plan for that Perseus-Medusa story I told you of, together with more notes on golden ratio, Fibonacci series, and logarithmic spirals than any sane writer will be interested in. My compliments. All that remains is for you to work out a metaphorical physics to turn stones into stars, as heat + pressure + time turn dead leaves into diamonds. I have in mind Medusa's petrifying gaze, reflected and re-reflected at the climax, not from Athena's mirror-shield, but from her lover Perseus's eye: the transcension of paralyzing self-consciousness to productive self-awareness. And (it goes without saying) I have in mind too the transformation of dead notes into living fiction—for it also remains for you to write the story! (652)

The transformation takes place as the author of *LETTERS* puts before us a voluminous array of scattered but interrelated notes and letters. Forced by this novel to watch ourselves read, and under pressure to transform the dead leaves of the text into a constellated textual system, we help make the connections. By doing so, we participate in the enactment of "textuality," as Homer Obed Brown defines it in a discussion of Richardson's epistolary novels, an emerging "sense of the encroaching circumstantiality of texts, their occasions, what was lost and what was gained in their becoming texts—their costly struggle to come into being, their dependence on others, and on several different orders of signifying chains, their recognitions of anteriority and exteriority, and also what is created *by* texts."[28] In LETTERS, these senses of the text are integrated with an understanding of history and the evolution of the self. Text, self, and history are then represented as a series of distended, cacophonous relations whose limits, as acts of interpretation, are written down. In this way, LETTERS imagines its own end while, paradoxically, projecting its own endlessness; it searches for its origin while stating as the condition of its existence its utter nonoriginality. What it loses by coming into being—innocence, perfection, silence, order—is replaced by its noisy, disorderly gains and its disruptive continuance. Barth's novel is, finally, a reconstructive narrative that offers side by side the hope of its beginning as well as the dread that narrative, and life, might be overwhelmed by the accumulations of a catastrophic past and of a tradition great with its own eminence.[29]

CHAPTER FOUR "A BOOK OF TRACES" *GRAVITY'S RAINBOW*

Trusswork is pierced by daylight, milky panes beam beneficently down. How could there be a winter—even this one—gray enough to age this iron that can sing in the wind, or cloud these windows that open into another season, however falsely preserved.

Thomas Pynchon, *Gravity's Rainbow*

I was the shadow of the waxwing slain
By the false azure of the windowpane;
I was the smudge of ashen fluff—and I
Lived on, flew on, in that reflected sky.

John Shade, "Pale Fire"

The nostalgic, false hope for an eternal life realized in the reflective language of John Shade's poem is radically revised in Thomas Pynchon's *Gravity's Rainbow*. While both Shade and Kinbote portray the desire of the self to "live on" in the mirrored sky of reflexive language, Pynchon creates a text, replete with descriptions like that of the rooftop hothouse cited above, that embodies the halfhearted hope for a fragile architecture which may survive to "sing" its tenuousness through the entropic, mutable growth it contains, rather than the world it shadows. Like the reconstructed house of Barth's *LETTERS*, the hothouse of *Gravity's Rainbow*, kept in London during World War II by a British officer obsessed with growing bananas, is a metaphor for textual construction. But while Barth's house is authorial, Pynchon's hothouse is cultural: the soil it humidifies is composed of the layered debris it contains—the "tracings" of our archaic existence.

Pirate Prentice's hothouse sits atop a "maisonette" originally built by

> Corydon Throsp, an acquaintance of the Rosettis' who wore hair smocks and liked to cultivate pharmaceutical plants up on the roof . . . a few of them hardy enough to survive fogs and frosts, but most returning, as fragments of particular alkaloids, to rooftop earth, along with manure from a trio of prize Wessex Saddleback sows quartered there by Throsp's successor, and dead leaves off many decorative trees transplanted to the roof by later tenants, and the odd unstomachable meal thrown or vomited there by this or that sensitive epicurean—all got scumbed together, eventually, by the knives of the seasons, to an impasto, feet thick, of unbelievable black topsoil in which anything could grow, not the least being bananas.[1]

The hothouse, "however falsely," conserves a cultural history of the inhabitants who have lived there, while it looks out upon the potential destruction of civilization caused by incoming V-2 rockets. In its precarious, transformative state, Prentice's "garden" is a redaction of the earlier hothouse of Pynchon's *V.*, which is viewed by the novel's historian, Fausto Maijstral, as a repository of the past: "Why use the room as introduction to an apologia? Because the room, though windowless and cold at night, is a hothouse. Because the room is the past, though it has no history of its own. Because . . . there must be a room sealed against the present, before we can make any attempt to deal with the past.[2] The second-born hothouse of *Gravity's Rainbow*, now warm and windowed, is an entrance to rather than an escape from the present. In reflecting a different epistemology for the cultural text of Pynchon's epic novel, this "hothouse" of narrative encloses the domestic waste that represents the supplementary text of a civilization known by its leavings.

As our contemporary "historical and cultural synthesis of Western actions and fantasies,"[3] *Gravity's Rainbow* presents an interpretation of culture in terms of what anthropologist Clifford Geertz calls "thick description." For Geertz, "thick description" is a way of talking about human existence that eschews representation by means of "symmetrical crystals of significance, purified of the material complexity in which they were located, and then [attributing] their existence to the autogenous principles of order, universal properties of the human mind, or a vast, a priori *weltanschauungen*." Rather, he suggests that culture is more accurately viewed as a palimpsest whose stratified, diffuse scribblings and erasures reveal the conflicting, half-conscious patterns of a civilization that works at cross-purposes to itself. Prevailing against the discovery of "the Continent of meaning and [the] mapping out [of] its bodiless landscape," "thick description" aptly describes the "archaeology" of *Gravity's Rainbow*.[4] For, in distinction from Nabokov and Hawkes, whose protagonists are primarily engaged in linguistic self-reconstructions, and from Barth, whose letter writers create an intertextual weave of documents that projects an intersubjective "history," Pynchon cultivates a linguistic landscape where the inscriptions of self and history are subsumed within the productions of a culture that reveals its narrative operations through myth, fantasy, and repression.[5] He achieves this, precisely, within the hothouse of a text that manifests the designs of Western, Faustian civilization by conserving the fragments it leaves behind. As Geertz's anthropology suggests, Pynchon's map of "material complexity" in *Gravity's Rainbow* quite literally traces out an interpretation of the self in culture that converts "being" into an archaeological sign and identity into the remnant of human action and desire.

If, as Tony Tanner notes of his early fiction, Pynchon's work is about "the whole human instinct and need to make tracks," then *Gravity's Rainbow* can be seen as a Book of Tracks, an encyclopedic account of the linguistic, informational, biological, thermodynamic, ballistic, historical, cinematic, and political discourses in which we find ourselves.[6] The postwar European landscape of the novel is populated by questers and mystics, Pavlovians and Hereros in exile, movie directors and rocket scientists, all implicated in the bureaucratic tangles, hothouse fantasies, and accidents of history that have conspired to bring them together and set them against each other. Existing without a conventional protagonist, only hundreds of seekers and trails that randomly meet and intersect, *Gravity's Rainbow* acts as a linguistic stenciling of interweaving discursive systems. A comparison with that other great accountant of plots and bureaucracies, Charles Dickens, shows Pynchon's more paranoid concern with "plot" as both the substance and the structure of his fictional world. For Dickens, in *Bleak House*, the entanglements of a many-stranded plot are woven together only to be disentangled as the solution to the novel's mystery is revealed and as the connection between all its disparate events, characters, and social classes is discovered by the questing reader. Dickens complexifies only, ultimately, to simplify. The telos of his novel is to make the crooked straight; in some sense, his fictive project is to reform the labyrinthine culture he describes by finding the simple truth, or the primary source of guilt and confusion, that lies behind all the seemingly disconnected manifestations of "plot."

In contrast, Pynchon's novel announces itself as "not a disentanglement from but a progressive *knotting into*" (3). It maintains an assemblage of material and imaginative debris which does not offer some single source of power or explanation for its fragmented state, not even the overwhelming force of gravity or the omnipresent War that some of its seekers incorrectly define as the culprits behind the plot. Instead, the novel's "knotting into" reflects Pynchon's vision of culture as an ungrounded, unending process of fragmentation and sedimentation that enacts a "molecular hermeneutics" wherein the labyrinthine quests for prime causes and elemental designs are doomed to repetition. As the description of Prentice's hothouse suggests, even the earth of *Gravity's Rainbow* is seen as an epistemic repository, "the cumulative deposit of all the material waste of ages past, buried stratigraphically, layer upon increasingly dense archaic layer."[7] The physical world here is constituted as a complex, asystematic process of exchange and transformation where the earth's wastes are changed into the machines of war and the plasticine luxuries of the middle class, only to return to waste again, broken down and stratified by the earth's gravitational pull. Everything in the novel, from rockets to the earth, is testimony to this unwieldy "plot" and its traces as it reflects how a cultural world is formed and "read" by its inhabitants.[8]

The twisted trail that connects the seemingly dispersed cultural debris or separated states of being in *Gravity's Rainbow* is exemplified by descriptions like the following, where domestic waste becomes military hardware:

> In the pipefitters' sheds, icicled, rattling when the gales are in the Straits, here's thousands of old used toothpaste tubes, heaped often to the ceiling; thousands of somber man-mornings made tolerable, transformed to mint fumes and bleak song that left white spots across the quicksilver mirrors from Harrow to Graves-end, thousands of children who pestled foam up out of soft mortars of mouths, who lost easily a thousand times as many words among the chalky bubbles—bed-going complaints, timid announcements of love, news of fat or translucent, fuzzy or gentle beings from the country under the counterpane—uncounted soapy-liquorice moments spat out and flushed down to sewers and the slow-scumming gray estuary . . . and isn't menthol a marvelous invention to take just enough of it away each morning, down to become dusty oversize bubbles tessellating tough and stagnant among the tar shorelines, the intricate draftsmanship of outlets feeding, multiplying out to sea as one by one these old toothpaste tubes are emptied and returned to the War, heaps of dimly fragrant metal, phantoms of peppermint in the winter shacks, each tube wrinkled or embossed by the unconscious hands of London, written over in interference-patterns, hand against hand, waiting now—it is true return—to be melted for solder, for plate, alloyed for castings, bearings, gasketry, hidden smokeshriek linings the children of that other domestic incarnation will never see. (130)

The "tracks" in this example of Pynchon's gloomy phenomenology of systems run from London to Cuxhaven, from the small mortars of mouths to the mortar fire of cannons, as the containers of hygiene and the instruments of a child's bedtime rituals are transformed into the instruments of death. The human community is unconsciously implicated within this process that, metaphorically, changes life into death and "caries into cabals" as the life-preserving defenses against tooth decay are made over into the remnants of war.[9] The tubes are squeezed into various shapes, "wrinkled or embossed," "written over in interference-patterns" which affect, even if infinitesimally, the process of transformation from tube to war machine. The human hands that squeeze the tubes inscribe an entire history of personal, habitual actions onto the metal that melts more slowly but melts nevertheless for the engraved designs of these domestic users. This is one among many anecdotal traces of human activity recorded in *Gravity's Rainbow*; together they reflect Pynchon's concern to wrench unlikely connections, analogies, and coincidences out of the disparate elements of cultural life. The route from the bathroom to the pipefitters' sheds is tortuous and full of obstacles; yet, here, a "plot" is revealed as a tracing of that route by which a strand of existence and the scattered human selves that unknowingly "weave" it are inscribed as cultural signs.

The description of the warehouse full of toothpaste tubes suggests that *Gravity's Rainbow* is essentially about a form of writing which, as Geertz shows, marks the interpretation of culture as a textual operation. A social anthropologist could conceivably read the stacks of tubes (or the dispersal pattern of a ship's mortar fire) for information about the people who used them.[10] The tubes' embossings could be seen as self-inscriptions that reveal something about the ritualization of dental hygiene. This is one of countless human acts that are interpretations and designations of the cultural self's discourse in the world—manifestations of those ghostly "interference-patterns" that mark, if only temporarily, the individual life. Indeed, the passage compels the uncomfortable reader to trace the horrific connection between bedtime cleansings and the screams of rockets. How is it possible that these innocent acts could lead to the mass destruction of "the children of that other domestic incarnation"? What psychology or mythology can we use to explain this labyrinthine, seemingly determinate movement from life to death?[11] In this scene of loss, where language itself—"bed-going complaints, timid announcements of love"—is metaphorically washed down the communal drain out to the sea upon which battleships float, Pynchon reflects doubly on the creation of cultural patterns and the production of fictions. These become, in this reflection, both acts of hyperbolic connectedness and the grounds for interpretation. As a countercurrent to the course of a culture's transformation of used tubes into bombs, entropy changed to aggression, there are the "lost words" of the children and the leprous, quicksilver mirrors which bear the marks of their brushings and half-articulated announcements. The inexplicable, natural, and human processes of exchange and transformation (whether these be known as "entropy" or as "progress") are both mirrored and resisted by the work of language which, as it imperfectly inscribes these processes, also "interferes" with them by generating the interpretable signs of their movement through history.

For Pynchon, language (conceived here as the embossings of tubes, the muffled voices of children, the spotted mirrors) semantically halts, in whatever minute ways, the death drive of modern culture. But language is also the primary conveyance of this drive, since words in *Gravity's Rainbow*, we shall see, articulate the fantasy and schema by which we may annihilate ourselves. Fictions parallel this linguistic/cultural dialectic since they, too, enact processes that work toward their own end or "death" while temporizing against that moment via the digressions of plot and figure.[12] The prospect that this view of language and culture presents is not as bleak as one might expect: true, in the scene of cultural writing I have been discussing, the movement is from the protection of life to its destruction, and the passage certainly allows for its interpretation as a sign of our thanatopic culture. But the loss here is not *all* loss. The passage successfully contains (like the mirror) the waste or leavings of the small selves it describes; it views their remnant as something which demands interpretation as a form of mutable preservation. Conversely, these "hieroglyphs" are dead, empty, and the children of the "other incarnation" are, through some labyrinthine tangle of plot, indirectly murdered by their tooth-brushing counterparts. The scene may thus be viewed equally as a sign of our hopeless condition, alongside an observation that, by these markings, we know who we are as beings who create stories from our cultural remains.[13]

"Cultural writing" in *Gravity's Rainbow* is represented in all its complexity by the novel's many labyrinths. Like the twisted route of transformation described above, they all perform a "knotting into," an enactment of cultural description as interference, complication, or entanglement. As a whole, *Gravity's Rainbow* may be seen as a construction of interconnected labyrinths that lack centers, though every Theseus of the novel imagines that a Minotaur lies within. Tyrone Slothrop, the novel's putative hero and the most prominent of its obsessed questers, frantically searches through postwar occupied Germany ("the Zone") for a secret rocket device he'll never find. On the way, he becomes lost within the labyrinthine underground of the German rocket factory at Nordhausen, the Mittelwerke, a punning name that sounds like "metal works" and means "middle factory." In this realm of the "middle," the construction site for the secret rocket, all the tunnels are formed in the shape of a "double integral," a mathematical symbol that looks like "the shape of lovers curled asleep" and "the ancient rune that stands for the yew tree, or Death" (302).[14] To Etzel Ölsch, one of the Mittelwerke's designers, the double integral "stood in [his] subconscious for the method of finding hidden centers, inertias unknown . . . imaginary centers far down inside the solid fatality of stone . . . thought of not as 'heart,' 'plexus,' 'consciousness,' . . . 'Sanctuary,' 'dream of motion,' 'cyst of the eternal present,' or 'Gravity's gray eminence among the councils of the living stone.' No, not as one of these, but instead a point in space, a point hung precise as the point where burning must end, never launched, never to fall" (302). The shapes of the tunnels thus configure a labyrinth that leads not to some unapproachable center but back upon itself as the maze becomes a Möbius strip. The Mittelwerke is "all" middle; the name for the shape of its twisting tunnels, if forced from its mathematical context to a more literal connotation, suggests a blinding paradox: how can something "integral," whole or complete unto itself, be doubled or reinscribed? As Slothrop approaches what he senses to be the "center" of the Mittelwerke and the object of his quest, he discovers only "amazing perfect whiteness. Whiteness without heat, and blind inertia: Slothrop feels a terrible *familiarity* here, a center he has been skirting, avoiding as long as he can remember—never has he been as close as now to the true momentum of his time: faces and facts have crowded his indenture to the Rocket, camouflage and distraction fall away for the white moment, the vain and blind tugging at his sleeves *it's important* . . . *please* . . . *look at us* . . . but it's already too late, it's only wind, only *g*-loads, and the blood of his eyes has begun to touch the whiteness back to ivory, to brushings of gold and a network of edges to the broken rock" (312; Pynchon's ellipses). For Slothrop, as for Ölsch, the "center" is an absence, lost as soon as it is approached, and one aspect of this scene's terrible familiarity may reside in its having been enacted by previous American questers such as Ahab and Pym. The labyrinth that leads to this absent center and the remnant of its nonmanifestation is "a network of edges" or a series of middles, though these exist, paradoxically, as inscriptions of the absent center's location.

The labyrinth of the Mittelwerke typically inculcates a desacralized "presence" analogous to writing as a sequence of hieroglyphic signs—

runes or "edges"—representing what leads to and remains from an impossible materialization of the center. This labyrinthine inscription is like those imaginative entanglements that a renegade Argentine submarine captain describes to Slothrop as the embodiments of a national mania: "In the days of the gauchos, my country was a blank piece of paper. . . . Fences went up, and the gaucho became less free. It is our national tragedy. We are obsessed with building labyrinths, where before there was open plain and sky. To draw ever more complex patterns on the blank street. We cannot abide that *openness*: it is terror to us. Look at Borges. Look at the suburbs of Buenos Aires. . . . Beneath the city streets, the warrens of rooms and corridors, the fences and the networks of steel track, the Argentine heart, in its perversity and guilt, longs for a return to that first unscribbled serenity" (264). For Pynchon, the obsession and fear are not just Argentinian but representative of all Western, written culture, which has somehow submitted to self-domination in the form of the century's annihilatory rocket.

Francisco Squalidozzi's parochial commentary concisely joins the textual and culture dimensions of the novel's labyrinthine analogies. These are expressions of a cultural language that inscribes an entire civilization's fear of nothingness as a series of crossings, twistings, curls, and loops that speak their difference from the blank page of pure absence by those scribblings. Stratification and graphesis are thus joined to articulate the sense of narrative and culture as "knotting into" themselves, escaping from the dread of the "not," ever moving toward yet around the point of origin. For J. Hillis Miller, this is to surmise the very nature of narrative, which functions to put into play what he terms "repetition": "Repetition might be defined as anything which happens to the line to trouble or even confound its straightforward linearity: returnings, reknottings, recrossings, crinklings to and fro, suspensions, interruptions, fictionalizings."[15] For Pynchon, the narrative "line" is transformed into a succession of centerless labyrinths manifesting a "world" made of honeycombed undergrounds and compost heaps while concealing, within, the semiotic operations of culture.

Everything in *Gravity's Rainbow*, from monolithic institutions to human selves, is conceived of as a form of language or, more precisely, as a collection of signs to be read, interpreted, and manipulated. The novel, according to Tony Tanner, is thoroughly "overdetermined" and speaks to a particularly modern dilemma: "Modern man is above all an interpreter of different signs, a reader of differing discourses, a servant of signals, a compelled and often compulsive decipherer. In Henri Lefebvre's use of the word, we do live in a 'pleonastic' society of 'aimless signifiers and disconnected signifieds' on many levels, so that you can see evidence of hyper-redundancy in the realm of signs, objects, institutions, even human beings. Wherever we look, there is too much to 'read.'"[16] Even the inanimate world in *Gravity's Rainbow* is viewed as a form of archaeological inscription made of interpretable signs which can be read by the novel's roving hermeneuticists, wandering through a wartime, bureaucratic labyrinth—"this lush maze of initials, arrows solid and dotted, boxes big and small, names printed and memorized" (76). The barbwire defenses along an English beach are described as "thick moiré" after a snowfall, as "black scrawl . . . etched in white" (91). An ancient mansion used by the Allied secret services, with its stark white, irregular walls, is referred to as "an architectural document, an old-fashioned apparatus whose use is forgotten. Ice of varying thickness, wavy, blurred, a legend to be deciphered by lords of the winter, Glacists of the region, and argued over in their journals" (72–73). The secret "00000" rocket, the sacred object of many quests which threatens to annihilate the world in a matter of seconds at the novel's end, is conceived by heretic Cabalists as a "Torah—letter by letter-rivets, burner cup and brass rose, its text theirs to permute and combine into new revelations, always unfolding" (727). Given this vision of the rocket as text, it hardly seems surprising when we are told by the novel's shadowy, infrequently omniscient narrator that at the German rocket-testing site, Peenemünde, the test stand "measured 40 × 40 cm, about the size of a tabloid page" (452).

The world of *Gravity's Rainbow* is, substantially and metaphorically, a text made of paper—a "linguistic wilderness," as Horst Achtfaden, a German rocket technician, acknowledges (455). Slothrop comes to a similar realization when he reflects on his ancestry and the family business, a paper mill: "Slothrop's family actually made its money killing trees, amputating them from their roots, chopping them up, grinding them to pulp, bleaching that to paper and getting paid for this with more paper. 'That's really insane.' He shakes his head. 'There's insanity in my family'" (553). Here, we see what is so "familiar" about the white center at the Mittelwerke, as Slothrop obliquely approaches the death-filled, bleached-out form and force of his ancestry. While Nabokov's textual world is largely composed of mirrors and glass, reflecting his concern to define the inscribed self as a refracted or shadowed image, Pynchon's is a labyrinth of paper, a textual bureaucracy that describes his vision of a writerly culture for which the medium of exchange is printed "texts." Everything in this world is a paper sign *for* something, as well as a representation of its own sign function; everything is consummately readable since it is already written.

Because his judgment about the insanity of this paper world is a matter of the text, Slothrop's comment on this state of affairs is tautological, though it indicates Pynchon's larger concern with the traceable roots of the connection to be made between bureaucracies, power, and cultural annihilation. Indeed, part of the novel's intention is to confirm this judgment: the massive paper chases of *Gravity's Rainbow* and of Western culture, however tortuously, lead to the overwhelming order of the rocket as the ultimate product of bureaucratic, linguistic, and textual operations. At the same time, while the world of *Gravity's Rainbow* is reduced to the substance upon which it is written, the text calls for the work of interpretation. The allowance the novel makes for a cultural self-understanding may be either a blessing or a curse: in reading, we may discover the hermeneutic power that enables us to make connections between the disparate semes of the text; we may also find that those connections determine our fate as readers, which is to be condemned to the inscribed determinacies this cultural encyclopedia imposes upon us.

The operations of language and interpretation are revealed at the deepest levels of Pynchon's paper world, within the subtext of the earth. As it is described in *Gravity's Rainbow*, in its geological and molecular structure, the earth is often seen as a language that people "read" as they search for the sources of the planet's organic, sedimentary power. Seeking and finding the earth's "trace" elements, these mineralogical textual critics recombine its primary shapes into the synthetic fuels and plastics that are the visible inscriptions of human desire. The report of a committee on molecular structure (one of the novel's hundreds of committees and bureaucratic cells) remarks on "how alphabetic is the nature of molecules" and insists on the analogy to be made between the creation of synthetic chemical chains and the alphabetizing of oral languages: "See: how they are taken out from the coarse flow—shaped, cleaned, rectified, just as you once redeemed your letters from the lawless, the mortal streaming of human speech. . . . These are our letters, our words: they too can be modulated, broken, recoupled, redefined, co-polymerized one to the other in worldwide chains that will surface now and then over long molecular silences, like the seen parts of a tapestry" (355; Pynchon's ellipses). This analogy is suggestive in several ways. It creates a bond between written language and chemistry that reinforces the novel-long argument for the connection to be made between the textuality of modern culture and its potentially disastrous technocracies. The vision is Orwellian: language can be manipulated in the same way that molecules are managed by chemists. Second, the analogy suggests that the operations of written language and chemistry are parallel in that their function is to recombine, differentiate, and shape a homogeneous "reality." As minerals are wrenched out of the earth's massive sameness, so the language inscribed in texts "redeems" from the "coarse flow" and "lawless streaming" of speech—words gone the instant they are heard—the preserved, formed letters of the alphabet that articulate the verbal "tapestry" of textual existence.

This analogy is reinforced by Lyle Bland, an American industrialist turned mystic who discovers late in life that "Earth is a living critter" and that gravity is "really something eerie, Messianic, extrasensory in Earth's mindbody." For him, the planet becomes a sacred text of sedimentary inscription, its wastes "hugged to its holy center" by gravity, "gathered, packed, transmuted, realigned, and rewoven molecules to be taken up again by coal-tar The Kabbalists . . . taken boiled off, teased apart, explicated to every last permutation of useful magic, centuries past exhaustion still finding new molecular pieces, combining and recombining them into new synthetics" (590). Bland expresses a hermeneutic fantasy in projecting the labor of recombination "centuries past exhaustion"—the kind of hopeful interpretive desire conveyed in Barth's concept of literary replenishment. This desire is implicated by the novel's compressing superimposed layers of history and geological strata, map parchments and skins, architectures and geometries, into a "metalanguage" that marks the promise of interpretability as a form of power and knowledge.

Significantly, the molecular committee's report appears in the "Kirghiz Light" section of *Gravity's Rainbow*, which Edward Mendelson has compared to the "Oxen of the Sun" chapter in Joyce's *Ulysses* as representing Pynchon's history of the English language.[17] The Kirghiz Light episode sketches the "civilizing" of some central Asian nomads, the Kirghiz Turks, through the introduction of the NTA—the New Turkic Alphabet; by this means, according to the molecular committee's analogy, an oral culture is transformed into a written culture and "redeemed." One product of this salvatory effort is the writing down of "The Aqyn's Song," which tells of the Kirghiz Light, a mystical emanation that is for these people "the face of God . . . a presence / Behind the mask of the sky" (358). The manifestation of the light is potentially another "center," like the radiant illumination at the Mittelwerke, imagined but not seen, inscribed by written language as a distancing or falling off: "If the place were not so distant, / If the words were known, and spoken, / Then God might be a gold ikon, / Or a page in a paper book" (358). A seeker after the light, Tchitcherine, a Russian officer sent to enforce the NTA, will see "It," but only as a vanishing prospect: "He is no aqyn, and his heart was never ready. He will see It just before dawn. He will spend 12 hours there, face-up on the desert, a prehistoric city greater than Babylon lying in stifled mineral sleep a kilometer below his back . . . someday . . . a purge, a war, and millions after millions of souls gone behind him, he will hardly be able to remember It" (359). Here, several layers of the novel's textual archaeology are excavated. The seeker, Tchitcherine, a representative man of Western, textual culture, searches for the light of presence but, lying atop the sedimented strata of prehistory, he must experience his vision as repression and "bare remembrance." If the place of this vision could be located in time and space, if the seeing of the light could be spoken in words, then, the aqyn's poem and Tchitcherine's experience tell us, God, presence, light—all become texts. The movement through history to written language is thus seen as a loss, but one that is also an awakening from the "stifled mineral sleep." History, as the story of culture, is an erection of paper and words that marks the passage out of nonconsciousness into the realm of signs, faulty memory, half-meanings, and the necessity of interpretation.

Writing, as the sign of culture in *Gravity's Rainbow*, represents a contradictory process that is the "mark" of interpretation. Every outcast seeker looks for the unattainable center and finds only the traces that denote each one's passage. Whether it is a benzene ring, the force of gravity, the unspoken name of the Torah, or the "word" from which all words and languages evolve, the novel's hermeneuticists seek the ultimate truth to which their language refers. In so doing, each exposes the limits of that language which, like a labyrinth, works only obliquely around this source or center. The interpretive riddle implicit in this view of the relation between inscription and truth is typified by Slothrop's hallucinations under the influence of Sodium Amytal, a "truth serum" administered by Tchitcherine. Slothrop has been programmed since infancy by an evil Pavlovian, Laszlo Jamf, to sexually respond to the presence of a certain plastic synthetic, Imoplex G. Without being conscious of it, he is obsessed with finding the "00000" rocket because it contains the Schwarzgerät, a secret device made of the plastic stimulus. Thus he is pursued throughout the novel by those, like Tchitcherine, who want the rocket for their own purposes and who perceive that Slothrop seems to know instinctively where it might be. The transcript of Slothrop's drug fantasy reveals what is behind all these quests:

> Black runs all through the transcript: the recurring color black. Slothrop never mentioned Enzian by name, nor the Schwarzkommando. But he did talk about the Schwarzgerät. And he also coupled "schwarz-" with some strange nouns, in the German fragments that came through. Blackwoman, Blackrocket, Blackdream. . . . The new coinages seem to be made unconsciously. Is there a single root, deeper than anyone has probed, from which Slothrop's Blackwords only appear to flower separately? Or has he by way of the language caught the German mania for name-giving, dividing the Creation finer and finer, analyzing, setting namer more hopelessly apart from named, even to bringing in the mathematics of combination, tacking together established nouns to get new ones, the insanely, endlessly diddling play of a chemist whose molecules are words. (390–91; Pynchon's ellipses)

The "insanity" recounted in this example, like that of Slothrop's paper empire—the "mathematics of combination" and "endlessly diddling play"—may be seen superficially as an ironic comment by the novel's author on the "mindless pleasures" of his text. More importantly, Slothrop's rhetorical flowering exemplifies the "growth" of language as a discontinuous movement outward from some unknown source—if we use gravity as the central metaphor, an endless process of attraction and repulsion or, if we use the Torah's sacred vessel, of gathering and dispersion.[18] Slothrop's naming, "dividing the Creation finer and finer," hearkens back to the nihilistic primal word "black," while generating out of that nothingness the recombined words which, as "coinages," are the currency of worldly, temporal human expression. It is not too fanciful to suggest that Slothrop's "Blackwords" literally represent inscriptions on the blank page of white text feared by the Argentinian Squalidozzi, which the labyrinth of print marks up. So Pynchon marks his own text as a scene of writing demanding the work of interpretation that, Frank Kermode argues, attends all narrative performances. These generate the quest for a single, original explanation for a "world" (metaphorized in *Pale Fire* by Kinbote's Zembla, in *Travesty* by Papa's car, in *LETTERS* by Bray's marsh, in *Gravity's Rainbow* by the Cabalistic center of the earth) that a given fictional language both foils and encourages, in a double process of "simultaneous proclamation and concealment."[19]

Within the many discourses of *Gravity's Rainbow*, each with its own originating truth or metaphor, all interlocking to form the textual culture of this massive book, the self as a cultural sign is to be found. The dynamics of the self in *Gravity's Rainbow* crucially reinforce (since they arise out of) the operations of language, interpretation, and culture that we have so far observed. By comparison, the image of the self for Nabokov is an embossed design that is clearly a self-reflection; for Barth, it is an anagrammatical language that names its own history and the larger History to which it bears witness. For Pynchon, the self can be compared to a cultural fragment or a readable hieroglyph—something that always belongs to a larger language and exists as a dispersed sign of that language.[20] The novel's selves, initially inscribed within an archaeological context as readable signs, then become readers who define their position within a cultural discourse through an act of literacy. Their labors are exemplified by Enzian, a messianic, expatriated Herero tribesman who searches through "the Zone" of post-war Germany for clues to a multinational conspiracy of powerful corporations that have cooperated to design the war. Enzian wishes to tap into this power supply for his own radical ends: "We have to look for power sources here, and distribution networks we were never taught, routes of power our teachers never imagined, or were encouraged to avoid . . . we have to find meters whose scales are unknown in the world, draw our own schematics, getting feedback, making connections, reducing the error, trying to learn the real function . . . zeroing in on what incalculable plot?" (521; Pynchon's ellipses). Enzian sees the world as a vast geopolitical circuit of information into which he must integrate himself so that he can, despite his revolutionary politics, become one more conduit of power, one more integer in a series.

Like all the novel's obsessed readers (including "the reader," who attempts to chart the novel's narrative schematics and feels like a participant in the same "plot convention" that Pirate Prentice attends in final paranoia), Enzian becomes yet another sign in its intricate, heterogeneous "system." The description of his search for the ultimate "00001" rocket conjoins mathematics and religion when he assumes the role of the questing function who sorts out information as he draws about him the coordinates of his search.[21] In the Zone—technically Germany but implicitly all the novel's desolate, entropic landscapes—the act of reading and the self as read take on bizarre dimensions while the frantic search for sources and routes of power unfolds. Counteragents with secret messages tattooed on their faces roam the Balkans, "their lips mere palimpsests of secret flesh, seamed and unnaturally white, by which they all knew each other" (16). A German refugee and drug addict engages in "papyromancy," "the ability to prophesy through contemplating the way people roll reefers—the shape, the licking pattern, the wrinkles and folds or absence thereof in paper" (442). An American soldier/barber who has the peculiar ability to "read" human shivers becomes an instrument of fate as he cuts a colonel's hair: "Each long haircut is a passage. Hair is yet another kind of modulated frequency. Assume a state of grace in which all hairs were once distributed perfectly even, a time of innocence when they fell perfectly straight, all over the colonel's head. Winds of the day, gestures of distraction, sweat, itchings, sudden surprises, three-foot falls at the edge of sleep, watched skies, remembered shames, all have since written on that perfect grating. Passing through it tonight, restructuring it, Eddie Pensiero is an agent of History" (643).

In each of these extraordinary, hyperbolic instances, the world and the self are known through their readability. Lips inscribed with the tattooer's ink, paper bearing the marks of human fingers and tongues, the cryptic pattern of a hairline, all reflect the sense of "self" as an incarnate sign that takes its place in a language created out of flesh and paper. Moreover, this semiotic self, manifested in the habitual motions of domestic culture or its disruptions, is seen in these examples as a form of interference or excess—the flesh protuberance of a scar or the "fall" from perfection evidenced in the "writing" of natural occurrence and human accident upon the colonel's scalp, "read" by the fateful barber. Like the world, the self in *Gravity's Rainbow* appears as an inscribed text which is an interpretation of other "texts"; these are, themselves, interpretations (falls from grace) in endless dispersion.

In this realm of the rocket, where "the trail of its components scattered on impact, or from in-flight explosion, provides a spoor of hardware, a text to decipher, leading at the end of the war back to the points of assembly," the self as written and as read often exists, like the Balkan spies, in the form of a palimpsest.[22] The novel's seekers seem to be patchworks or assemblages of the cultural debris they have scavenged on their quests. Tchitcherine, for example, is "more metal than anything else" (337), a collection of steel plates and ligatures picked up during various wars. As he travels through the Zone, Slothrop assumes a series of personae ranging from a British correspondent, "Ian Scuffling," to "Plechazunga, the Pig-Hero," to "Rocketman" in his search for the plastic fragment buried in his programmed past. These self-assemblages reflect the status of the self in *Gravity's Rainbow* as a construction problematically defined by Rollo Groast, who is a member of "The White Visitation," an Allied intelligence section comprised of parapsychological acrobats. Groast writes to his father of a strange experiment at The Visitation involving Gavin Trefoil, a man able to change the color of his skin "from the most ghastly albino up through a smooth spectrum to very deep, purplish black" (147). Groast theorizes that Trefoil achieves this remarkable transformation as a form of writing and interpretation:

> We do know that the dermal cells which produce melanin—the melanocytes—were once, in each of us, at an early stage of embryonic growth, part of the central nervous system. But as the embryo grows, as tissue goes on differentiating, some of

> these nerve cells move away from what will be the CNS, to migrate out to the skin, to become melanocytes. They keep their original tree-branch shapes, the axon and dendrites of the typical nerve cell. But the dendrites are used now to carry not electric signals but skin pigment. Rollo Groast believes in some link, so far undiscovered—some surviving cell-memory that will, retrocolonial, still respond to messages from the metropolitan brain. (147)

This evolutionary fantasy unites the inner and outer worlds of *Gravity's Rainbow*, for as culture arises through a process of scattering and stratification, so the genetic development of Trefoil's chameleonlike nervous system is a dispersion from the source, a "differentiation" that infers a "retrocolonial" link back to the unknown center.

Groast's description of the genetic self links the biological, textual, and political layers of the novel's thematic strata. Trefoil's nervous system is perceived as an evolutionary battleground, where the freed, independent melanocytes still hearken back to the "mother country" of the CNS. His body appears as a text upon which this dialectical molecular struggle is inscribed as he changes color; furthermore, the individual melanocytes "keep their original tree-branch shapes," the sign of the natural source of the novel's paper empire, presented here in a revolutionary drama that moves from "ghastly albino" to "deep, purplish black," which are the "colors" of inscription. The passage allies the differentiating operations of technological culture and the evolved human body with those of writing. It suggests that the "self," in its bodily as well as noncorporeal senses, is one in a universe of echoing texts that describe the condition of "textuality" as a fall from the "original" in endless dispersion. This bodily "text," Groast goes on to say, is "part of an old and clandestine drama for which the human body serves only as a set of very allusive, often cryptic programme-notes—it's as if the body we can measure is a scrap of this programme found outside in the street, near a magnificent stone theatre we cannot enter" (147–48). Groast's analogy invokes, again, the relation between inner and outer as the connection between fragment and center. He conceives of totality as an assemblage of "notes" where the known self is an explanatory passage which the seeker for total self-knowledge can use to gain admission to "the whole show." But like the evolved melanocytes, the self in Groast's vision exists as a dispersed note or trace (with the sinister implication of being "programmed") known by its separateness. Here, the self is figured as a textual message written into a larger cultural encyclopedia, within which the sign of the self is both lost clue and corresponding annotation.

Groast's version of the self's genesis infers a disturbing concept of the self as determined by the cultural system of which it is note and part. If the act of locating the self in culture is paralleled in *Gravity's Rainbow* to a quest for connections between traces, then the corresponding fear is that of the paranoid: one is always part of some half-seen, predetermined "plot." This is usually the case for selves entangled in the plots of fiction, but the broader deterministic implication of Pynchon's novel is that culture itself reads just like a novel, so that the operations of narrative are made continually analogous to the operations of culture. The novel's various languages, from the bodily to the metaphysical, comprise the interpretable signs of culture, but they are often monolithic and self-destructive in their complex evolution. The quest for meaning, connection, or the "truth" behind traces, Pynchon seems to say, leads to those kinds of epiphanies represented by the final inscription of repressed cultural fantasies in the novel's omnipresent rocket. The rocket is known by its trail as it rises from the earth and falls back again; its "end" is a return to origins and a confirmation of the covenant we have made with nature in bringing about mutual destruction. According to the novel's imposing logic, the transformation of spoken language into alphabetic letters, or the evolution of the human cellular structure, is directly parallel to the compartmentalization of civilization into dispersed bureaucratic cells that unknowingly cooperate in producing the "gathering" of the rocket.

This massive entangling of cultural developments accounts for the quality of fatalism that darkens much of Pynchon's fiction. For even if we think we have some control over our political destinies, up to this point, we certainly have never had much to say about the development of the central nervous system in humans. And if our political systems—indeed, our need for "system" itself—can be so closely aligned to some form of cellular centralization on the microscopic level, then our sense of destiny or purpose within this schema of hyperbolic naturalism is reduced to the level of a physiological dialectic that belies our hierophanies and our economies. In terms of the self-fulfilling prophecy that the novel vigorously promotes through its overdetermined analogies, the self becomes the most literal cipher of its own biological desire to regress back to the "center." Stripped of its mystical or political trappings, this movement traces the desire for a form of preexistence or death of consciousness toward which, paradoxically, the differentiations of our evolution in culture and history have steadily led us.

Yet this is to read the irony of Pynchon's dialectical novel in only one way. The very quality of differentiation which may lead to the destruction of oral cultures and the proliferation of bureaucratic death cells also constitutes the sign of the novel's "life." Struggling against the novel's centralizing systems are its "preterite," who, like the most important seeker in *Gravity's Rainbow*, Slothrop, are witches, sensitives, outcasts, and freaks acting as "interferences" that impede the flow of information in discursive systems. Repelled by the systematic destruction of war and the obsessiveness of his infant programming, Slothrop gives up his personal rocket quest without finding his grail, his mind "jammed" by too many signals from too many directions: rocket plots, syntheses, and searchers for the key to synthesis seem to be everywhere in the Zone. There, Slothrop becomes more scattered as he participates in other plots that intersect with his own, until he appears "lying one afternoon spread-eagled at his ease in the sun, at the edge of one of the ancient Plague towns . . . a crossroads, a living intersection" (625). He becomes a legend; he evolves into a floating signifier to the world's outcasts, who "look for him adrift in the hostile light of the sky, the darkness of the sea" (742). Quester transformed into grail, Ahab become the whale, to the preterite readers Slothrop is both Oedipus and Christ, scapegoat and savior, his the sign of scattering, crossing, and interference.

In one sense, Slothrop stands for the unimaginable possibility of the random, asystematic, nonlinguistic realm excluded in Pynchon's world of overwhelming linguistic orders.[23] Outside of the centripetal processes of language and culture, no matter how oppressive they may be, lie the disorder of "scattering" and the disappearance of the self, since language like "repression gives us individuality and culture, a collective history, as gravity gives the earth form and configuration."[24] Yet Slothrop, as an embodiment of the novel's preterite outsiders, can also be seen as the unassimilated fragment that *causes* the evolution of culture and the restructurings of language necessitated by the desire for connections to the scattered trace. After his "disappearance," a community springs up which believes that "fragments of Slothrop have grown into consistent personae of their own. If so, there's no telling which of the Zone's present-day population are offshoots of his original scattering" (742). Like a broken vessel, like the earth itself, Slothrop becomes a kind of signifying diaspora that ever gravitates toward its origin—perhaps home, perhaps silence, perhaps death; these are metaphors for the "work" of language in its role as a signifying system that represents its own proliferation and call for order. Around his legend, a new "brotherhood" is created, with its own counterculture, countermythology, and attendant rituals:

> Let the village idiots celebrate. Let their holiness ripple into interference-patterns till it clog the lantern-light of the meeting hall. Let the chorus line perform heroically: 16 ragged staring oldtimers who shuffle aimlessly about the stage, jerking off in unison, waggling penises in mock quarter-staffing, brandishing in twos and threes their green-leaved poles, exposing amazing chancres and lesions, going off in fountains of sperm strung with blood that splash over glazed trouser-pleats, dirt-colored jackets with pockets dangling like 60-year old breasts, sockless ankles permanently stained with the dust of the little squares and the depopulated streets. Let them cheer and pound their seats, let the brotherly spit flow. (743)

Behind this obscene parody of the community of men in Stevens' "Sunday Morning" is the notion of "counterforce," a systematic reaction against ruling systems. Opposed to the domination of the rocket is the disorderliness of the preterite, organized into a language and a ritual ruled over by the lost, scattered presence of Slothrop. The dissemination of life becomes a resistance to the organization of life into systems, but this resistance, in its enactment, becomes organized into a chorus, language, and culture.[25] Out of the dialectical clash between the repressive and preterite orders of language arise cultures and countercultures where the self is read into crisis and history. Like Barth, Pynchon suggests that there is nothing outside of culture and discourse and that the possibility of self-annihilation is near. We can't help being profoundly disturbed by the tyranny and deceptiveness of language in *Gravity's Rainbow* when we observe that the "double integral" of difference and the sign of sleeping lovers can also be viewed as double lightning bolts, the sign of the German SS. Language has this power and ambivalence: it can inscribe our death as well as our life. But Pynchon projects the contradictory hope that the noise of cultural resistance, inscribed by the disseminatory aspect of writing, might be heard above the horrendous scream of rockets and the pluming of their trails across the novel's blank sky. It is by this resistance and its contrary movement toward the impossible center that the self, for Pynchon, revises the language of its history of struggle for self-recognition as a variation amidst the interstices of linguistic orders. Thus, he offers a tracing of our being in language and our subjection to culture as the fruit of our interpretive labors.

CHAPTER FIVE THE WORLD DACTYLIC

FLANNERY O'CONNOR'S *WISE BLOOD*

If there is too much uncontested meaning on earth (the reign of the Angels), man collapses under the burden; if the world loses all its meaning (the reign of the demons), life is every bit as impossible.

Milan Kundera, *The Book of Laughter and Forgetting*

Unlike Thomas Pynchon, who exists in the public eye as the imaginary creation of an absconded author, Flannery O'Connor has made her intentions regarding her fiction well known. The first novel of this southern Catholic writer with a penchant for the charismatically grotesque is most often viewed just as O'Connor wished it to be: as the odyssey of a modern-day Antichrist who becomes a "Christian *malgré lui*."[1] The contrast between Pynchon's and O'Connor's authorial presences points out what I wish to argue is the crucial hermeneutic battle enacted in *Wise Blood*—a battle where the singularity of an authorial intention is placed against the ironies generated by the signs O'Connor employs in fulfilling that intention. The cultural dialectic of *Gravity's Rainbow* becomes, in *Wise Blood*, a dialectic of authority, as the novel puts into question the intentions of its author's prefatory remarks and asks us to consider another dimension of the desire for meaning. Here, and in *The Franchiser*, we may observe the extremities of interpretation: on the one hand, the desire for a validated and validating "authority" who provides the dominating certainty of a singular order; on the other, the invalidations of an unauthorized, radical pluralism. While neither novel privileges one of these alternatives over the other, each tests the limits of certainty and uncertainty by making problematic the rhetorical intentions of gods, fathers, and authors.

As an anagogy or a vision of ends and means, *Wise Blood* dramatizes the contest figured by Milan Kundera in the epigraph, that between the "angelic" spirit of absolute certainty and the "demonic" abolition of all meaning. O'Connor's world is constituted by what Frederick Asals calls "the language of extremity," reflecting an "insistence on duality, dissociation, splits, paradox, and the tension of opposites"—an either/or chiaroscuro realm electrified by the arcing oppositions of monism and meaninglessness.[2] Typically, her protagonists either engage in a Calvinistic quest for some cosmic certification of salvation or reject all signification and its savage source of authority. Between the rock of certainty and the abyss of meaninglessness, signification itself founders, signs fracture and split, as O'Connor's most concentrated reflection upon the act of interpretation formulates a semiosis located within the dualistic realm of certain saints and ironic demons.

The "Christian *malgré lui*" of *Wise Blood* is Hazel Motes, just returned from a tour of duty in the army and possessed with the idea of establishing an anti-church, "the church of truth without Jesus Christ Crucified."[3] Hazel comes to the city of Taulkinham in order to found his nihilistic ministry, where he preaches that "the blind don't see and the lame don't walk and the dead stays that way" (105). Once in the city, he does manage to organize a ministry, but in a manner far different from what he had intended, as he is slowly transformed into an unwilling savior/victim in a demeaned environment. Hazel is an obsessed literalist in a sign-filled world looking for the one, ultimate "truth" (even if it is that there is no truth) to which each sign points; he is yet another preacher in this city of talk, where every character frantically gesticulates and shouts out the unique message which each has providentially been given.

With its sidewalk hawkers, wandering preachers, chronic economic depression, racism, and provincial "grotesque" atmosphere, Taulkinham bears the marks of a typical city in the Deep South of the forties and fifties. Similar to the Atlanta of "The Artificial Nigger" or the urban tangle of "Everything That Rises Must Converge," Taulkinham is also, allegorically, the "City of Man." From O'Connor's explicit theological perspective, the city is the result of worldly ambition and vanity, where the wandering, alienated soul is lost, its life threatened by the allure of profane enchantments. Significantly, most of O'Connor's stories take place in rural locations, where the light of revelation is seen all the more clearly for the absence of city lights.

Thus, one of her few "city" stories, "The Artificial Nigger," concludes on an affirmative note as the protagonists—grandfather and grandson—return from the inferno of the city to the relative paradise of their familiar, rural cabin, there to enjoy the new-found intimacy and understanding that their urban trials have conferred upon them. *Wise Blood* contains no parallel return to nature, though Motes arrives at Taulkinham having traveled from the desolation of his rural family home in Eastrod. The profane city of the novel perforce must also serve as the site for any sacralizations that Hazel's spiritual odyssey will reveal.

For the reader inclined to unquestioningly accept O'Connor's stated pronouncements about *Wise Blood*, Taulkinham can be seen as a series of mundane inversions of the natural world that present to the pilgrim, Motes, a succession of earthly travails to be endured on the road to salvation. There is, for example, the city zoo that employs Enoch Emery, who plays the role of parodic, bestial Antichrist to Hazel's scapegoat/savior. The zoo is an antiparadisiacal realm containing absurdly humanized bears "facing each other like two matrons having tea, their faces polite and self-absorbed" (93), reviled hyenas, and a godlike owl whose eye appears to be "in the middle of something that looked like a piece of mop sitting on an old rag" (95). Motes unwillingly journeys through the zoo to the "heart of the city," a room in the local museum where Enoch forces him to view the remains of a mummified pygmy. For Enoch, the room is a sanctuary, the mummy its idol, and he its guardian—notions he hilariously realizes when he steals the mummy and sets it up in the mock tabernacle of his own transformed room. For Hazel (or, rather, for the reader forced to observe Hazel in this carefully constructed symbolic world, since he is largely noncommittal about his experience), each place—zoo, museum, concert hall, boardinghouse, used-car lot—becomes a trap from which he must escape, a mirrored profanity by which his self-ascendancy can be measured. Hazel's appearance at the city concert hall can be seen as a comic analogue to the story of Christ whipping the Philistines in the temple: there, in "a large building with columns and a dome," fronted by "stone lions sitting on pedestals," he reviles a crowd of exiting theatergoers with proclamations of the Church without Christ Crucified and scatters religious tracts about the sidewalk (48–49). Hazel's later visit to the zoo can be compared to a hell-harrowing journey through an absurdist, bestial underworld. In one view, then, the city, like all concrete manifestations of the novel, is composed of "signs that are pressed outward on things from within" Hazel's own being.[4] Taulkinham potentially exists as the symbolic arena where the inner conflicts of the wayfaring stranger are exteriorized and where his personal destiny becomes the world's fate.

Yet to see Taulkinham in this light is to accept it, and *Wise Blood*, as a rather heavy-handed allegorical portrait of the Christian *malgré lui*. Certainly against O'Connor's stated intentions, Taulkinham may be more interestingly viewed in an unsuspected context: it bears a striking resemblance to one of the cities of *Gravity's Rainbow*, paranoiacally imagined by Tchitcherine while hallucinating a gigantic, providential finger that points the way to the novel's founding conspiracy, the rocket cartel: "It appears to be a very large Finger addressing him. Its Fingernail is beautifully manicured: as it rotates for him, it slowly reveals a Fingerprint that might well be an aerial view of the City Dactylic, that city of the future where every soul is known, and there is noplace to hide" (566). Taulkinham, as the topos of *Wise Blood*, is this prefigured "city of the future" reified, a realm of gesture and epiphany where everything is objectified under the omniscient gaze of a judgmental authorial eye. This suggests that the one-eyed owl at the zoo and all the novel's "eyes" are interesting representations of authorial self-parody. Rhetorically, the narrated world of *Wise Blood is* the pointing finger of Tchitcherine's vision, wherein the heroic function becomes a hermeneutic game of hide-and-seek as Hazel attempts to avoid, misread, and finally accept the fate constructed for him at the outset. He cannot evade the dictates of his "wise blood" as he walks the streets of Taulkinham, which progressively route him more directly toward his end as savior and sacrificial victim. Though he struggles to escape the information conveyed to him by the signs of the world—a struggle by which exteriority is converted to self-knowledge—Hazel becomes, himself, the sign of his own apotheosis, prefigured by the arranging, pointing hand of the "god" who constructs his narrative.

The city of *Wise Blood* is thus a tautology; it "knows" its protagonist from the outset; the "process of discovery" enacted here is merely a matter of Hazel's matching his own self-recognition (or those of others who exist as characters in Taulkinham) with the overwhelming evidence presented by the novel's outer layer of object and reference. Indeed, since we know if something has affected Hazel only by means of his jerky, unexpected reactions or his sudden, hysterical outbursts, self-recognition itself is a matter of objectification in the novel. Hazel is thus the obverse of *Travesty*'s Papa, who adjusts the world to a theatricalized self-image; in *Wise Blood*, there is no "self," only an overwhelming, authorized world. John Hawkes has referred to the constraining authorial stance he sees in all of O'Connor's fiction as "reductive or diabolical," a case of the "pure creation of 'aesthetic authority,'" by which he suggests that the directorial view which leads Motes to his preordained fate levels the novel's world to a single, dominating intention.[5] To demystify Hawkes' demonic metaphor, we can see the novel as a "city dactylic" which presents a vision similar to that contained in the plot summary of a movie viewed by Enoch Emery: "The first picture was about a scientist named The Eye who performed operations by remote control. You would wake up in the morning and find a slit in your chest or head or stomach and something you couldn't do without would be gone" (138). "The Eye" objectifies and removes what is hidden; its healing is a loss. The "eye" of the novel, embodied by the narrative stance of "aesthetic authority," struggles to remove and hold out for our inspection the "mote" which threatens the clarity of its monocular vision. Hazel Motes, as itinerant irritant, recapitulates this process in his own shortsighted quest to understand and interpret that singular destiny which, pursued to its end, the city will reveal to him.

As the topographic representation of *Wise Blood*'s entangling and disentangling of evidence, authority, and interpretation, Taulkinham is a realm of repetitive referentiality. Like the confusion of road markers Alice encounters as she traces her path through the labyrinth of Wonderland, Taulkinham appears as a collection of signs pointing in all directions but condemning the worldly traveler, Motes, to pursue the "one way" of his fate. Even before he enters the city, Motes seems compelled to invest a great deal of authority in written signs. On a visit to his family's empty, ruined homestead, he puts in each drawer of the only piece of furniture untouched by vandals, a "chifforobe," this note: "THIS SHIFFER-ROBE BELONGS TO HAZEL MOTES. DO NOT STEAL IT OR YOU WILL BE HUNTED DOWN AND KILLED" (26). Hazel's ludicrous sign, which is more an incitement to theft than a prevention of it, predicts his own fate, for it is he who will be "hunted down and killed" by the "ragged figure" who imposes upon Hazel his unwilled vocation. More importantly, the sign declares ownership; in this place of lost and ruined origins, upon a coffinlike object repeated elsewhere in the images of a real coffin (Hazel's mother's), a train berth, the backseat of a car, and a burlesque show "pit," Hazel confers a sign of possession as a displacement of his own nonexistent selfhood. Even the comic, dialect name he gives the object, "shiffer-robe" (in French and German, "chiffre" can mean "cipher"), suggests a kind of gesticulating exteriority, a "shifting garment," inscribed on a piece of paper contained inside the hollow drawers of a dresser standing inside an empty house. What is "outside," the sign, made ironic here by its placement "inside," refers to the ungrounded representation of an objectified exterior while, simultaneously, pointing toward the hollowness within. This literalistic, displaced semiology, we shall see, is "all" that comprises the world of the novel's city.

Our first view of Hazel in the city is this: "When he got to Taulkinham, as soon as he stepped off the train, he began to see signs and lights. PEANUTS, WESTERN UNION, AJAX, TAXI, HOTEL, CANDY. Most of them were electric and moved up and down or blinked frantically" (29). The rhetoric of this passage cataloging the city's signs is both suggestive and duplicitous. Hazel, ever seeking confirmation of anathema or transcendence, would naturally be looking for "signs and lights," but in the profane city the only signs he sees are those advertising corporeal satisfactions (peanuts, candy), worldly transcience (Western Union, taxi, hotel), and the demeaned name of a Greek hero known for his size, beauty, and suicidal impulses. Furthermore, these electric signs are not constant; taken *as* signs, they blink frantically (a flinching gesture repeated numerous times by the novel's "eyes") or move up and down. Not only are they signs of transience but signs *in* transience. They serve as demarcations of slippage and are, thus, alienating signs to Hazel Motes, the intransigent seeker after the certainty of nothingness. From the authorized perspective of the novel's preface, these are the signs of the world that Hazel should ignore in his pursuit of a higher destiny. Instead, they are the signs conferred upon him by the narrating, aesthetic authority who assembles them before us as the concrete representations of his being. Since they are signs that mean "nothing" to him, they speak doubly to his alienation and to the certain fate that is his—a fate he will "possess" at the novel's end as the ironic reward for his labors.

We might wish to go further in interpreting these signs for their inherent meaning, but we are always forced to return to the tautology of the signs themselves, which stand for the preordination of Hazel's destiny. "Peanuts" and "candy" may indicate that Taulkinham is a circus or a zoo, but these meanings only reemphasize the presupposed profanity of the city and, in retrospect, serve merely as repetitious prefigurations of the zoo where Enoch Emery works. Similarly, "Ajax" and "taxi" are nearly anagrams, indicative of the repetitive, monotonous verbal conveyances of this world. In this sense, all the novel's signs refer to their own axiomatic predications, so that Hazel's ignoring of them is a moot point: whether he "reads" them or not as being indicative of where he should go or what he should do makes no difference, since they refer only to themselves or to what is "already there," awaiting him in the future. Impatient with this literal iconography and wanting "a private place to go" (30), Hazel, in a city where no one, especially the city's signified, can hide, follows a sign indicating the men's room to a graffitied "welcome" sign on one stall door. Inside, a scrawled address on the wall leads him to a prostitute, Leora Watts. This is only the beginning of his journey, but here Hazel is properly initiated into the antihermeneutic quest which guides him, seemingly by accident, but altogether inevitably on the one road he must follow.[6]

What these early signs forecast is a world where the protagonist may be given two choices that lead to the same end: either read and interpret the signs you are given, under the pretense that the world is constructed as a series of available meanings relevant to you, or ignore the signs (as Hazel largely does) and proclaim the world meaningless. In *Wise Blood*, the roads to paranoia and nihilism are parallel because the signs themselves are evidences of a referential mania where everything gesticulates outward, to some one thing or to nothing at all. This "one thing" can be viewed as a version of empirical "reality" which, in all its weight and concrete exteriority, taken to its end, becomes a singular, monolithic monument to its own absurdity. While Hazel walks the streets of Taulkinham "along downtown close to the store fronts but not looking in them," the narrator's monotone ominously describes the "black sky [which] was underpinned with long silver streaks that looked like scaffolding and depth on depth behind it were thousands of stars that all seemed to be moving very slowly as if they were about some vast construction work that involved the whole order of the universe and would take all time to complete" (37). Who observes the cosmos in this passage? Surely not Hazel, who does not even see the lighted interiors of the stores as he passes by them. This "construction" is an authorial certification of the novel's vast "order" (the teasing "as if" aside), which is erected upon the "scaffolding" underlying a cosmological "work in progress" (the novel we are reading) whose "depths" appear as an optical illusion painted on canvas or an advertising billboard. This image of the night sky can be compared to the novel pointing its finger to itself and to us. Dactylically, it commands us to observe its "truths" as a matter of its own rhetorical constructions, indicated by the signs of its ad campaign, which refer to their own making as an imposed order of significance that will be revealed in the metonymic distance of "all time."

Beyond this, the night sky's depthless depth is either all or nothing: a cosmic unfolding of meaning that will take an eternity to reveal itself or an absurdist façade upon which is inscribed the meaningless, one-dimensional signs that belie, as fake stars, their own revelatory power. Like all the novel's signs, the stars over Taulkinham are ciphers, possibly emptied of meaning in this iconoclasm, embodying that one meaning which is a matter of self-reference, the stars' fortune: a = a; the depthlessness of the sky implies the "soullessness" of this profane world. In short, there is no real distance between signs and their referents in *Wise Blood*, as if, in a parody of the omniscient author, the entire world existed in the single mind's eye of the narrating aesthetic authority. The novel suffers from what might be called a "semiotic collapse," where the relation between a sign and what it means is erased, leaving only the monolithic signs themselves as the concrete, "objective" demonstrations of the world's meaning.

For Paul de Man, in the literary modes of allegory and irony, such a collapse is unthinkable: "in both cases [of allegory and irony] the relationship between sign and meaning is discontinuous, involving an extraneous principle that determines the point and the manner at and in which the relationship is articulated. In both cases, the sign points to something that differs from its literal meaning and has for its function the thematization of this difference."[7] This "difference" or distance, filled by the element of temporality in narrative, allows pluralistic meanings to emerge. Barth's *LETTERS*, for example, is largely given over to a self-conscious expression of narrative temporality and its relation to the process of interpretation. The history of A. B. Cook VI may repeat, in some ways, that of A. B. Cook IV, but it is the Heraclitean difference over time and the changes in historical contexts that allow them to be more than mere repetitions of each other; instead, they are meaningful echoes of and metonymical supplements to each other. But in *Wise Blood* there are, imaginatively, no interpretations and no temporality. The "whole order" of the novel's universe, which will "take all time to complete," casts the work into an anagogical mode, which represents an order of eternity already complete (all the signs are already in place) yet ever in the process of becoming.[8] The attempted rejection of temporality can be seen in Hazel's frequent and futile attempts to rid himself of his past, embodied in the image of the "ragged figure" who pursues his dreams or in the closed spaces of the novel, which are all repetitions of his seeing his mother in her coffin. That overdetermined vision literally erases time as it unites, in one image, birth and death, the coffin and the womb. When he creates his new church, Hazel significantly declares that time does not exist for his disciples: "Where you came from is gone, and where you thought you was going was never there, and where you are is no good unless you can get away from it" (90). His nihilism is expressed as a flight from time; it betrays a deep temporal anxiety that fears the difference between thought and experience, expectation and fulfillment, place and projection—the mutual inadequacies from which the possibility of interpretation arises. In one sense, O'Connor's fiction is not a novel but a gospel or, more precisely, a send-up of a gospel that does not announce the "good news" of incarnation where the word has become flesh and signs have been welded to their significances. Rather, the novel generates an exteriorized, empirical world; it is a "shiffer-robe" of a fiction where signs are collected to reveal, as absurd concealments, a "reality" inscribed on canvas or paper.

Thus, Hazel roams Taulkinham observed by a narrator who observes the signs he ignores, thereby authorizing their potential "meaning." Beneath a sky that was like "a piece of thin polished silver with a dark sour-looking sun in one corner of it," he enters a used-car lot designated by the sign "SLADE'S FOR THE LATEST" (68). There, as the sky tells us, Hazel succumbs to Mammon by mistaking a worldly vehicle, his "rat-colored" car, for more spiritual considerations and transports. He does so under the sign of Slade, an evil-sounding name that suggests a murdering of the spirit, whose apocalyptic "for the latest" either connotes a profane faddishness or defines his customers as the last who, eventually, shall come first. (But notice how the authorial pressure frames even this ironic sign: would Slade sound quite as "evil," would the biblical gloss be relevant or recognizable, were this not a novel about a Christian *malgré lui*?) In any case, the sign tells us that Hazel is taking a wrong turn in buying the car. The judgment is confirmed when it is destroyed later in the novel, signifying Hazel's growing concern with more ascetic matters. As he drives the car away from the lot, with a "feeling that everything he saw was a broken-off piece of some giant blank thing that he had forgot happened to him" (74), Hazel encounters the inevitable graffiti painted upon a boulder along the highway—"WOE TO THE BLASPHEMER AND WHOREMONGER. WILL HELL SWALLOW YOU UP?" and in smaller letters at the bottom, "Jesus saves" (75). The two possibilities the future holds for him, damnation and salvation (which, in a sense, are one, since to be damned by the world is to be saved by God in the novel's schematics), are thus starkly inscribed upon his "blankness." Hazel is written upon, made into a hieroglyph like that which greets his vision in the novel's "heart." Enoch Emery takes him to the sanctuary of the museum, but only after passing the sign of the "FROSTY BOTTLE," where Enoch partakes of a ritual, parodic "communion" as he drinks his daily milkshake. At the entrance to the museum's "holy of holies," both Enoch and Hazel gape at a mysterious inscription: "A concrete band was over the columns and the letters, M V S E V M, were cut into it" (96). Enoch misreads the sign as " Muvseevum," which appears as a palindrome interrupted by the middle letters "S E E," commanding the viewer to see the literal, meaningless repetition on each side. The museum sign, like all the novel's signs, including Hazel, is an imperative to read the inscriptions "cut into" the text, but in a manner which can only observe their archaic, one-dimensional presence, rather than interpret their differential plurality of meanings.

In this way, with these signs, O'Connor represents the "real," concrete, tactile world of her fiction—a grotesque world "without a transcendent context" but one which, paradoxically, stands for eternity.[9] Hazel and his quixotic partner have these signs imposed upon them, try as they might to ignore or misread them. Often unwillingly, they become sign processors as they fulfill their seemingly disparate but parallel destinies. In observing their own destinies, Enoch and Hazel become proficient typologists as they match their roles to the types or antitypes that preordain them. Enoch's path leads him to first steal the mummy from the museum and enshrine it as a "new Jesus." Then, when this god proves false, he transforms himself into the ape/god or "rough beast" whose final act is to stand gazing at the skyline of Taulkinham, ready to descend upon a new millennium. Enoch's anxiety, throughout, is revealed in his hermeneutic caution: "he was not a foolhardy boy who took chances on the meanings of things" (131). Thus, his shedding of his ordinary clothes and his assumption of the ape suit seem the logical ends to his quest for a certain salvatory role in existence. Rejected by Hazel and obsessed with the elements of ritual idolatry in a nontranscendent world, Enoch becomes what he must become, a parodic avatar, a literal "new Jesus" who brings, rather than redemption, fear and hilarity into the world. He is the ludicrous sign of the false prophet, a desacralized John the Baptist who precedes Hazel's apotheosis as a nihilistic Christ.

Hazel, also, does not like to take chances on the meanings of things but follows a slightly different path. Rather than making himself over into a ludicrous objectification of the world's transcendental failures, he attempts to reject the meanings of all signs and, thereby, abnegate his own being. His quest leads him through a series of denials of false "Christs"—the blind preacher Asa Hawks, the oily street preacher/con man Hoover Shoats, and his cohort Solace Layfield, who acts as Hazel's alter ego. Each of these, for Hazel, is a form of self-denial. At bottom, Hazel is an obsessive literalist who rejects any possibility of a sign's plurality, a gesture that, in the world of Taulkinham, seems redundant. His hilarious exchange with Hoover Shoats (also known as Onnie Jay Holy) shows the extremity of his literalism, compared to that of Shoats, who, like any good con man, knows that words and signs can sometimes be made to mean what you want them to mean. Shoats attempts to convince Hazel to join him in promoting "the Holy Church of Christ without Christ." Hazel responds to this "blasphemy": "My church is the Church without Christ . . . I've seen all of you I want to" (157). To Hazel's nominative finickiness, Shoats replies, "It don't make any difference how many Christs you add to the name if you don't add none to the meaning, friend" (157).

For Shoats, language is a commodity that additively, supplementarily generates "meaning." For Hazel, who insists that the "new Jesus" of which he speaks—the non-Christ—is just an expression, "nothing but a way to say a thing . . . No such thing exists" (159), language is a system of signs pointing to that which does not exist. Both views of language may be equally shortsighted, but Hazel's conception makes him especially susceptible, albeit unwillingly, to the authorial impositions of the text since, for him, the signs of language and of the world contain "nothing." The world, like Hazel, is a façade, a blank; the inscriptions of its meanings are just "expressions," "nothing but a way to say a thing," which suggests that the semiotic collapse discussed earlier is, appositely, a total sundering of the relation between sign and signified. The signs of the novel stand by themselves in Hazel's vision, and as mere ciphers they are available to the impression of any meaning that any "authority"—God, author, fate, repression—may want to force upon them. Like these signs, Hazel is also a "blank," a cipher, not interpreter but interpreted. At the end of the novel, for Mrs. Flood, his landlady, who like us is a reader looking for the purpose or meaning of Hazel's blinding and self-crucifixion, he becomes a sign of nothingness: "she sat staring with her eyes shut, into his eyes, and felt as if she had finally got to the beginning of something she couldn't begin, and saw him moving farther and farther away, farther and farther into the darkness until he was a pin point of light" (232). Unlike Enoch, who appears on the verge of descending down to the city in his costume as the sign of his own comic, devolutionary rebirth, Hazel recedes into an infinite distance, beyond origins, the merest speck of light in the dark pupil of Mrs. Flood's/the reader's/the novel's eye, and an antitranscendent sign of his own inner collapse. In a sense, he becomes a pure sign in the end, "a pin point of light" that reflects nothing but its own disappearance; literally, Hazel becomes an illuminated period.

In the either/or world of *Wise Blood*, inner being and the outer world are concretized as a singularity; linguistically, what I have cited as the novel's semiotic collapse is an erasing or fracturing of the relationship between signs and meanings. In the novel, the hero's subjectivity is exteriorized and scattered across its pages as the tangible signs of "reality." Conversely, everything in the novel is a fractured reflection of Hazel's obsessive quest for spiritual truth. Thus, the image of his face, which had "a fragile look as if it might have been broken and stuck together again, or like a gun no one knows is loaded" (81), suggests his potentially explosive personality and his nature as a patchwork assemblage of insignificances, a shattered and reconstructed mirror of the "broken-off piece of some giant blank thing." The ultimate effect of O'Connor's literalistic creation is the setting forth of a flat, controlled, outer-driven narrative that attempts to cast out that which is uncertain, noisy, or multiple. And expulsion is the fate ordained for the problematic "mote" of the novel, who never fits into this world, who acts as an irritant to it, because he threatens it as a fragmentary reflection of its own groundlessness.

The reductive world of *Wise Blood* is a "mundanization," a term developed by the Swiss psychoanalyst Ludwig Binswanger in describing the paranoid visions of his patient Lola Voss. This tragic, obsessive personality perceives existence to be a vast book of signs, written just for her, in which she reads "by a continuous interrogation of 'fate'" her sense that she is doomed by some exterior, alien force to a singular destiny: this is the "meaning" of her life. Binswanger writes, "In the case of Lola, we could observe in extreme degree the phenomenon of what we call mundanization [*Verweltlichung*], a process in which the Dasein is abandoning itself in its actual, free potentiality of being-itself, and is giving itself over to a specific world-design." Lola's construction of a "world-design" stems from, in Binswanger's analysis, a linguistic desire to control existence by means of a "net of verbal combinations that she throws over the Uncanny." Her "interpretation" of existence, then, is a validation or an authorization of an inner need for certainty that reduces the world to the single, definable "meaning" already inscribed in its skies and read in its stars. Thus, Lola says during analysis, "I see in the signs all the time that *I ought to be cautious* (since I don't know what may happen)."[10] As for Hazel, this fear of the unknown, the "uncanny" strangeness or paradoxical nature of existence, is really a fear of temporality, since for Lola time prospectively spreads out before her in the interminable future; it is this temporal flood that she attempts to dam up into a single source or stream. By casting her verbal net, she negates time. All the signs stand in place, ready to speak to her in the proper terms she has designated as arising from her own "reading," while she follows that single, timeless path which the signs "tell" her is her destiny.

Lola's monomania is an incorporation of the outer world into the self as the internalized necessity for certainty becomes exteriorized.[11] O'Connor's portrayal of Hazel Motes is the obverse of Binswanger's portrayal of Lola Voss, but with similar results. While Lola consumes the world, then spews it out again as a scattering of preexistent signs, Hazel's being, before *Wise Blood* even "begins," has been spread across the cosmos as the signs which will mark his self-development. At the novel's end, he is merely a reflection of those exteriorizations which have existed from time immemorial and which he joins as "a pinpoint of light," another star in the eternal sky. In both cases, the world is objectified, vacuumed of its temporality, and collapsed into the singular, reduced concreteness (self made world or world made self, outer made inner or inner made outer) that manifestly *is* its "meaning." Binswanger's translator, Jacob Needleman, makes a crucial comparison between Lola's self-referential system of signs and what he refers to as the dangers of empiricism:

> May we not, therefore, draw the analogy between what we described as the homogeneity of symbolic reference in the mentally ill and the dangers of overreductionism in explanatory systems? In both cases we find ourselves faced with an impoverishment of world, a price paid by the psychotic for the lessening of feelings of anxiety and paid by the overreductive system of explanation for comparable certainty. In both cases this impoverishment of world can be viewed as a loss of freedom: the psychotic is surrendered over (*ausgeliefert*) to his world-design, he is ruled as if from without by a world of his own essential structuring ("projection"); the overreductive system cannot return to the phenomena it has reduced; it finds itself committed to a world that no longer is the one it sought to understand; it cannot "let the world be."[12]

Needleman's formulation is problematic in that it posits, against empiricism, "letting the world be," a form of phenomenological passivity that implies the kind of self-negation, from the other side, that the reduction of the self in a totalized explanatory system portends.

Yet Binswanger's conception of "world-design" illuminates the world of *Wise Blood*, where signs, organized into a referential homogeneity, are projected as if from above rather than from within. The effect of this projection is to create an authorized world of inscribed destinies and dactylic gesticulations that betray a narrative anxiety about the uncertainties of interpretation. Like Hazel, we cannot ignore these signs, try as we might; we must read them as expressions, even generators (since one sign leads to another) of his fate. *Wise Blood* inculcates a dramatic textual desire to create a certain, certified impression, an "explanatory system" that will persuade us to accept the conditions of the protagonist's destiny, no matter how extreme. How else to explain the nearly scandalous amount of critical material written on the comparatively small body of O'Connor's work which, I would argue, poses throughout the problems of interpretation and certainty played out in *Wise Blood*? Critics flock to O'Connor, I suspect, largely because they seek to "explain" and, often, to justify the imposed authorizations her work promotes—as if the critics, themselves, wished to participate in this certainty of expression. From this view, *Wise Blood* appears as an ode to empiricism. The novel attempts to "prove" itself as a projection of a heroic progress that unfolds as a series of prefigured patterns, which leads to the conclusion that this "proof" preordains. Hazel, driven by half-concealed motives toward ends he never recognizes, becomes what he was meant to be within the system of signs that have existed "for all time" in the novel's sky: the victim/savior, the textual predicate, "despite himself."

Yet, if *Wise Blood* was satisfied to rest here, in certainty, it would lack the obvious humor and the powerful sense of the absurd that arise as an antistrophe to the novel's pronouncements. The text may struggle to impose its signs upon us as an expression of an authorial anxiety concerning hermeneutic multiplicity, but it cannot repress the "*malgré lui*" or the elements of surprise and trickery that occur at odd places in the novel.[13] What has been cited by one critic as evidence of O'Connor's sadism—her brutality to characters such as the family of "A Good Man Is Hard to Find," who, despite their foibles, hardly seem to deserve mass murder—might be seen, instead, as a form of textual disruption that discomfits any easy moral assessment of her work and undermines its dominating empiricism.[14] The cogent, authorized worlds her protagonists dwell within often seem to explode in their faces in the form of practical jokes, accidents, or unexplainable natural occurrences. It is possible to regard such "surprises" from a theological perspective as evidences of divine mystery's intrusion into a profane world. However, as is the case in *Wise Blood*, that world is imposed upon us as a graduate of the hero's "spiritual progress"; thus, the text's "surprises" may also be viewed as intratextual resistances or outworkings that struggle against its own impositions. Enoch Emery evinces a startling example of textual surprise when he remembers a childhood accident while observing a poster of Gonga, the ape/man he will become:

> Enoch was usually thinking of something else at the moment Fate began drawing back her leg to kick him. When he was four years old, his father had brought him home a tin box from the penitentiary. It was orange and had a picture of some peanut brittle on the outside of it and green letters that said, A NUTTY SURPRISE. When Enoch had opened it, a coiled piece of steel had sprung out at him and broken off ends of his two front teeth. His life was full of so many happenings like that that it would seem he should have been more sensitive to his times of danger. (178)

Here, several layers or undercurrents of the text seem to be at odds with each other as the "nutty surprise" is revealed. The incident explains why Enoch is so cautious about "the meanings of things," since his whole existence, like Hazel's, is dedicated to eliminating the recurrence of the unsuspected or the unexplainable. The hackneyed trick that limes him works because he is the perfect victim: a naïf who believes that signs and pictures mean, literally, what they say or depict. In one sense, the sign on the peanut brittle can is "correct" because what is contained within *is* a bad joke; but since it leads the literalist to believe that the words on the can represent the pleasant surprise depicted by the picture of the candy, the sign is also "incorrect." The two senses of "surprise" work against each other, and this semiotic conflict is placed in the larger context of a classical trickster (Fate) or demon (Satan, as the coiled snake) whose activity explains the presence of this surprise.

To accept such explanations would be to see Enoch as Oedipus or Christ, while everything in *Wise Blood* tells us he is a parody of these figures. The "nutty surprise" works to deepen the parody by subjecting him to a hardly disastrous trick of fate, but it also works to interject, in this totally determined world, a bad joke. Insofar as Enoch's odyssey is a profane replication of Hazel's story, the "serious" dimension of the novel is subjected to the nonsensical tautology of the surprise (which is, but then isn't, what it says it is). As if the signs were laughing at themselves in this passage, encouraging our laughter and suspicion at their play and malevolence, the "nutty surprise" works to "break up" the novel's overwhelming linguistic order. Peering out of this textual fissure is the visage of *Wise Blood*'s "aesthetic authority" pointing to itself as the Fate who kicks Enoch in the seat of the pants or the snake which jumps at him. This is exactly the effect of a surprise Enoch encounters earlier, in a daze of possession, knowing that "he's going to do something" on this day of antiheroic pursuits, but not what. Sitting at a soda fountain, he studies the menu, particularly "a picture . . . of a Lime-Cherry Surprise, a special that day for ten cents" (136). What ensues is one of a series of Enoch's laughable encounters with women in the novel as the waitress attempts to foist a stale Lime-Cherry Surprise upon him, while he is only able to mechanically repeat, "Something is going to happen to me today" (137). The waitress incorrectly interprets Enoch's obduracy as displeasure at her attempt to con him and thus makes him a fresh Surprise, but to no avail; he leaves without touching it: "'I got to go now,' Enoch said, and hurried out. An eye caught at his pocket as he passed the popcorn machine but he didn't stop. I don't want to do it, he was saying to himself. Whatever it is, I don't want to do it: I'm going home. It'll be something I don't want to do. It'll be something I ain't got no business doing" (137). Again, several interpretive contrasts reveal themselves in this scene. Enoch is on the verge of his comic apotheosis and so is compelled to act in ways he does not understand by the constraints of his unwilled role as comic god to Hazel's scapegoat. He thus observes the signs around him, but he is not allowed to read them, though they might mean something to him.

For the reader, the sign of the Lime-Cherry Surprise is potentially significant, since it is by blood and lime that Hazel will crucify himself and thus attain *his* apotheosis. In this regard, the scene of the Surprise is comically overdetermined; everything here is an exotic, tawdry reduplication of the sacrificial colors. The "red-headed waitress" wears "a lime-colored uniform and a pink apron" while working behind a counter composed of "pink and green marble linoleum" (136), as if the "aesthetic authority" felt it necessary to inundate us with the visual significances of the scene. The sign of the Surprise may serve either as a prediction of Hazel's fate or as a humorous gesture that points out the inappropriate, exotic destiny that awaits the surprised Enoch as Gonga reborn. On the one hand, we are given a mechanical, fated antihero; on the other hand, we are invited to interpret a ludicrous sign of the hero's destiny—each serves to parody the structures of meaning conferred within and upon the text. While Enoch wanders off, unable to interpret even the most obvious signals (the eye which "caught at his pocket" as he passes by the popcorn machine echoing the owl eye at the zoo and preceding, by minutes, Enoch's viewing of "The Eye"), the narrative authority of *Wise Blood* is busy throwing up a dense screen of signs which frantically point to parallel destinies but which, at the same time, undermine the dactylic authority of signs. These colorful "surprises" jump out at us in the novel's rigid, black-and-white world, compelling us to engage in a hermeneutic activity similar to those of Hazel and Enoch. We can make something of the signs by translating practical jokes and envisionments of lurid corporeal delights into significations, no matter how demeaned, of what will eventually happen. Or we can ignore them as meaningless incidents that take place in the odd, absurd, caricature world of the southern grotesque. To recall the hermeneutic oppositions of *Pale Fire*, we feel compelled, as readers, to side with the party of Shade or Kinbote, despite our knowledge that one "reading" of reality or another, poem or commentary, is not the whole story. Analogously, as readers of *Wise Blood*, we become either typologists or nihilists. Such inclinations, however, will not allow us to escape the self-conscious embarrassments that an encounter with these textual surprises inspires as disruptions of the novel's predictive semiotic arrangements.

I have been dwelling on what may appear to be two insignificant scenes from *Wise Blood* precisely because they exist on its margins as evidence of "comic relief" but have the crucial function of giving the lie to the hermeneutic argument that the weight of the novel poses. While so much of *Wise Blood* is given over to proving, by event and symbol, what all the signs initially dictate, these deviations disprove its tautologies and undermine, as jokes or nonsense, its certainties. To reiterate, the novel proposes an either/or world where everything means something (all the signs point toward and "convince" Hazel to accept his burden as Oedipus/Christ) or nothing (all the signs indicate the meaninglessness of existence, fulfilled in Enoch's assumption of the role of beast/god and Hazel's fading into oblivion). Everything in *Wise Blood*—signs, names, topographies, scenes, occurrences—potentially demonstrates those predestined outcomes and *a priori* assumptions upon which the text is founded. The "nutty surprises" generate a both/and alternative. They are signs that can exist as self-validating "proofs" of their own position in the text, as predicators of what is to come, and as iconoclastic descriptions that point to themselves as ambiguous, ridiculous divergences from the "real story." Their effect is to reintroduce into the novel its riven, temporal dimension. For the signs of surprise create gaps or unassignable spaces within the narrative order; they produce "surprise"—that element of the uncanny so feared by Lola Voss—in a monolithic environment. As hermeneutic obstructions, they generate a lag between sign and meaning which the text has unsuccessfully attempted to repress and which now must be filled by the self-conscious, temporal work of interpretation.[15]

When Enoch ignores all the omniscient "eyes" of his existence, while Hazel constantly gazes into the falsely blind eyes of Asa Hawks, looking for the truth of his fraudulence, an incongruency is established which forces us to question the status of the novel's "eye signs." Are they visual jokes? Are they signs of the "aesthetic authority" about to kick its creations from behind? Or do they indicate Hazel's paradoxical progress toward a vision which requires his self-blinding to achieve, a movement that recalls and reinterprets the eye imagery of literature from *Oedipus Rex* to *The Great Gatsby*? The difference between possible interpretations encouraged by puns on the word "eye," or the "nutty surprises" which play hermeneutic tricks on the reader as they play bad jokes on the protagonists, permits the text the ironic pleasure of commenting on its own semantic activity. In this way, *Wise Blood* undoes the singular condition it has assigned to itself and, thereby, allows for the possibility of interpretation, albeit as a countercurrent to the novel's "stated intention," which is to "mean" exactly what its signs tell us.

In "The King of the Birds"—that stunning essay that commemorates her hobby, raising peacocks, which has become an emblem for her life and work—O'Connor writes: "I intend to stand firm and let the peacocks multiply, for I am sure that, in the end, the last word will be theirs."[16] O'Connor's peacocks are, literally, only her pets; but they might also be her progeny, her stories and novels, and she the authoritarian "king" who "stands firm" while they regenerate, eventually becoming autonomous enigmas: the "last word," theirs. The figure she draws can be seen as an analogy for the authorial enforcements and rebellions of *Wise Blood*, where the drama of interpretation unfolds as the conflict between certainty and uncontrolled signification ("surprise"). The peacocks will have the millennial last word or ultimate statement about the nature of things, but their multiplicity—their power as signs—comes about as a corollary to the author's standing firm: a significance arising out of certainty. Whatever else they may mean, the peacocks, taken as signs, may stand just for themselves, those vainglorious birds whose appearance is both miraculous and scandalous, and whose most notable physical trait is a fan-shaped tail which displays a multiplicity of "eyes."

As representations of created objects, O'Connor's peacocks become a multitude of "I's" raised up by the single, rectitudinous "I"—O'Connor—who nurtures them, then proclaims their eschatological authority. The expressed desire in this image is for the author to establish and regenerate her own authority; yet, she seems to imagine that the outcome of this desire guarantees multiplicity and the freedom of peacocks, works, and signs to, figuratively, speak for themselves. The inherent contradiction of these twinned concerns informs the conflict of interpretation and the ironies of textual strategy that are the "subjects" of *Wise Blood*. The novel is, manifestly, an anagogy, a revelatory fiction that speaks of last things through a system of signs which dictates the apocalyptic, salvatory fate of the hero as a matter of the "reality" he finally recognizes in the moment of self-blinding. The heroic movement in the anagogy of *Wise Blood* is the gradual recognition of self and other as implicated within an established design, whether that design is regarded as theological, satanic, or existential. Less obviously, *Wise Blood* tears its own narrative fabric as an expression of a desire that signs speak for themselves. They inculcate a "reality" that is allowed to contain the uncanniness of temporality, where everything is not given over to a single, end-directed significance but is permitted "to be" as divergence, surprise, or frayed plurality. In generic terms, *Wise Blood* exists between its formation as a parodic gospel (but with the serious intention of making a statement about the function of saints in fallen worlds) and its knowledge of itself, partially brought about through parody, as a fiction. Its certainties, then, are fractured by the very signs which are indicative of certainty. For it is in the power of signs to stand both arbitrarily for themselves and for the distance between their manifestations and their meanings. While O'Connor's strained yet meticulous effort is to validate a singular world that reveals the problems of certitude in fiction, Stanley Elkin's *The Franchiser* celebrates, while questioning, the validity of pluralistic worlds and interpretations. There, we shall see, the "proper" realm of fiction is presented as a heterogeneous assemblage of voices raised in conversation or as a centrifugal flight of signs outward from their disinherited, authorial sources of significance.

CHAPTER SIX THE WOR(L)D MADE FLESH

STANLEY ELKIN'S *THE FRANCHISER*

. . . language has its true being only in conversation, in the exercise of understanding between people. This is not to be understood as if that were the purpose of language. The process of communication is not a mere action, a purposeful activity, a setting-up of signs, through which I transmit my will to others. Communication as such, rather, does not need any tools, in the real sense of the word. It is a real process in which a community of life is lived out. To this extent, human communication through conversation is no different from the communication that goes on between animals. But human language must be thought of as a special and unique living process in that, in linguistic communication, "world" is disclosed. Linguistic communication sets its theme before those communicating like disputed objects between them. Thus the world is the common ground, trodden by none and recognized by all, uniting all who speak with one another. All forms of human community of life are forms of linguistic community: even more, they constitute language. For language, in its nature, is the language of conversation, but it acquires its reality only in the process of communicating.

Hans-Georg Gadamer, *Truth and Method*

[My] task . . . consists not—of no longer—treating discourses as groups of signs (signifying elements referring to contents or representations) but as practices that systematically form the objects of which they speak. Of course, discourses are composed of signs; but what they do is more than use these signs to designate things. It is this *more* that renders them irreducible to the language (*langue*) and to speech. It is this "more" that we must reveal and describe.

Michel Foucault, *The Archaeology of Knowledge*

Ben Flesh, the roving protagonist of Stanley Elkin's *The Franchiser*, is, like the talk-show host of Elkin's *The Dick Gibson Show*, a communications expert and a facilitator of conversations. Typically, for Elkin's bad men, con artists, bail bondsmen, and merchants of the quotidian, Flesh is a raconteur of shaggy-dog stories and an assembler of cultural connections. Above all, he is a dialogist whose fervor to perpetrate upon the world the similitude of his franchises—Holiday Inns, Radio Shacks, Fred Astaire Dance Studios—is tenuously balanced against his quest for the multiplicity of existence—the thousand shades of house paint or the myriad arithmetical permutations of the world's thirty-one flavors. His prime interest exists in the discovery of a language that can articulate, by naming, the sheer abundance of America's material production. Simultaneously, he attempts to forge a language that states the underlying causal, analogical connection between all the materializations of physical desire. Flesh is an archaeologist of the ordinary and the mass-produced, alternatively sensitized and desensitized to the tactile quality of the world's goods by dint of the chronic illness he suffers from, multiple sclerosis. According to William Gass, Ben is also an author, since his is a "scribbler's sickness; [Ben] is MS'ed up, to put it as poorly as possible."[1]

What *The Franchiser* franchises through the discontinuous voice of its talkative subject is language, but not molded, as in *Wise Blood*, into an assemblage of preemptive signs. Rather, the language of Elkin's novel implicates the "more" of discourse that Foucault describes, the "communications" of a cultural field or *arche* which, replete with its own discontent and the eruptions of the uncanny into the ordinary, conserves itself within the inscription of the human world as the "conversation" of that world. The self, here, is no merely stable "subject" or preordained commination of value and need. In contrast to the fated subject of *Wise Blood*, the self of *The Franchiser* is "unauthorized"; it is the mutable, groundless intersection of the languages that it speaks and is determined by. Whereas Pynchon sees the linguistic relation between "self" and "culture" as polarized into a dialectical struggle, Elkin is concerned to portray this relation as a noisy "conversation" that defines our refractive relation to the incorporated objects of existence. "Being" becomes, in Elkin's world, a mode of interpretation expressed as a form of glossolalia, wherein multiple significances are simultaneously affirmed and shouted down. Yet, too, *The Franchiser* attempts to establish the limits of human discourse by miming and mocking its sonorities and by suggesting, within the framework of speech's enslavement to silence and life's to death, its finite variety.

Flesh's self-narrated story is told as a series of interlocking journeys the franchiser makes through "the packed masonry of states" (3) as he audits and modifies his various movie theaters, dry cleaning operations, and ice cream concessions. Driving across state lines, remarking the discourses of business, love, and illness that arise within the "packed masonry," Flesh views himself as an eternally transgressive, liminal figure who, because of his very marginality, is highly attuned to the "ordinary" world in all its massive homogeneity and noisy variety. Alternatively undergoing attacks of his disease and inconsistent periods of remission, Ben roams the world with a double death sentence hanging over his head: that decreed by the slow progress of his multiple sclerosis, and that ordained by the rising interest rates of an America moving through the energy-rich fifties to the inflationary seventies. For Ben, who is an orphan, has inherited from his godfather, Julius Finsberg, "the prime interest rate"—not money or land but their ghostly revaluations, the fiction of interest, which guarantees his right to borrow capital from the Finsberg fortune for his various enterprises at the best available rates. Ben is thus disinherited from estate or place while made heir to the phantom fluctuations of a market economy. As a franchiser, he *is* his itinerary. This route is guided by the rise and fall of interest, making Ben an "economy factor" as he continually crosses the boundaries of the states' chiseled edges. Ben's positionless position thus offers him the opportunity to perceive and to affect, parasitically, the orders of the quotidian which he articulates, in fantastic embellishments, as a language of common desire and dread.

From his privileged perspective, Flesh sees the world as an endless catalog of particulars, to be apprehended "without" as a system of knowable generic codes and "within" as an inexhaustible dissemination of specific varieties. Observing a group of conventioneers parading past him in the lobby of a Kansas City hotel, he elaborates on the contemporary styles of the businessman's uniform:

> Their sport coats are the nubby textures and patterns of upholstery from credit furniture supplements in Sunday newspapers. They are crosshatched, double knits, drapery, checks like optical illusions, designs like aerial photographs of Kansas wheat fields, Pennsylvania pastureland, or the russets of erosion in western national parks. The pockets of their blazers are slashed, angled as bannister. Change would fall out of them, he thinks. The flaps are mock, shaped like the lower halves of badges. Their notched, pointed collars ride their shoulders like the conferral of wide, mysterious honors, the mantles of secret orders—and Flesh supposes they belong to these. He has never seen such shoes. Many are glossy white loafers, the color and sheen of wet teeth in ads. Gratuitous, useless buckles vault the white piping that rises from their shoes like welts. The jewelry and fixtures in the center of their false straps could be I.D. tags, or metal tablets, or slender sunken scutcheons. He sees no belts in the tight cuneiform-print trousers, in the plaids like colored grids, like cage, windowpanes, that climb their legs like ladders. The pants hold themselves up, self-supportive, a flap of fabric buttoned to a rim of itself like flesh sealed to flesh in operations. He marvels at their bump-toe shoes, their thick fillets of composition heels like shiny mignon or rosy cross sections of pressed geology. (73)

In this explosion of pun and verbiage, Flesh relates a profusion of details that typify the appearances of apparel as a language which "conventionalizes"—culturally articulates—these conventiongoers. The designs of their suits appear as the patterns of landscape seen from the air or as the substrata of the earth's archaeological layerings. In succession, their lapels are perceived as "mantles of secret orders," their coat pocket flaps as "badges," the metal buckles of their shoes as "scutcheons," suggesting their entrance into a mercantile knighthood where a coat, rather than a coat of arms, is the sign of identity and the hieroglyph of self-protection. Even the detail of the "cuneiform-print trousers" suggests a cultural uniform which inscribes the wearer within several linguistic orders—commercial, religious, legal, genealogical, geological—as a signal within a complex system of communication or a variation within that uniformity.

We might well wonder what, beyond the superficial referent of "men's clothing," binds aerial survey to heraldry to sedimentation as the imitative, intersecting languages used to describe these apparels. The passage is replete with references to the patterned designs typical of Elkin's catalogs: "crosshatched," "double knits," "checks," "plaids," "grids," "cage," "windowpanes," "ladders," "fillets of composition," "rosy cross sections of pressed geology." The overdeterminations of design suggest that what is at issue in such passages is "design" itself. For Flesh, at this moment, the world is perceived as an interweaving and manifestation of inscribed, arranged tracings (a "cuneiform"); individuals within this world are viewed as "arrangements within arrangement" or identifiable, self-displayed collections of available signs. We have seen a similar understanding of the "self" in relation to the "world" in *LETTERS* and *Gravity's Rainbow*, but in *The Franchiser* there are added elements in this relation which I will discuss shortly: voice and body, conversation and corporeality. For now, we can notice that Flesh's catalog articulates this small piece of the world as a "convention" of languages whose extremities reside in an utter homogeneity that falsely hides a secret ("Rosicrucian") order scattered in a diversity of signs, shapes, and heterogeneous discursive arrangements. This linguistic design of sameness and difference defines the "work" of language in *The Franchiser*, where the knowable and the visible coincide as the exteriorizations of the human need for pattern, order, and communication.

Ben compiles another, more sensual catalog when he describes the olfactory qualities present in a dry cleaning franchise:

> He loved the shop, the smells of the naphthas and benzenes, the ammonias, all the alkalis and fats, all the solvents and gritty lavas, the silken detergents and ultimate soaps, like the smells, he decided, of flesh itself, of release, the disparate chemistries of pore and sweat—a sweat shop—the strange wooly-smelling acids that collected in armpits and atmosphered pubic hair, the flameless combustion of urine and gabardine mixing together to create all the body's petty suggestive alimentary toxins. The sexuality of it. The men's garments one kind, the women's another, confused, deflected, masked by residual powders, by oily invisible resins of deodorant and perfume, by the concocted flower and the imagined fruit—by all fabricated flavor. And

> hanging in the air, too—where would they go?—dirt, the thin, exiguous human clays, divots, ash and soils, dust devils of being. (112)

In this elaborate, Rabelaisian analogy, human secretions are transformed into a grammar of the self's exteriorizations. Corporeal substance and the apparel Flesh has observed at the convention are here made over into a common "fabrication" that both reveals and hides the exuding bodies within. While the bodies are present in terms of the sensory residue they leave behind, they are really absent from these garments which, folded or on hangers, appear as only the dummy shapes of their incorporations. This catalog of smells effects a discourse that simultaneously unites and disperses: the "dust devils" or floating traces of the human race disguised and arrayed in its cultural makeup are similar to those physical trace elements—bodily odors—that deodorants are supposed to conceal and the dry cleaning process to expunge.

As is the case with many of Elkin's "cultural interiors," the dry cleaning plant is an artificial world. Its purpose is seen in a centripetal/centrifugal operation which is at work in these rituals of masking and cleansing, parallel to the operations of a "collective" language that acts as the garment and exudation of our corporeal being. Humans sweat; in order to cover up this common manifestation of the physical self, they manufacture a diverse profusion of coverings and disguising scents. These proliferate and combine with the smells of dry cleaning agents to create the unique assortment of odors Ben appreciates in the shop—a difference returning to sameness as soon as the odors and traces of this human "progress" have been erased by the successful conclusion of the cleaning process. *The Franchiser* argues that this circular movement is, analogously, cultural and linguistic and that it has a singular referent, the human body, which assembles about itself as a language these diverse signs of the desire to be acculturated; conversely, this cleaning is also an expression of the body's desire to erase the marks of its own physicality. Sharon Cameron, discussing the body in Melville and Hawthorne, suggests that exhibitions of "body language" are reflections upon human identity as a relation of "inside" and "outside," "body" and "world," since "in the simplest sense, the world can neither be had nor known, the proper object of anatomization must be the self."[2] For Elkin, the catalog is a tracing of this relation, a self-manifestation in which the categories body/self/world are not conjoined into a monolithic, signified unity but are represented as a dispersion of signs that describe the ultimate incompletion and unknowability of these "categories." The list of human odors and fabricated smells made to disguise them (along with the languages of advertising generated out of this process) is, potentially, endless; the body, in its parts and coverings, is a heterogeneous multitude. Yet the point of the catalog is to assemble differences and to suggest the analogical relation between human and chemical substances, between the body and the "world" of elements that reveal the body's desire to disguise its presence. This, then, is a language of the self or a narration of the self's implication in the languages of the world—an implication that is represented as a collection of the self's remnants and a masking of its unseen, corporeal inwardness.

The anagogic conception of language in *Wise Blood*, seen as an inscription of signs whose meaning determines the relation between a "known" world and an elemental self, is countered in *The Franchiser* by the view of language as catalog and the world inscribed therein as a collection of bodies that exteriorize their relation to each other. While visiting one of his Fred Astaire Dance Studio franchises (on the verge of bankruptcy for lack of customers), Ben induces a motley collection of exiting moviegoers, innocent bystanders, and streetwalkers to attend a free dance and feast in his ballroom. He takes on the role of MC and, ever the appreciative observer of pattern and disorder, studies the dance floor upon which someone has accidentally dropped a bottle of ketchup:

> . . . he perceived from the various footprints, the rough male rectangles and female exclamation points, where each couple had been . . . From these and other signals he felt he understood why what they did was called the "conversation step." It was a conversation of spatial displacement, the ebb and flow of presence, invasions, and polite withdrawals . . . [a] minuet of hitherings and yonnings, the lovely close-order drill of ordinary life. So civilized. So gentle were the men. He explained this to them over the loudspeaker, explained how it was possible to re-create from the ordinary schmutz of a broken ketchup bottle, not just where the dancers had stood, but where

> they had stood in *time*, that movement was nothing more than multiple exposure. (61)

Here, Ben transforms a cultural manifestation, dancing, into a readable, narrative language that is both a patterning of the dancers' diachronic movements "in time" and a recognition of their synchrony or "multiple exposure." The dancers perform the "conversation step" beneath a huge revolving mirrored globe that throws off a galaxy of reflections which mime their movements. Within this restrictive, artificial cosmos, Ben metaphorically overhears the human "conversation" whose subject is our bodily positioning in space and time. *The Franchiser* might be seen as a book of such conversations: the world viewed as the transcription of languages, bodily or vocal, communicating with each other about the form and ends of communication, just as the notable imprints of the dancers bespeak the dance's pattern and missteps. This "conversation" of bodies is also a process of conversion. The intangibilities of human energy and movement are translated into a visible language which traces the desire for relation and the need to dance. In this way, Flesh oversees what he might well call "the miracle of communication," whose task seems to be to generate relations and mark them. The dozens of physical and verbal conversations that take place in the novel and their endless verbal transformations—bodily movement become patterned signals; sweat, fabric, and cleaning fluid mingling in the process that will eradicate other "signals" of this sexual dance—become fused into a novel-long exchange of discourses. *The Franchiser* orchestrates signs, patterns, patois, lists, and messages into what Mikhail Bakhtin, defining the nature of the novel, cites as "an active polyglossia and interillumination of languages."[3] The dance figured here is thus the "dance" of *The Franchiser*'s many languages, which (as MC) it conducts and forges into the discourse of narrative, marked by "Flesh."

Collectively, almost every conversation, catalog, and observation in *The Franchiser* is a decodable communication, its "world" a switching station of long-distance calls, a clutch of crossed messages. During one of his journeys, Ben attempts to stay in the vanguard of a massive power shortage moving slowly across the Midwest during one spectacularly hot summer. Perusing his maps, scrutinizing his car's heat gauge, he tries to "read" the seemingly erratic path of the brownout's progress as he frantically attempts to avoid being caught up in the American entropic nightmare:

> The pumps would not work where the electricity failed, and whenever he came to one of those zones of remission—the heat, constant everywhere, did not in itself insure a brownout; rather the land and towns, invisibly networked with mad zigzag jigsaw power grids, grids like crossword, secret-coded with electric messages he couldn't break . . . had been mysteriously parceled; agreements had been made, contingency plans had gone into effect, Peter robbed here to pay Paul, there permitted to hold his own, a queer but absolute and even visible (the lights, the lights) negotiation and exchange like the complicated maneuvers of foreign currency, the towns seeming to have grown wills, a capacity to conspire, to give and to take; he had an impression of thrown switches, jammed buttons, broken locks. (140)

If Flesh's map world is a vast system of communication, then his flight from its apocalyptic failures reveals its extremities. Remembering that these brownouts are the direct result of the human desire to artificially control an erratic environment, we can observe Ben confronting the polarities of order and disorder, progress and entropy as he reads the outage's inner, encoded message. Whole towns are implicated in some negotiated conspiracy that seems to allocate power willy-nilly for its own unknown reasons: the "pattern" of the brownouts is the communication of this message. The hidden conduits of power are transformed into a language (a "crossword, secret-coded") that designates a concealed system of exchange (a "foreign currency") which Ben must learn to read in order to survive and escape.

In this way, Elkin connects randomness and order as the extremes of a language that fuses sameness and difference, design and unweaving, inner and outer. The extremes reveal the epistemological alternatives of this language: radical certainty opposed to radical doubt; utter similitude brought up against utter dissemination; the secret, "inner" order wrought into, seemingly, a random scattering of "outages." While the readable codes of *Gravity's Rainbow* demarcate similar polarities, they are caught up in the tautological, either/or structure of that novel's embattled dominant and submissive orders; furthermore, the master referent of these codes is metaphorically assimilated as an underlying political or religious "plot" that orders the world and its Manichean conflicts. For Elkin, the languages of catalog, connection, and itinerary alternatively force the coalescence and bring about the dissolution of these extremes. The referent of these languages (power, the body) is not any substantial order or entity; rather, as Ben discovers, the referent is a corporeality or energy known only by its transformations *into* language, the marked routing of its transitions and conversions. A more concentrated discussion of the self in this world of sign systems suggests that what is at stake in *The Franchiser* is the groundless figuration of a polyphonic discourse whose "subject" (Ben Flesh) is the result, or physical marker, of its movements and its disinherited point of origin.

Similar to *LETTERS*, the genealogical concerns of *The Franchiser* inform the definition of the self and its presence, or absence, in language. While *LETTERS* equates textual and biological regeneration in an attempt to examine the entrance of texts and selves into history, *The Franchiser* more literally views the self as a fleshly "signal" in the "communication systems" of existence. *Gravity's Rainbow*, too, represents the body as a sign, but usually only instrumentally, as a response to a certain providential or scientific "program." Ben Flesh, seen as a symptom and a reader of signs, is at once within and without the discursive systems that articulate the novel's world. Physically a "stray signal" as he roams about the nation, Ben is the product and transmitter of a "miscommunication." His potentially faulty gene structure bears the bad news of his illness, MS, the symptoms of which, in his case, reveal themselves as an inability to correctly distinguish between different tactile surfaces. At times, he is a damaged receiver of the world's sensual message. But in his periods of remission, resensitized to the wondrous heterogeneity of touch and smell, he becomes a celebrant of the ordinary, at the center of the mundane, possessing the ability to tune in on any frequency of sensation with appreciative clarity.

Ben is thus an infrequently accurate reader of signs: much of his energy is used up by long periods of illness and misconstrual. Furthermore, as a transmitter of language—as salesman, storyteller, conversationalist—Ben is the sign of inconsistency. At certain points, he seems able to weave even the most ordinary, unnoticeable particularities into a fabric of connections that convinces us to believe (to resurrect Barth's phrase in *LETTERS*) that "everything reflects everything else," giving the world a relational quality nearly mystical in its sheer connectedness. Then again, as he stands in a revolving bucket perched atop a sign advertising his new fried chicken franchise, Ben indulges in a long-winded shaggy-dog story about a country rube coming to town that can only be seen as a comic replay of the verbal logorrhea which generally afflicts Elkin's talkative protagonists. In *The Franchiser*, Flesh's "self" exists as a barometer of the extremes of language figured as the relation between connection and discontinuity, order and dissemination, clarity and noise. Appropriately, Flesh does not, in his own speeches or itinerary, resolve these polarities; rather, he encompasses them in his "ecstasy attacks" (the sure symptom of a remission's approaching end) as the adjacent extremes of reading and speaking.

Ben is indirectly related, as "god-cousin," to the strange family whose patriarch is Julius Finsberg, a ruthless kingpin of the theatrical costume industry. Finsberg has conferred upon Ben both his vocation and the means to fulfill it. Subsequently, Ben takes over the role of stepfather to Finsberg's survivors and additionally becomes, over time, lover to each Finsberg daughter. He is also the family interpreter, for it is only Ben who can tell the identical Finsberg progeny apart. His description of the Finsbergs' remarkable physical similarities approaches a parody of the family likeness: "There were eighteen, nine boys and nine girls. Identical triplets, identical twins. But not just discretely identical, the part in each set identical to the other part or parts of each set, but identical to each other set too, somehow equal to and collateral with the whole. Each girl slightly favoring the father and each boy the mother, so that even their sexual differences seemed to cancel out the very notion of difference, and they looked, the boys and girls, like one person" (40). Ben locates the source of this incredible genetic replication in Finsberg, Sr., whose "very sperm, his very *genes* had become like a single minting of dimes, say" (41). But this outward manifestation of absolute sameness conceals the inner particularity unique to each Finsberg, the symptom of one of eighteen exotic maladies with which each is afflicted. Their perfect genetic symmetry is paradoxically matched by what Ben calls their "freak's ruined genetics, his terrible telegony and dark diathetics" (85). A sampling of the family illnesses might include Cole, who "had a tendency to suffer from the same disorders as plants and had a premonition he would be killed by Dutch elm blight"; Gus-Ira, who "as a nail biter was allergic to his own parings"; and La Verne, whose "organs lined the side of her body, her liver and lungs and kidneys outside her rib cage" (86). Ben naturally attributes these symptomatic manifestations of identity to Julius, who marries late in life and thus confers upon his progeny the residue of his exhausted being: "It was Julius, set in his ways, throwing himself like an ocean into Estelle's coves and kyles, till all that was left of his genes and chromosomes was the sheath, the thread of self like disappearing cheshire garments resolved at last to their stitching. Obsessive, worn out, he had made hemophiliacs of the self-contained and self-centered. Julius' progeny—that queer wall of solidarity and appearance, that franchise of flesh—were husks, the chalices in which poisoners chucked their drops and powders" (85).

The Finsbergs' collective fate reveals an old dichotomy between form and content or appearance and essence. Their corporeal "husks" are the illusory manifestations of similitude which cover the inner, radical difference that results from an old man's obsessiveness.[4] Julius is a progenitor who has worn out the "self" through his self-centered empire building, an activity whose beginnings lie in his act of cheating his business partner, Ben's father. His offspring seem biologically condemned to bear the marks of the father's sins—peculiar genetic tracings of their common exhausted source—just as Ben's scattered, failing franchises (failing because of the rise in the very "interest" that is the source of *his* power) exist as the disseminated remnants of the Finsberg dynasty. The movement from consolidation to dispersal, reflected as an inner/outer dialectic in the bodies of the Finsberg children, is imagined by Flesh as the bad transmission of a message or as the unraveling of the "thread" of the self's "cheshire garments," whose remnant is only "sheath" and "stitching." The message of the chromosomes, in this case, is a sign without a referent, a hieroglyph of being consumed which transmits only a genetic husk bearing the determinative stamp of the "selfless" father. The identity contained within as Finsberg's absence is figured as a miscommunication or a freakish physical extravagance. In one sense, the generation of Finsbergs seems to inversely repeat the extremities of language that, we have seen, mark the world of *The Franchiser*; indeed, their generation is a parodic recapitulation of narrative "labor": the story of their birth is an unweaving, a reduction to "stitchery" of the seams (semes) whose binding function becomes meaningless. But the Finsbergs also successfully communicate, physically, their father's guilt. Their corporeal symptoms can stand for the element of determinism in Elkin's worldly discourse justified by the constant vision of desire transformed into flesh, fabric, and architecture as the sign of passing generations. Alternatively, the Finsbergs can be viewed, semiotically, as the riving of inside and outside, sameness and difference, sign and design which, we are convinced elsewhere, can converge in catalog and conversation.

For Ben, the Finsbergs are a readable language that inscribes the scattered signs of the family patriarch's exhausted sexuality; similarly, for him, the world is a graph charting the transformations of human energy and desire into highways and franchises, power lines and cities. Because "he went extensively beyond externals," though always on the periphery himself, Ben achieves an "insight" into the Finsbergs' manifest identicality: he is "as certain of their differences as a geologist of landscape, of fault, strata, and where the ice age stopped, hunching the mineral deposits, informed-guessing at the ores and oil fields, water-witching what was—forget age, forget sex, forget names even . . . their infirmities, their mortalities distinct to him and strident as the graffiti of factions" (84–85). Ben's comprehension of the Finsbergs' differences takes two opposite directions. He is acutely conscious of their peculiar mortalities, which, elsewhere, he defines as signs of the self's beginning ("Everyone carried his mortality like a birthmark and was a good host to his death" [290]). But he also continually comments upon their common source, the "deposit" of Finsberg's semen and money, which their genealogical exfoliations sublimate *as* a difference, with interest.

Ben thus "reads" the Finsbergs as the dissemination of a failing sexual energy which has been used up because of Julius' obsessive empire building. Each child bears the outward mark of Julius' patriarchal impression and the inward mark of, to paraphrase Emily Dickinson, "internal difference / Where the meanings are." They are, Ben notes, the result of a "franchising" activity which he attributes to an idealized conception of Howard Johnson, originator of another kind of human "chain": "He had assumed that a man named Howard

Johnson made ice cream, an ice-cream scientist, someone with a visionary sweet tooth, a chemist of fruits and candies, a larky alchemist who reduced the tangerine and the mango, the maple and the marzipan to their essences, who could, if he wished, divide the flavor of the tomato and the sweet potato from themselves, a tinkerer in nature who might reproduce the savor of gold, the taste of cigarette smoke" (46). Here, as with Julius Finsberg, the source of a hundred scattered "progeny" is envisioned as a simultaneous movement toward reduplication and division. The self of family or franchise is thus located in a discourse—sexual or chemical—that inscribes the desire of the self's origin to scatter or reproduce itself. That, in the case of Julius Finsberg, this desire is perverted or, in the case of the mythical Howard Johnson, alchemical, "unnatural," is not a point to be missed: for these are the desirous inscriptions of patriarchal power, the maker's mark. Like all the languages of *The Franchiser*, this discourse of the father marks its own systematic processes. It inscribes the routes by which the ends of desire mark themselves as the extreme, paradoxical movements of splitting and reduplication, unraveling and reduction. For the Finsbergs, the ends of these movements lie in their beginnings. The symptoms of their mortality are their birthmarks stamped, from the start, with the father's name ("*fin*"), which exist as the incarnated phonemes of his mortal, assimilatory language.

In its extremes, this patriarchal, authorial discourse is either a mere repetition of origins that results in deformity or a mania for the creation of explanatory "world-designs" similar to that which afflicts Lola Voss. One of Julius' offspring, Patty Finsberg (known as "the Insight Lady"), joins Ben on one occasion in Colorado Springs, where he effects a temporary escape from the entropic heat wave that tracks his itinerary. In a city where Ben had "a sense of connection, the roads that led to Rome, of nexus, the low kindling point of filament, of globe and tubing, as current poured in from every direction . . . the city like the exposed chassis of an ancient radio, its embered tubes and color-coded wire" (154), he suffers Patty's remarkable ability to consolidate disparate cultural phenomena. What seem, at first, to be astoundingly imaginative connections—she notes, for example, that chandeliers "must have come in with the development of lens astronomy at the beginning of the seventeenth century. I should think it was an attempt to mimic rather than parody the order of the heavens, to bring the solar system indoors" (181)—become more parodic and farfetched as she goes on:

> Men's ties are a sort of male brassiere, of course. In the phallic sense of *straightening* the chest. I don't go much for the plumage theory. What's more interesting is that ties complete the circle of the throat, much as a priest's collar does. Shirts, open at the throat, are arrows to the genitals. Do you suppose there can be a correspondence between the tie and the hangman's noose? Idiom says "necktie party," but the operative world is "party," I should think, with its comic insistence on the collaboration between the celebrational formality and seriousness of death. Then there's the notion of the knot, a clear adumbration of the Adam's apple. But overriding all is the tie's tattoo symbolism. . . . Marvelous. And to do it in silk, wools, the softer cottons. Pleasure/pain. Velvet bondage. *God*! (182–83)

A true child of Julius, Patty attempts to assimilate everything, through this discourse on "ties," into a single, connected language that "adumbrates" human desire. This example of her comic monologue, which lasts the entire weekend and is to be heard even amidst the throes of her lovemaking with Ben, might be seen as a humorous rendition of the dark dialectic enacted in the Finsberg family line, where beginnings and ends are intimately connected. Patty "talks out" the connections with Ben, who is reenacting another version of the dialectic as he momentarily escapes from a heat wave that produces random displacements, or blackouts, which conceal a secret progression. Ironically, he escapes to this city of connections lying in the shadow of a quite unnatural mountain which contains NORAD, the nerve center of America's defense command. The implication at this point in the novel is that all scattered manifestations of reality are connected into a single discursive system. Patty only scratches the surface, but here endless metonymies suggest infinite interconnection.

Furthermore, it seems impossible to escape this monolithic discourse with its secret, thanatopic origins and ends. Even when Ben and Patty escape "into nature" (but on Cheyenne Mountain), their conversation seems condemned to repeat the obsessions and extremities of the acculturated discourse that has heretofore defined "life" as the sign of death and transformed a domineering desire into unnatural clonings and malformations:

> . . . no place to hide in nature save in the wonderful. He meant the bizarre, he meant the awful, strangenesses so odd, so alien, they were religious. Vouchsafed to die of his disease, it was as if here, in nature, where everything was a disease, all growth a sickness, the mountains a sickness and the trees a sickness, too, with their symptomatic leaves and their pathological barks, the progress of his disease could leap exponentially, travel his bloodstream like the venom of snakes or the deathbites of killer spiders.
>
> "I heard," he said quietly—was this praying? was this some crazy kind of prayer?—"I heard of a man who had a bedspread made of wolves' muzzles. He kept them in a freezer in St. Louis until he had enough for his tailor to stitch them together." (199)

Connection, in this "idyll," is the sign of death, of nature denatured and woven into a "product." As the Finsbergs' diseases mark the language of their mortality, as Ben's disease is symptomatic of his own nerves' unraveling, so both nature and culture in *The Franchiser* appear in their signifying chains, successions, and similarities as the reversible, teleological languages of their own beginnings and ends. Even the "uncanny" in Ben's reflection partakes of this signifying illness as the abnormal is converted into a sign of the referent—death—which is the end of all the interwoven manifestations of existence he describes. The self in these languages, thus far defined, discloses its identity in the repetition of its genetic source and as a scattering of the source's seed or an entropic fraying of its paternal thread. This is Elkin's vision of the self in story or the self *as* the story—woven, stitched, or unraveled—of its inheritance. Here, the self is a sign in a monolithic, analogical discourse that connects everything together in a fabrication of the desire that seeks, while signifying, its own death.

The authoritative discourse of *The Franchiser* may be viewed in many ways: as the writing of logocentrism, of Western civilization, even—if we use Peter Brooks' analysis of narrative as inscribing, while deferring its own end—of narrative itself, which weaves plots and makes connections in order to finish itself off.[5] Yet, set alongside this mortal interpretation of existence is a conception of language and self which Julia Kristeva, reading Bakhtin, calls "carnivalesque." The carnival in literature, she argues, represents a scene of writing that brings together the "ends" of language—"repetition," "nonexclusive oppositions," "distances," "relationships," "analogies"—not connected in a linear, hierarchical manner (as replication leads to utter dissemination for the Finsbergs) but absorbed into an alogical, riotous "whole."[6] The desire implicit in such a nonanagogical discourse is for what lies between all of the novel's stated oppositions. It is a nonoriginary discourse of the middle, though it is framed in *The Franchiser* by the birth of Flesh's vocation and his death from multiple sclerosis. While this other conception of language is not an escape from its own beginnings and ends—any more than Ben can finally escape from heat waves or the progress of his own disease—it is an "outworking" or eruption within the confines of life and death, sameness and difference.

The "conversation step" that Ben observes in the ballroom is an example of this language of middles, as it inscribes a pattern in the mess and tells of a dialogic exchange between partners about the mutable relationality of their positions. Another example occurs when Ben describes to Lorenz Finsberg the "miracle" of the world: "Drive up and down in it as I do. Look close at it. See its moving parts and its cranes, car parks and theater districts. It can't be. It could never have happened . . . The complicated ports with their forklift trucks and winches. All the hawsers, tackle, sheets, and guys. All the braided, complex cable. All the gantry, all the plinth . . . The planet's rigging like knots in shoes. The joists and girders, trivets, chocks. Oh, oh, the unleavened world. Groan and groan against the gravity in stuff" (257). What Ben describes in yet one more catalog is the creation of the world as an opposition to the leavening power of gravity, whose force is both assimilatory, as it pulls everything unto itself, and differential, as it stratifies or marks into layers the eruptions of antigravitational forces. This may be seen as a figure for language and narration in *The Franchiser* or those evidences of them existing in the catalog and shaggy-dog story which form opposing discourses to Julius Finsberg's end-directed genetic messages. Knot and braid, cable and winch might be seen, analogically, as the entanglement of language which is also its labor: not merely connection but knotting, not only a fraying but a plying of work in progress. Again, this discourse does not escape its ends, any more than does the "unleavening" of the world as the construction of civilization in, according to the passage, pyramids and oil refineries, both monuments to death and extinction. Yet, as a kind of semiotic "life" within these ends, Elkin suggests a view of the corporeal self and voice generated by language as a noisy resistance, a celebratory filigree, or a meandering itinerary.

Near the end of *The Franchiser*, his money running out and his health failing, Ben Flesh opens his last franchise, a Travel Inn located in Ringgold, Georgia. The Inn is an immediate financial disaster because Ben has failed to correctly read and prophesy the intertwinings of his patrons' needs, human habits, and historical events. Having carefully traced the popular routes from major Midwest cities to Disney World in Florida, Ben has placed his Inn in this telling location because he calculates that it will be the most convenient stop in a two-day journey between points. But only months before the Inn's opening, America suffers the Arab oil embargo, spiraling inflation, and the lowering of speed limits: a two-day trip becomes a three-day trip, and Ben's Inn cannot attract enough customers to break even. Disenfranchised, foiled in this final attempt to make connections, Ben roams the corridors of his half-filled Inn and, suddenly, while voyeuristically listening in on the conversations taking place behind the flimsy motel doors, discovers a "conversation" of lovers: a discourse of erotic desire overheard and displayed in all its comic, subversive varieties. The scene is, precisely, an example of the "carnivalesque" in its transgressive yet paradoxically inhibitory panorama of lovemaking as Ben moves from room to room. The vision causes him to have an "ecstasy attack" and an insight about his place in the represented world of a wall map:

> He rises, intending to go to his room, when his eye is caught by the map on the big display board opposite the registration desk. The concentric hundred-mile circles make the states between them a sort of target, twelve hundred miles of American head seen through a sniper-scope. He goes up to the map, to dartboard America, bull's-eyed, Ptolemaic'd Ringgold. He examines it speculatively. And suddenly sees it not as a wheel of distances but of options. It's as if he hadn't seen it

> properly before. Though there are dozens of road maps in the glove compartment of his car, he has rarely referred to them. Not for a long while. Not since the Interstates had made it possible to travel the country in green straight lines. Why, there are signs for Memphis and Tulsa and Chicago in St. Louis now. Signs for Boston and Washington, D.C. in the Bronx. Seen in this way, in swaths of hundred-mile circles like shades in rainbows, he perceives loops of relationships. He is equidistant from the Atlantic Ocean and the Gulf of Mexico and Pine Bluff, Arkansas and Centralia, Illinois. He could as easily be in Columbus, Ohio, as in Petersburg, Virginia. New Orleans rings him, Covington, Kentucky, does. He is surrounded by place, by tiers of geography like bands of amphitheater. He is the center. If he were to leave now, striking out in any direction, northwest to Nashville, south to Panama City, Florida, it would make no difference. He could stand before maps like this one in other Travel Inns. Anywhere he went would be the center. He would pull the center with him, the world rearranging itself about him like a woman smoothing her skirt, touching her hair. (332–33)

Arguably, this passage is a flagrant example of egotistic self-centeredness—a return to the Finsberg model—as Ben appears to view himself at the center of the universe. But another reading suggests that Ben is still marginal, a displaced center in this final vision, in the middle of a nonlinear world perceived as a "wheel . . . of options," "loops of relationships." Seen mystically, it is a world without ends, since all the roads appear to circle back on themselves; seen ironically, it is a world whose subject, Flesh, labors under a death sentence as the "bull's-eye" of its center. And Ben, as the "floating middle" of this map universe, is conceived not as a generating presence but as a repository of relationships, like Slothrop, an intersection of possibilities continually undergoing rearrangement. This "middle ground" is produced by the carnivalesque conversation of lovers, whose many languages refer to their common desire and activity. Positioned in relation to these, Ben is the displaced receiver, the "connection" who comprehends and transmits their message.

Ben literally becomes the mediator for the lovers' discourse when he broadcasts, over the Inn's intermural telecommunications system, the details of his discovery: he has witnessed "love's detritus on posted land, everywhere the flotsam and jetsam of concupiscence scattered as beer can, common as litter" (328). His message inspires other innkeepers (other receptacles of this common, "inward" desire and its voicings in lovers' languages) to converse over the telex lines about their own exposure to the "scatterings" of sexuality. Acting as a conversationalist in this passage, Ben becomes an interchange between these voices who speak of these disseminations wrought into a common language of desire. As he is at the center of the map, so he is, analogously, in the middle of this discourse, its interpreter and interpretant, marveling at the wonder of his position: "And ah, he thought, euphorically, ecstatically, this privileged man who could have been a vegetable or mineral instead of an animal, and a lower animal instead of a higher, who could have been a pencil or a dot on a die, who could have been a stitch in a glove or change in someone's pocket, or a lost dollar nobody found, who could have been stillborn or less sentient than sand, or the chemical flash of someone else's fear, ahh. *Ahh*!" (342).

Ben lapses into the inarticulate after this scene of recognition because what he is, as the "subject" of the novel and of his reflection, cannot be named. He is not to be defined in terms of some representation; he is not, merely, an analogous sign or only the vehicle of his own end. He may be seen as constructed in language, as the nodal point and transmitter of desire's conversation, or as being at the center of random yet contingent possibilities, but he is not the origin of these. Instead, he is originated by them. He will die, but he is not merely a symptom of his own death, "a dot on a die," or a self-inscription, "a pencil," or a determined reaction, "the chemical flash of someone else's fear." Like his catalogs, Ben's "self" in the end may be seen as a design, but one that refers to its own groundlessness and displaced otherness as an interweaving of routes, an echoing of voices. But unlike Slothrop, who dissolves into the larger movements of a cultural counterforce, Ben Flesh retains his identity as a mediation of crossed messages and competing languages. The irony of Elkin's novel prevents any amelioratory conclusions about this self-conception, which reflects the inherent risks of Flesh's liminal, multiple state of being. For here, identity is temporalized in a minute-by-minute struggle to sustain the sense of "marginality" under a constant death sentence. Put another way, *The Franchiser* convinces us to accept Flesh's version of "reality" as groundless and indeterminate, while arguing that "life" is, precisely, the quest for the ground of being. Ben finds the potential for this semiotic self-conception relational rather than patriarchal, mediatory, erotically conceived within its dead ends, and nothing short of miraculous, as well as ultimately inarticulable. He is the ironic focus of a narrative which, poised against its own beginnings and ends, renders its protagonist as an entangling of and a digressive witness to the world's "text" or, to foreshadow the next chapter, an inconstant reader.

CHAPTER SEVEN ENTANGLEMENT THE READER IN CONTEMPORARY FICTION

All modern interpretation that is not merely an attempt at "re-cognition" involves some effort to divorce meaning and truth. This accounts for both the splendors and the miseries of the art. Insofar as we can treat a text as not referring to what is outside or beyond it, we more easily understand that it has internal relationships independent of the coding procedures by which we may find it transparent upon a known world. We see why it has latent mysteries, intermittent radiances. But in acquiring this privilege, the interpreters lose the possibility of consensus, and of access to a single truth at the heart of the thing. No one, however special his point of vantage, can get past all those doorkeepers into the shrine of sense. . . . The pleasures of interpretation are henceforth linked to loss and disappointment, so that most of us will find the task too hard, or simply repugnant; and then, abandoning meaning, we slip back into the old comfortable fictions of transparency, the single sense, the truth.

Frank Kermode, *The Genesis of Secrecy*

Throughout these six readings of contemporary fictions and the dialogue which introduced them, I have been implicitly concerned with what Kermode has punningly called "the reader's share"—his parcel and parsing of the text, her exchange with or implication within it.[1] Scattered through my explications are the loose ends of a discussion I wish to gather up here about the "reader," a being who construes while being construed by the text which is engaged. Since I have been so concerned with the concept of the semiotic self as conceived within contemporary narrative, perhaps this final movement toward the discussion of the reader's self may appear, on the surface, to be both obvious and redundant. For the two selves (that of the text's subject and that of the reader) can be seen as Faulkner envisions them in *Absalom, Absalom!*—dark brothers, each other's doubled shadow, sharers in the secret of the text. These two are, analogously, in a relation like that represented by the successive pools of Quentin Compson's famous metafictional image, each "*a different temperature of water, a different molecularity of having seen, felt, remembered*," yet all "*attached by a narrow umbilical water-cord*," thus each differently repeating, in ripple effect, the unseen fall of a pebble into the first pool in the succession.[2]

This complex image of repetition and difference, of reflections and echoes that refer back to an unseen origin, retains numerous inferences in the context of Faulkner's novel. For my present purposes, Quentin's analogy defines the operation of narrative language I have been discussing all along, as well as the interpreter's antigenealogical "place" in that language: as neither the source nor the receiver of the text's (absent) authority or origin but as a refractive element that is both its witness and its perpetrator. What readers uncover in the act of interpretation is, partially, themselves reading. More importantly, by becoming a signifying force in the semiosis of the text, they reconstitute its semantic field or, in other words, tell the interpeter's story within the larger interpretive history of the text. That this story, as Kermode poignantly discerns in the epigraph, is one of loss—each interpretive reconstitution of meaning a further distancing from the "original" text and its unrecoverable intention, a deeper entanglement in the history of its meanings rather than a glimpse of "the text itself"—is only one side of the coin. The obverse is equally true. The loss of transparency is a gain in relationality where (to use a phrase initiated by the shadowy narrator of *Absalom, Absalom!*) "some happy [and noisy] marriage of speaking and hearing," leading inevitably to "paradox and inconsistency," is generated as the reader produces, steals, or mistranslates a hermeneutic discourse out of the relation to the text.[3] The remainder of what I have to say will be directed toward an understanding of the reader's relation to the book being read. This relation can appear, at one extreme, as a labyrinthine inwardness that traces out only the reader's solipsistic reflection and, at the other, as an untenable objectification of the text and of the reader as a relation of observer to specimen. In between the extremes, I will suggest, the reader finds a place and a being as reader.[4]

Let me begin, again, by stating what is not solely at issue here: the reader as implicated construction, as responsorial voice, as a loosely affiliated member of a community of interpreters, or as a determined seeker after the text's "truth."[5] While each of these separate conceptions may be found, usually parodically, in the novels I have discussed, together, they promote a definition of the reader as *the understanding of his or her relation to the text*. This general statement is one I hope to make more useful by specifying its complexities through example and commentary. My emphasis, clearly, is on the constructions and discontents of those relations that produce meaning from reading ("the act of interpretation"), as well as how that production, in turn, constitutes the reader's self. For Charles Kinbote, in *Pale Fire*, the relational function of the reader appears to result in awestricken silence when she or he gazes passively upon the theatricalization of the author's verbal pyrotechnics:

> I wish you to gasp not only at what you read but at the miracle of its being readable (so I used to tell my students). Although I am capable, through long dabbling in blue magic, of imitating any prose in the world (but singularly enough not verse—I am a miserable rhymester), I do not consider myself a true artist, save in one matter: I can do what only a true artist can do—pounce upon the forgotten butterfly of revelation, wean myself abruptly from the habit of things, see the web of the world, and the warp and the weft of that web. (289)

While he wishes "the reader" to appreciate the legibility of his authorial commentary, Kinbote projects himself as a "true artist" in the role of a reader who celebrates his own ability to make the world readable. In contrast to the conception of the artist as magician and mimic, Kinbote proposes that his particular artistic gift lies in the ability to precipitate the world's design, its interior looming, and to find the Gnostic, immemorial key to its mysteries ("the forgotten butterfly of revelation") through a process of defamiliarization ("wean myself abruptly from the habit of things"). That he imagines himself as a collector who captures, kills, and pins the metamorphosed avatar of "revelation" suggests that this instance of "true artistry" partakes of a mortal hermeneutic, a "mystery" hunted down and caught in the dead letters of the text. Using the image of the spider's web, that favorite trope for texts, plots, and the work of fate, Kinbote sees the text of the world only in the form of a singular explanation or as a vehicle of foreseen revelations. There is something "behind" this world and the alphabetic letters that inscribe it, something between the lines which, once deciphered, will appear to be a transparency of meaning, the dead revelation captured and displayed, ironically, as a still life. In short, Kinbote perceives himself as a scientist and the world as a textbook of anatomy. What induces this perception is his tortured desire for the validity of his own self-conception, which he *must* comprehend for the sake of his own artistic survival as already, "originally" inscribed in Shade's poem, rather than merely read into it. His obsessive activity is precisely to confirm his "reading" of the world, as if the act of interpretation was a mere decoding of the distanced relationship between the reader and the text, represented by a preordained, magical, but thoroughly imitative fictive language that never doubts its revelatory powers.

Of course, *Pale Fire* compels us to see the folly of Kinbote's efforts and the tremendous loss that these bring about. It visibly parodies the effects of alchemy-cum-empiricism as Kinbote tries to objectify the geography of his imagination. By negation, the reader of Kinbote's readership is cast into a state of doubt about the competence or validity of any interpretation of *Pale Fire*. Every effort to get at its mysteries, including my own, which dwells upon the mysterious origins of the self as the absent source of the novel's exfoliations seems doomed to the same reductiveness characterized by Kinbote's commentary on the poem. As Marc Chénetier has observed of any interpretive gestures that might be made toward the novel: "Could it not be that Nabokov . . . manages to offer a bone to all and any pursuer of critical inquiry: from information theory (noise) to deconstruction (shade, haze, and trace) via psychoanalysis and linguistic (oppositions) or semiotic (X, Y) investigations, via also all sorts of psychological theories and decodings of artistic objects? By which I mean that the text itself would make well-nigh impossible—and this programmatically—any one hermeneutic handling; all hermeneutics being then of course but a muted spin-off of the original thing, and the critical act a 'pale fire' indeed."[6] Read in this way, *Pale Fire* is undermined by its own limitations and the parodic trials it undergoes on Kinbote's account, who will attempt any theory of interpretation in order to validate (or "discover") his own image within the text of "Pale Fire." Still, as more skeptical Kinbotes ourselves—but Kinbotes nevertheless—we are often caught up in his game, since our "natural" inclination, as we move from poem to commentary and back again, is to confirm or deny his hypotheses about the poem's meaning. Yet, as Kinbote's understanding of interpretation as "defamiliarization" tells us, this inclination is no more natural than any other way of reading; it is a learned, empirically based process of trial and error that assumes the existence of preexistent, transcendent truths hidden under the protective covering of the text's literal inscriptions.

Reading in this way, the reader projects certain hermeneutic values—validity, priority, transparency—that are at odds with those promoted by, in Roland Barthes' terminology, a "multivalent text," which attempts to undermine these values: "A multivalent text can carry out its basic duplicity only if it subverts the opposition between true and false . . . if it flaunts all respect for origin, paternity, propriety, if it destroys the voice which could give the text its ('organic') unity."[7] At once, in reading *Pale Fire*, we attempt to establish or deny the authenticity of Kinbote's voice—a voice obsessed with its own origins refracted in the text—while experiencing the vertigo that the novel, as a multivalent text, produces. The epistemological paradox of the novel, which may be summarized as a radical doubt in search of certainty, recapitulates the extremes of interpretation mentioned earlier. As Kinbote scans the text for the objectification of his own narcissistic image, the reader is caught between an unacceptable reduction of the text to a self-validating critical approach and an equally unacceptable subjectification of the text ("it can mean anything we want it to") or a radicalizing of its doubtfulness ("since it doesn't mean anything in particular, it means nothing").

From a distance, *Pale Fire* might be viewed as rejecting the dialectical extremism of this readerly entrapment—an extremism which, interestingly, the dactylic world of *Wise Blood* promotes—where we must establish either certain clearly defined parameters of interpretation or none at all. Closer in, we are fatally attracted to the novel's bait in our desire to diminish the void between the reader and the text, expressed as an unfulfilled need to make its language a transparent, perfectly revelatory medium of its truths. The irony of this desire lies in its ends: insofar as we hermeneutically "empathize" with Kinbote by attempting to efface the distance between ourselves and the text, we actually reincorporate this distance in viewing the text as an observable object, thus viewing ourselves as extractors of the text's information, "outside" it. This obsessive, "readerly" desire opposes the knowledge that the gap between readers and texts or, within *Pale Fire*, between poetic original and commentary is the space of interpretation. For only through its "gaps"—its mistranslations, false leads, skewed prefigurations, and laughable digressions—are we allowed at all to enter the novel as readers with a task to perform.

The space of interpretation, which can be understood as a relation between readers and texts experienced as a doubt-filled abyss, is graphically figured in a contemporary novel I have not yet considered, one that shares *Pale Fire*'s concern with the invalidities of the interpretive act. William Golding's *Free Fall* portrays the autobiographical quest of its artist hero, Samuel Mountjoy, for the "patterns" of his existence implicated in the design of the self remembered, which will explain the tragedies that have befallen him. He is particularly anxious about coming to terms with his experience as a prisoner of war in a darkened cell and with understanding where his responsibility lies for the mental breakdown of his former mistress, Beatrice Ifor. In the prefatory remarks to this "graph" of his life, Mountjoy despairs at his inability to communicate to the reader the ineffable properties of Beatrice's beauty or the horror he has experienced in the cell:

> My darkness reaches out and fumbles at a typewriter with its tongs. Your darkness reaches out with your tongs and grasps a book. There are twenty modes of change, filter and translation between us. What an extravagant coincidence it would be if the exact quality, the translucent sweetness of her cheek, the very living curve of bone between the eyebrow and hair should survive the passage! How can you share the quality of my terror in the blacked-out cell when I can only remember it and not re-create it for myself? No. Not with you. Or only with you, in part. For you were not there.[8]

The narrator of *Free Fall* does not ask the reader to marvel at the "readability" of his story. Instead, he admits that the chasm which opens up between the reader and the text—an abyss doubled by the temporal space that exists between Mountjoy's experience and his inscription of it—can be bridged "in part" only by coincidence, only through the most mechanical correspondence between the writer touching the keys of the typewriter and the reader turning the pages of the book. Language is viewed in this passage as "filter and translation." It is an assemblage of black ciphers which implicitly seem to mark what Beatrice is not and which foil the attempt to communicate even the barest architectural sign—the "living curve of bone" of her appearance. Mountjoy insists upon what Gabriel Josipovici refers to as the "double nature of written words," which are both "black marks on a white page" and, not unproblematically, the "utterance of a person": "Without the black marks all would be sheer occurrence, endless flux; yet to imagine that these black marks somehow hide meaning and permanence within themselves . . . is to fall into as great an error as imagining we can do without the marks at all."[9] For this reader, randomness and necessity define the polarized boundaries of inscription as, at one end, purely arbitrary tracings and, at the other, a paradoxically opaque transparency that somehow contains the "thing itself." Within these boundaries there is an indeterminate space where the forcibly self-conscious reader roams, trapped between the extremities of mark and immanence. This errancy emphasizes the distance between the act of reading and the sundered meanings of the text's inscriptions. And yet, it is across this distance, because of it, that we are enabled as readers. To again paraphrase Ricoeur, we seek, like Mountjoy, signs scattered through the world or the text. Through the "passage" of the text from the writer's to the reader's hands, we attempt to trace the pattern of its scattered, repeated images while accounting for its accidental qualities, its uncanniness. Our interpretation then becomes an attempt to close the gap between the reader and the text by means of an "arrangement" where we check derived significances against the word signs that express them. In so doing, we are continually exposed to the mismatch between, for example, image and idea or made conscious of the verbal residue that remains after we have plumbed a passage for its significance.

Mountjoy's complaint underscores the crucial self-critical aspect of our hermeneutic labor. Predictably enough, the enchantments of collection and arrangement are enhanced by the linguistic games and elaborate narrative systems of such novels as *Pale Fire, Gravity's Rainbow*, and LETTERS. Yet no reader can be thoroughly comfortable while ferreting out, for example, the pattern of 8's in Barth's novel or explicating the theory of thermodynamics that informs Pynchon's encyclopedia. In both cases (and this, as Herbert N. Schneidau has pointed out, is a general symptom of reading any narrative)[10] the hermeneutic gesture may be fascinating for the involved reader, but there is always an accompanying sense of embarrassment: what other response could there be to one's Kinbotishness in reading *Pale Fire* or to the critical industry that has already sprung up around *Gravity's Rainbow* in a parody of paper chases that has been bureaucratized to the point *of* parody? What may seem a form of freedom for readers in their indeterminate "space" as they play games, uncover the underlying assumptions of a textual design, or reconstruct some conception of self inscribed in the text may well turn to a form of paralysis in the infinite regress of their self-awareness as sign-gathering hermeneuticists. Here, we cannot help but doubt our abilities to read and question our participation in the interpretive excesses that contemporary narratives engender as a result of our desire to see meaning everywhere.

William Gass would seem to celebrate the joys of the reader's self-determination, rather than the paralyzations of self-awareness, when he writes of the perceiver's latitude in discerning the world's shapes and patterns: "When I peer at the web of a spider, I can choose to see there geometry; I can discover sine curves on shells or in love affairs angles of ninety degrees. On the other hand, I can also find shell shapes in my sine curves, sexual sinuosities, my geometry can seem haunted and covered with webbery."[11] Gass emphasizes the delights of structure and the interchangeability of geometries; applied to the act of interpretation, this passage becomes a commendation of the reader's ability to detect designs within and relations between such disparities as the emotional chaos of a love affair and the calculable precision of a sine wave. For Gass, one pulls things together in language, thereby engaging in "combinational delight." But this essentially structuralist conception of the reader's activity is attended by a linguistic self-consciousness that permeates Gass' geometry. The string of sibilants insinuates itself in the passage to the extent that we as readers, peering at the writer marveling at the intricacies of "webbery," realize that we have been trapped by or designed within a web of language: for aren't spiders' webs, sine curves, shells, and sex related as much by sound and the similarity of their initial inscriptions as by any inherently similar qualities they may share "in nature"? Isn't this relation alphabetically, phonetically, and etymologically conscripted as well as a product of playful manipulation?

Gass' description takes with one hand what it gives with the other when it suggests that the constructor of linguistic geometries is equally constructed by them. One senses behind the alphabetic determinism of his perceptual metaphor the quixotic hope of Robert Coover's tribute to Cervantes as he, too, celebrates the attractions of design: "The return to Being has returned us to Design, to microcosmic images of the macrocosm, to the creation of Beauty within the confines of cosmic or human necessity, to the use of the fabulous to probe beyond the phenomenological, beyond appearances, beyond randomly perceived events, beyond mere history. But these probes are above all—like your Knight's sallies—challenges to the assumptions of a dying age, exemplary adventures of the Poetic Imagination, high-minded journeys towards the New World and never mind the nag's a pile of bones."[12] Coover's metaphor is authorial rather than readerly, but it projects the same kind of self-critical awareness about the act of writing that Gass' statement does about the act of perception. One can't help but "mind," in the self-conferred, illusory freedom which accompanies the conception of fabulous designs and probings beyond the "real," that "the nag's a pile of bones"—that the vehicle of the imagination's sallies, the language of narration, is partially determined by its archaicisms and its history. For Gass and Coover, both among a handful of the finest stylists in recent literature, the concept of "design," which may be seen as the product of the reader's or the writer's playful, imaginative desires, raises "an epistemological problem, a question of hyperbolic doubt."[13] The doubt, in this case, is caused by a self-conscious separation between the desire for a free-standing imaginative construction and a skepticism regarding the available material, language, which is saddled by its etymologies and its alphabetical histories.

Alternatively, we can observe Italo Calvino's lighthearted skepticism regarding hermeneutic labors when he portrays one of eight readers reading in his encyclopedia of interpretation, *If on a Winter's Night a Traveler*:

> Reading is a discontinuous and fragmentary operation. Or, rather, the object of reading is a punctiform and pulviscular material. In the spreading expanse of the writing, the reader's

> attention isolates some minimal segments, juxtapositions of words, metaphors, syntactic nexuses, logical passages, lexical peculiarities that prove to possess an extremely concentrated density of meaning. They are like elemental particles making up the work's nucleus, around which all the rest revolves. Or else like the void at the bottom of a vortex which sucks in and swallows currents. It is through these apertures that, in barely perceptible flashes, the truth the book may bear is revealed, its ultimate substance. Myths and mysteries consist of impalpable little granules, like the pollen that sticks to the butterfly's legs; only those who have realized this can expect revelations and illuminations.[14]

The smugness of Calvino's reader belies his assumption that if the interpreter behaves as a kind of antigeometer, breaking apart the text, isolating its "minimal segments," and observing its "lexical peculiarities," he will have access to the book's inherent truths via these "apertures." The metaphorical fissures of this reader's text may be seen as a parodic, inverse gloss on James' "house of fiction" or Barth's reconstructed domicile. Instead of an architecture, there is a void, to which the reader has access not as a roamer of rooms or a helpful handyman but as a wrecking agent who "isolates" and decontextualizes textual peculiarities or a hopeful anatomist who microscopically inspects the small, seemingly disconnected textual granules for a metonymic glimpse of the book's "whole truth." The ungraspable fluidity of Calvino's analogy, which moves from atomic, to hydraulic, to optical metaphors for the text, mimes the impalpability of the text itself, which is a void, vortex, particular nucleus, or fissured mystery. Yet, whether the relation of the reader to the text is, in Gass' analogy, a form of metamorphic transformation or, in the view of Calvino's reader, a disseminating scrutiny—whether the interpreter's work is "reconstructive" or "deconstructive"—the reflection on this relation yields a difference between rather than an identification of the reader and the text. This difference may be the result of the self-critical regard in which the players of linguistic games and the partially determined constructors of sign systems must hold themselves. Or it may be a disparity enforced by a conception of the text as the hieroglyphic tracing of its own alphabetical combinations.

In either case, the act of reading takes place within and as the perception of this difference.

To put the matter in other terms, readers of the fictions I have discussed are constrained to witness themselves reading: this reflexive "witnessing" constitutes their relation to the text, which necessarily involves their self-construction as testimonial readers. John Barth's *LETTERS* is replete with examples of self-witnessing, self-constructing readers; however, one of the most striking instances of this readerly activity in Barth's fiction appears in an earlier novel, *Giles Goat-Boy*. I will first quote the passage from the novel, then provide a context for its exemplification of the reader's activity:

> The pimpled maid, thin and udderless as Mrs. Rexford but infinitely less prepossessing, looked over her spectacles from the large novel she was involved in and said with a careful clarity—as if that question, from a fleecèd goat-boy at just that moment, were exactly what she'd expected—"Yes. A stairway goes up to the clockworks from this floor. You may enter it through the little door behind me." All the while she marked with her finger her place in the book, to which she returned at once upon delivering her line. Mild, undistinguished creature, never seen before or since, whose homely face I forgot in two seconds; whose name, if she bore one, I never knew; whose history and fate, if any she had, must be *lacunae* till the end of terms in my life's story—Passage be yours, for that in your moment of my time you did enounce, clearly as from a written text, your modest information. Simple answer to a simple question, but lacking which this tale were truncate as the Scroll, an endless fragment.
>
> "——*less fragment*," I thought I heard her murmur as I stooped through the little door she'd pointed out. I paused and frowned; but though her lips moved on, as did her finger across the page, her words were drowned now by the bells of Tower Clock.[15]

The narrator of this encounter is the novel's hero, George Giles, who is in quest of his "herohood" and is about to embark upon the final stages of the mythic hero's progress as defined by Lord Raglan and

Joseph Campbell, with emendations by John Barth. This scene occurs in the library of the "west campus" (read "the Western world") immediately before Giles' third and final descent into the belly of WESCAC, an enormous computer that runs the university and is the womb of Giles' emergent heroic being. Giles comes to the library information desk fresh from an extended debate with several "rabbinical" scholars over the definitive version of the Founder's Scroll, the sacred text of the university. The scholars have attempted, with his help, "to reconstruct, from the shards of the Founder's Scroll (actually several scrolls, overlapping, redundant, discrepant), the parent text, until then hypothetical, from which all known variants had descended and on which their authority was ultimately based."[16] Giles, anxious to reenter WESCAC, escapes from the group of scholars by scattering the fragments of the Scroll about the room; he then proceeds to the information desk, where he asks the young woman, reading, for the available route of "passage" to the computer.

It is clear from the cited passage that the large novel the librarian is reading while she points the way is the same one we are reading, *Giles Goat-Boy*, since her murmured "——*less fragment*" follows directly upon Giles's reflection that his "life's story," without the information the woman provides, would be "truncate as the Scroll, an endless fragment." The effect of this passage goes beyond, simply, the inversion or "story within a story" effect present in fiction since the beginnings of the novel and common in all of Barth's later work. For the woman is a reader (a reader within the text) who gives vital information to the hero, thus directing his performance.[17] Since the conclusion of *Giles Goat-Boy* suggests an infinite series of heroic cycles or stories and retains, like *Billy Budd*, partial interpretations of Giles' autobiography, the young woman reads a book whose end is a collection of fragments, no less "truncate" or full of "lacunae" than the scattered shards of the disputed Scroll. The relation between the woman and the text she is reading which is literally produced while she reads it, and our perception of her reading the text we are reading forms a model for the paradox of the fictionalized reader in the novels under question in this book. The reader, observing this woman, is compelled to witness his or her own ironic signifying activity. Like the librarian, the reader brings information to the text and "directs" the hero's antiauthoritarian, disseminatory performance; yet, like the woman, the reader is only part of the story woven into its larger design, only an actor in a minor episode lip-reading one of the novel's endless fragments. Designer and designed, the reader in Barth's literate analogy is bound to this ventriloquized text as she mimes or echoes its partial syntax, her resonant murmur the sign of her fragmentary contextualization as reader. The reader *of* Barth's novel realizes that against the constructions he or she may impose upon the text as the signification of a desire for the book to be interpretable, there is the facticity of "the text itself," spelled out in words on the page which cause a predictable movement of the lips, an interlinear repetition. Once again, a gap opens up between the reader and the text, figured here as the ironic mirroring of the book within itself and the reader's witnessing its being read.

Taken together, these readerly analogies of Barth, Gass, Coover, Calvino, and Nabokov display a series of oppositions concerning our desire and activity as readers, between which lies the no-man's-land I have nominated "the space of interpretation." The desire for transparency, or perfect communication, is crossed by the knowledge that the medium of communication, writing, is opaque, arbitrary, hieroglyphic. The desire for imaginative freedom, à la Gass, is hedged by the prescribed, historical sinuosities and alliterative qualities of the language the author must use and we must read. The reader desires to interpret ("Let me play now," says Shreve, in *Absalom, Absalom!*); yet this playfulness is condemned to what is there in black and white and bounded by what Gayatri Spivak has called the logocentric desire of language itself: "the metaphysical desire to make the end coincide with the means, create an enclosure, make the definition coincide with the defined, the 'father' with the 'son'; within the logic of identity to balance the equation, close the circle."[18] The double consciousness that the oppositions of desire and ironic knowledge inculcate in the reader accords with Paul de Man's definition of "literature" as a mediating divergence from the transparency of expression that we comprehend as "empirical reality":

> Literature . . . is the only form of language free from the fallacy of unmediated expression. . . . the truth emerges in the foreknowledge we possess when we refer to [something] as a *fiction*. All literatures, including the literature of Greece, have always designated themselves as existing in the mode of fiction; in the *Iliad*, when we first encounter Helen, it is as the emblem

> of the narrator weaving the actual war into the tapestry of a fictional object. Her beauty prefigures the beauty of all future narratives as entities that point to their own fictional nature. The self-reflecting mirror-effect by means of which a work of fiction asserts, by its very existence, its separation from empirical reality, its divergence, as a sign, from a meaning that depends for its existence on the constitutive activity of this sign, characterizes the work of literature in its essence.[19]

The "sign" of fiction, de Man asserts, is its deconstitutive relation to the "reality" that stands behind it and to the meanings that attend this "reality." Helen's story in the *Iliad* is the history of her weaving, just as the story of de Man's reading of this episode is an unraveling of her design in order to expose its preemption of "reality" and its ungrounded designedness. The artificiality of the literary construction is foregrounded in de Man's example, so that its interpretive possibilities are occluded by that very artificiality: its relation to history is neither necessary nor sufficient. Yet the arbitrariness of the fictive design is not total or unbounded, for it is only as a divergence from the constituted significances of "reality" (a "reweaving" of these) that it is known as a "fiction." This divergence or difference, which, for de Man, is the sign of fiction and, in my terms, distinguishes the space of interpretation, has its thresholds and limits. Fiction's reflexive mirror reflects, variously, the narrative's signification of itself *as* narrative, its "history" as a story among other stories, and the visage of the potential reader, who contributes to the history of the narrative's interpretation while gazing upon the reflection of the self as reader. These effects take place within the language of fiction which is known, as the act of reading is known, by its difference from the "constitutive activity" of signs welded into a discourse that creates the illusion of a transparent "reality" or a singular "history."

I have been defining the relation between the reader and the text as a gap or void—a blank page, like Ambrose Mensch's water-message—because in reading the novels I have discussed, we are constantly made aware of their "fictionality," which is expressed by the arbitrary, multivalent nature of our interpretation yet is determined by letters. We regard with a sardonic eye the imposed, singular design of the obsessed artist in *Travesty* or revel in the seemingly infinite interlocking designs, clues, and histories of *LETTERS*. But in both instances, whether the artistic design we engage is claustrophobic or cosmic, we are ever conscious of our own compulsion to render an interpretation which may not be too different, in its symmetries and consolidations, from Papa's manic artistry. Though we understand that there is none, we still search for the single code that will reveal *the* connection between all the selves and discourses of Barth's epistolary encyclopedia. We desire meaning; we desire our readerly being or participation in the text, yet we are in some sense isolated from the book we cannot take "at face value" and distanced from the self-significations—Papa's, Ben Flesh's, Kinbote's, Mensch's—produced by acts of reading which our own can only mock or repeat. What is at stake in this succession of paradoxes, as within the stories themselves, is our being as readers. Our role, in the broadest sense, is existential; our reading act, in its potency and invalidity, brings under question the nature of "being" itself.

In *Being and Nothingness*, Sartre discusses the idea of "being" as a witness to its own limitations and possibilities, an activity roughly equivalent to what I have been defining as the work of the reader. This self-witnessing, he insists, is one of the primary functions of consciousness:

> Being has its possibility outside of itself in the pure regard which gauges its chances of being; possibility can indeed be given *to us* before being; but it is *to us* that it is given and it is in no way the possibility *of* this being. The billiard ball which rolls on the table does not possess the possibility of being turned from its path by a fold in the cloth; neither does the possibility of deviation belong to the cloth; it can only be established by a witness synthetically as an external relation.[20]

For Sartre, the idea of being's "possibility" (which can be seen to parallel the potential interpretations of a text) exists separately from "being itself" or something that comes into play under the gaze of the witness, "the pure regard which gauges its chances of being." The distinction between that which is within the field of play and constitutes its "scene"—the billiard balls, the table—and the player who posits possible courses of action is analogous to the model of the reader I have been constructing thus far: that entity who, by reading, gives rise to the interpretive possibilities of a text, who, by observing the emerging inscription of the heroic self and the fictionalized reader within the scene of writing, makes way for the entrance of design and meaning in the fictional world. Furthermore, as a witness who "synthesizes" textual possibilities, the "reader," in Sartre's conception, testifies to its design, thus becoming a partial maker of it. Again, such self-construction in the novels I have considered is a matter of "design." The arrangement of textual signs into signifying patterns, or the unraveling of these in order to explore and explode the assumptions of the text, constitutes the testimonial activity of the reader which results in the construction of the reader's textual "self."

That the reader's position in this view is as an "external relation" does not suggest a return to an empirical view of the reader's role. The reader does not merely observe some framed objectification of a fictive design "out there," something to be judged in terms of its reified values or its mimetic affiliations with "reality." Rather, we are externalized as witnesses to the internalization of our being as readers in the text, as if, observing that reader in *Giles Goat-Boy* who mouths the words we read or Kinbotishly attempting to detect the linguistic design of *Pale Fire*, we were reading over our own shoulder. Across the chasm which exists between the reader *in* the text (who doubles the hero as reader) and the reader *of* the text there can be heard an echo between, in Sartre's terminology, being *pour soi* and being *en soi*. Our being as readers, thus defined, is doubled and split: we exist as reading selves to be questioned and interpreted and, at the same time, as the self who reads, questions, and interprets. Interpenetrating these two existences, Sartre suggests, is the nothingness which is the foundation and "hemorrhage" of our reading/being, the void or space of interpretation which splits "us" in two. Upon this space, inevitably, we inscribe the alphabetic designs of the reading self's relation to the text, which is both an adjacency and a schizophrenia that allow us to read.

The double consciousness of the reader's being is interestingly defined by Georges Poulet as a form of "self-alienation," where the reading self is seemingly possessed by the "consciousness" of the author:

> Whenever I read, I mentally pronounce an *I*, and yet the *I* which I pronounce is not myself. This is true even when the hero of a novel is presented in the third person, and even when

> there is no hero and nothing but reflections or propositions: as soon as something is presented as *thought*, there has to be a thinking subject with whom, at least for the time being, I identify, forgetting myself, alienated from myself. "*Je* est un autre," said Rimbaud. Another *I*, who has replaced my own, and who will continue to do so as long as I read. Reading is just that: a way of giving way not only to a host of alien words, images, ideas, but also to the very alien principle which utters them and shelters them.[21]

For Poulet, the reading self, somewhat romantically, becomes interfused with some alien "other," a foreign intruder who is not the biographical author but the authorial "thinking subject" of the text. This theory of the relation between the reader's and some form of authorial consciousness assumes that hidden within the text's alphabetic inscriptions there is a kind of ghostly subject who inhabits the house of fiction, to which we have access, in some sense, by giving up "ourselves." Both Sartre's view of the self as witness to itself and the contemporary scenes of writing and reading I have represented here would argue against Poulet's conception of the haunted reader. They insist that what we encounter in reading is, indeed, seemingly alien and other, but that it is also ourselves as readers performing in an analogous way to those semiotic protagonists who assemble and force the scattered signs of the world into patterns of recognizable significance. In reading, we are continually thrust back upon ourselves as the being who participates in the construction of a fiction and who witnesses this construction. We become, at once, Narcissus, who gazes at his own solipsistic image, and Echo, who is the dissemination of and the reciprocal response to the "other." Thus, in reading, we become the paradoxical sign of utter similitude and utter difference, a sign *of* reading that forms the bridge between these opposed qualities. The alien "other" who is born in the text, then, is that self-consciousness which defines our function as beings who read.

In short, the reader's activity is semiotic. The reader as witness constitutes the interpreted patterns and designs of the text; at the same time, the librarian, the "other" reader reading, is constituted by those patterns. The reading process of this double consciousness can also be seen, according to Mikhail Bakhtin, as social or as constitutive of a "psyche" which is in a marginal relation to the social world:

> *The reality of the inner psyche is the same as the reality of the sign.* Outside the material of signs there is no psyche; there are physiological processes, processes in the nervous system, but no subjective psyche as a special existential quality fundamentally distinct from both the physiological process occurring within the organism and the reality encompassing the organism from the outside, to which the psyche reacts and which one way or another it reflects. By its very existential nature, the subjective psyche is to be localized somewhere between the organism and the outside world, on the *borderline* separating these two spheres of reality. It is here that an encounter between the organism and the outside world takes place, but the encounter is not a physical one: *the organism and the outside world meet here in the sign*. Psychic experience is the semiotic expression of the contact between the organism and the outside environment. That is why *the inner psyche is not analyzable as a thing but can only be understood and interpreted as a sign.*[22]

Bakhtin's formulation is doubtless problematic (not the least difficulty being the instrumentalist assumptions underlying the rhetoric of the passage, which may be partially attributable to the translation), but this redefinition of subjectivity in semiotic terms has important implications for the conception of the reader's relation to the text. This relation is neither wholly private nor transparent, at least not for the reader of those fictions which work to subvert these readerly fantasies. The idea of the reader, alone, bent over the book and ciphering out its concealed meanings is, metaphorically, a form of nostalgia that contemporary narrative continually questions for its innate egotism and its privileging of the romanticized, reading "self." Yet it must be said that this is a nostalgic relation reinforced by a novel like *Gravity's Rainbow*, which is solidly in the tradition of those anatomies that spur on the Faustian reader while, simultaneously, parodying that reader's efforts to encompass all knowledge. In place of the romanticized reader's "self," we can assert the conception of the reader as a sign, as a participant in the unfolding language, or sign system, of the book being read—at once its witness, its mediator, and one of its referents.

Bakhtin's statement suggests that the "subjective psyche" is in between the physical being of the subject and the "outside environment"; more precisely, subjectivity is the point of contact between the body of an individual and the world in which she or he eats, travels, lives. Analogously, the reader's self might be said to be the point of contact between the inscriptions of the text and the larger "reality" in which both readers and texts are "inscribed." This contact point, we have seen, is also a gap from which interpretation springs. The reader as message sorter, Theseus or Helen, Narcissus or Echo, entangled disentangler, signifier signified—all these are terminologies which suggest the position of the reader in relation to the text as an interpreter who, in the act of interpreting, becomes part of the textual design. It is this awareness of the reader's self that informs the final realizations of Elkin's Ben Flesh when he celebrates, adjacently, his "centeredness" as a signifying force in the world and his realization that he is inscribed within a history and a culture that marginalize his being. Thus, we are led back to the prefatory statement that the human "self" is, by nature, a reader. Our subjectivity, rather than being a place, quality, or agent, is a process of interpretation. It is a continuous intentional movement through history and language, not toward some ultimate self-realization, which could only be a form of death, but within the emerging discourses that make up our "reality" and that—knotted, partial, indistinct—demand interpretation.

"We live," Wallace Stevens writes in this century's finest reflection on self-extinction,

> . . . in an old chaos of the sun,
> Or old dependency of day and night,
> Or island solitude, unsponsored, free,
> Of that wide water, inescapable.[23]

The puzzle of these lines is reflected in the paradox of readers, who are chained to the text at hand but who can interpret as they will. The novels of interpretation I have considered convince us that our readings are "unsponsored," unauthorized, not patronized by any scribbling, authorial construction who would oversee our readerly self-creation as a god would his muddy incorporations. Yet this hermeneutic freedom has its mortal limits. Roland Barthes may indulge in a fantasy of some ideal, "writerly" text "based . . . on the infinity of language," a text which "has no beginning; it is reversible, we may gain access to its several entrances . . . the codes it mobilizes extend *as far as the eye can reach*, they are indeterminate (meaning here is never subject to a principle of determination, unless by throwing dice)."[24] However, this nonexistent text is beyond interpretation, only a matter of chance, and as much an end product of our desire to read and engage in endless play as of the contrary desire to gain immediate access to the text's mysteries. Transparency and *jouissance* may be seen as other terms for the limits of interpretation, an activity that takes place within and as an echoing response to the text we scan. We read within history: both the history of the language in which the text is written and the history of our self-conceptions. But when we read, we are not merely the product of these histories. Since we contribute to the emerging interpretational history of the book we read, we make ourselves, as readers, part of that history.

Merleau-Ponty states the point in crucially different terms: "space and time are not, for me, a collection of adjacent points nor are they a limitless number of relations synthesized by my consciousness. . . . I am not in space and time, nor do I conceive space and time; I belong to them, my body combines with them and includes them. The scope of this inclusion is the measure of my existence; but in any case it can never be all-embracing. The space and time which I inhabit are always in their different ways indeterminate horizons which contain other points of view."[25] Merleau-Ponty's metonymic indeterminacy, unlike that of Barthes, is not infinite, for it is bounded by the intentionality of the perceiver or interpreter, who belongs to a given temporal/spatial world and who contributes to the emergence of its horizons while being entangled in its heterogeneity of viewpoints. As readers, we are "free" within the limitations of the language in which we conceive our reading, yet this freedom is subtended by the temporal nature of the language we read. This language is loaded with, according to the inscriptions of *Pale Fire* or LETTERS, the importations of its (and our) passage through time; its "meaning" is the alphabetization of its archaeologies. These limitations, in turn, are indeterminate because we continually change language through the supplements of our interpretations. As with the interdependency of day and night, so in our self-conceptions as readers we hang upon the text and the text upon us.

The recognition of the reader's relation to the text I have disclosed in this chapter has come about as the result of an analysis of six contemporary American novels. But, implicitly, this recognition may be induced in reading any narrative; it is intrinsic to the narrative "genre" whose prime quality is its mutability. It may be, as Wolfgang Iser asserts, that modern narrative incorporates a greater degree of indeterminacy than "older narrative" because, increasingly in modern novels, "one detail appears to contradict another, and so simultaneously stimulates and frustrates our desire to 'picture,' thus continuously causing our imposed 'gestalt' of the text to disintegrate."[26] However, I suspect that this descriptive statement reveals a desire more to view the history of narrative in diachronic and evolutionary terms than to see the actualities of narrative's discontinuous, surprising "progress." Certainly from the perspective wrought by a theory of narrative that suggests that novels are "about" their own self-questioned origins and the origins of the self, the novel has by fits and starts made novelty, or "contemporaneity," its subject from the beginning. What may be more characteristic of the contemporary novels I have been concerned with (though not exclusively so) is their ability to bring about, in the reader, the state I have termed "passionate doubt." For these books seduce us into their reading: by their alphabetical correspondences and hermeneutic games, their flirtations with history and their renderings of the semiotic self, they coerce us into the labor of interpretation in demanding the conferral of meaning upon them. Yet this passion for significance is always attended by its ironic dismissal. Contemporary narratives make it clear that the "ends" of signification lie in either an unacceptable reduction of the text to its validated meanings or an equally unacceptable leap into its yawning *mise en abîme*—a thoroughly solipsistic, relativized infinity of meanings. In setting up this tension, contemporary narratives question the nature of significance itself; they scrutinize the conditions (their own) under which meaning may be produced, and they assert as "meaningful" this scrutiny.

Since I have been suggesting that these fictions are sign systems that question their own semiotics, perhaps it is appropriate that their "contemporaneity" is viewed as a sign of the times. At some future point, should we survive, our age might be seen as one which, as every episteme must, redefined the concept of "boundary," not as a limitation but as a horizon, not as a separation between opposed factions or entities but as a condition which allows for their adjacency. In the field theory of modern physics, in the development of an epistemology of paradox, in the current reconceptualizing of "difference," in the revisions of and reactions to romanticism which characterize the movement from modernism to postmodernism, we can see a common attempt to redefine such concepts as "meaning," "value," and "identity" arising out of the very indeterminacies that they fortify themselves against. Contemporary narrative is part of this effort; indeed, it may be seen as this effort's "story." The novels I have discussed are, if only generally, representative of this work in its various manifestations. They ask us to question where meaning begins and ends and in what ways we inscribe ourselves as reading subjects in that movement. In this long moment of extreme peril that we have, with hopeful irony, named "postwar," these novels signify our well-founded anxiety about the nature of certainty itself which, formulated into disputes over certain boundaries and, supposedly, clear ideologies, has led us to a deadly impasse. Less apocalyptically, these fictions of interpretation insist that we accept the doubt in the nature of our being human, while inciting our insatiable desire for a book and a world filled with significance. We dwell between the determinate and the indeterminate, we read these books, and we witness the emergence of a world which, by design, is a matter of interpretation.

NOTES

Preface

1. I appropriate the phrase from the preface to Jonathan Culler, *Structuralist Poetics: Structuralism, Linguistics, and the Study of Literature* (Ithaca: Cornell University Press, 1975), p. viii.

2. The range of works that study the semantics of narrative grammar and structure runs through structuralism to deconstruction, sparsely represented by the following: Tzvetan Todorov, *Poetics of Prose* (Ithaca: Cornell University Press, 1977); A. J. Greimas, *Structural Semantics: An Attempt at Method*, introd. Ronald Schleifer, trans. Daniele McDowell, Ronald Schleifer, and Alan Velie (Lincoln: University of Nebraska Press, 1983); J. Hillis Miller, *Fiction and Repetition: Seven English Novels* (New York: Oxford University Press, 1982) and "Ariadne's Thread: Repetition and the Narrative Line," *Critical Inquiry*, 3 (1976), 57–77; and Barbara Johnson, *The Critical Difference: Essays in the Contemporary Rhetoric of Reading* (Baltimore: Johns Hopkins University Press, 1980).

3. Fredric Jameson, *The Political Unconscious: Narrative as a Socially Symbolic Act* (Ithaca: Cornell University Press, 1981), explores how the "unconscious" structures of narrative are also "social" structures. The essays collected in Robert Con Davis, ed., *The Fictional Father: Lacanian Readings of the Text* (Amherst: University of Massachusetts Press, 1981), variously discuss how the "word" or verbal constructions of the "father" haunt the structures of literary texts. Tony Tanner's *Adultery in the Novel: Contract and Transgression* (Baltimore: Johns Hopkins University Press, 1979) explores the underlying analogies between narrative's hidden orders and those configured in marital and extramarital relations.

4. "Intertextuality" is, perhaps, the most widely discussed topic of contemporary criticism—a discussion which can be found in theorists as diverse as Harold Bloom, Jacques Derrida, and Mikhail Bakhtin. A succinct and useful definition is provided by John Carlos Rowe in *Through the Custom-House: Nineteenth-Century American Fiction and Modern Theory* (Baltimore: Johns Hopkins University Press, 1982): "Intertextuality may be made explicit in such mixed forms as the novel or criticism, both of which operate as shameless thieves, but intertextuality does not belong exclusively to literature. Language itself is a ceaseless activity of crossing, translating, transgressing that makes possible the passage between apparently exclusive realms of divided territories" (194). It is this linguistic rather than generic or authorial

concept of intertextuality that informs my implicit consideration of the topic throughout this book.

5. The phrase is Jacques Derrida's, which he uses in his discussion of the sign in "Différance," *Margins of Philosophy*, trans. Alan Bass (Chicago: University of Chicago Press, 1982), p. 9.

6. Walter Benn Michaels, "The Interpreter's Self: Peirce on the Cartesian 'Subject,'" *Georgia Review*, 31 (1977), pp. 395, 401 respectively.

7. For the discussion of the self in contemporary fiction from a formalist perspective, see Manfred Pütz, *The Story of Identity: American Fiction of the Sixties* (Stuttgart: Metzler, 1979). Charles Caramello, *Silverless Mirrors: Book, Self, and Postmodern American Fiction* (Tallahassee: University Presses of Florida, 1983), brings a deconstructive perspective to bear on the presence of the self in classic and postmodern American texts, arguing that the latter, curiously, retain a nostalgia for the "self" of modernism. In *The Performing Self: Compositions and Decompositions in the Languages of Contemporary Life* (New York: Oxford University Press, 1971), Richard Poirier conceptualizes the "postmodern" self as a self-constructing and -destructing artifice.

8. Tony Tanner, *City of Words: American Fiction 1950–1970* (New York: Harper and Row, 1971), is concerned with the self as a linguistic and textual operation in his survey of contemporary American fiction. My scope is somewhat narrower than Tanner's, since I eschew survey in favor of extended explication, and I more doggedly pursue the specific conception of the self as a conflation or scattering of signs produced within the text by the processes of narrative. But I wish to properly acknowledge the influence, on my own readings, of Tanner's book, which remains the most comprehensive theoretical discussion of contemporary fiction.

9. For an alternative, modular view of "contemporaneity" and self-scrutiny within the contexts of modernism, see Alan Wilde, *Horizons of Assent: Modernism, Postmodernism, and the Ironic Imagination* (Baltimore: Johns Hopkins University Press, 1981). Wilde distinguishes between kinds of reflexivity in twentieth-century literature based on his division of modern works into "modernist," "late modernist," and "postmodernist" phases. Each stage reflects an increasing concern with the nonreferential aspects of fictive language as they are informed by the uses of irony. Wilde's paradigmatic conception of modern literature is especially helpful in explaining postmodernism's apparent turn to a language of surfaces as, simultaneously, a return to the depth and "immediacy" of actuality by forsaking the authorial control over language (cf. pp. 127–88). See also Robert Alter, *Partial Magic: The Novel as Self-Conscious Genre* (Berkeley and Los Angeles: University of California Press, 1975), who regards fictional self-scrutiny generically and historically.

10. Alan Wilde, "Acts of Definition, or Who Is Thomas Berger?" *Arizona Quarterly*, 39 (1983), 315. See also Wilde's "'Strange Displacements of the Ordinary': Apple, Elkin, Barthelme, and the Problem of the Excluded Middle," *boundary 2*, 10 (1982), 177–99.

11. For some of the major work on the ideology and history of "postmodern" fiction, see Caramello, *Silverless Mirrors*; Raymond Federman, ed., *Surfiction: Fiction Now and Tomorrow* (Chicago: Swallow Press, 1975); Ihab Hassan, *The Dismemberment of Orpheus: Toward a Postmodern Literature* (New York: Oxford University Press, 1971) and *Paracriticisms: Seven Speculations of the Times* (Urbana: University of Illinois Press, 1975); Jerome Klinkowitz, *Literary Disruptions: The Making of* a *Post-Contemporary American Fiction*, 2nd ed. (Urbana: University of Illinois Press, 1980); Robert Scholes, *Fabulation and Metafiction* (Urbana: University of Illinois Press, 1979); and Larry McCaffrey, *The Metafictional Muse: The Works of Robert Coover, Donald Barthelme, and William H. Gass* (Pittsburgh: University of Pittsburgh Press, 1982). For a crucial work on the politics and aesthetics of postmodernism in general, see Jean-François Lyotard's recently translated *The Postmodern Condition: A Report on Knowledge*, trans. Geoff Bennington and Brian Massumi (Minneapolis: University of Minnesota Press, 1984). While I am not as concerned with postmodern aesthetics as these works (which, in their radicality and energy, beg the question: why the driving need for a postmodern aesthetics?), much of what I have to say about the self and narrative is informed by them. I would like my discussion to be seen, rather than as repeating or opposing the "findings" of these critics in one way or another, as adjacent to them, a next-door neighbor pacing behind the blinds. Given the reconsiderations of intertextuality and influence that recent theory has conducted, the position of adjacency seems the only proper one in relation to those critics with whom I've thought along similar and different lines.

12. This "social" conception of the reader is based on Raymond Williams' understanding of the social self in *Marxism and Literature* (New York: Oxford University Press, 1977), especially pp. 11–71.

Introduction

1. Henry James, *The Art of the Novel: Critical Prefaces*, ed. and introd. R. P. Blackmur (New York: Scribner's, 1934), p. 136.

2. Maurice Merleau-Ponty, *Phenomenology of Perception*, trans. Colin Smith (New York: Humanities Press, 1962), p. 136.

3. Paul de Man, *Blindness and Insight: Essays in the Rhetoric of Contemporary Criticism* (New York: Oxford University Press, 1971), pp. 42–43.

4. Barbara Johnson, "The Frame of Reference: Poe, Lacan, Derrida," *Yale French Studies*, 55/56 (1977), 503. I pursue the discussion of the reader's "self" more formally in chapter 7 of this book.

5. Geoffrey Hartman, *Saving the Text: Literature/Derrida/Philosophy* (Baltimore: Johns Hopkins University Press, 1981), p. 149.

6. Jorge Luis Borges, *Labyrinths: Selected Stories and Other Writings*, ed. Donald A. Yates and James E. Irby (New York: New Directions, 1964), p. 26.

7. Edward Said, *Beginnings: Intention and Method* (1975; rpt. Baltimore: Johns Hopkins University Press, 1978), p. 12.

1. *Pale Fire*

1. Mikhail Bakhtin, "Epic and Novel," in *The Dialogic Imagination: Four Essays*, introd. Michael Holquist, trans. Caryl Emerson and Michael Holquist (Austin: University of Texas Press, 1981), p. 10.

2. See Alter, *Partial Magic*, for a historical/critical account of reflexivity in the tradition of the novel. I am, as any commentator on present-day fiction must be, indebted to Alter's discussion, though I am more concerned here than he with the semiotic ramifications of reflexivity in *Pale Fire*. For a larger, anthropological conception of reflexivity as a self-critical concept, see the special issue of *Semiotica*, 30 (1980), on the reflexivity of signs in culture, ed. Barbara A. Babcock, and her introductory essay, "Reflexivity: Definitions and Discriminations," pp. 1–14.

3. As with the notion of reflexivity in fiction, the fictive presentation of the self has always been an integral part of narrative traditions. For relevant critical discussions of the history of self-presentation in Anglo-American literature, see Stephen J. Greenblatt, *Renaissance Self-Fashioning: From More to Shakespeare* (Chicago: University of Chicago Press, 1980); Arnold Weinstein, *Fictions of the Self: 1550–1800* (Princeton: Princeton University Press, 1981); Robert Langbaum, *The Mysteries of Identity: A Theme in Modern Literature* (New York: Oxford University Press, 1977); and Poirier, *Performing Self*. Again, my discussion dwells more on a semiotic conception of the self than these, as does a recent analysis of the self as sign in nineteenth-century American literature to which I am indebted, John T. Irwin, *American Hieroglyphics: The Symbol of the Egyptian Hieroglyph in the American Renaissance* (New Haven: Yale University Press, 1980), especially pp. 114–235.

4. Both Lucy Maddox, *Nabokov's Novels in English* (Athens: University of Georgia Press, 1983), p. 29, and Marilyn Edelstein, "*Pale Fire*: The Art of Consciousness," in J. E. Rivers and Charles Nicol, eds., *Nabokov's Fifth Arc: Nabokov and Others on His Life's Work* (Austin: University of Texas Press, 1982), p. 218, mention in their discussions of *Pale Fire* that Nabokov is interested in the presentation of the self as a written sign, but they do not pursue the subject to the point of discussing how self-inscription and textuality form parallel concerns in the novel.

5. David Walker, "'The Viewer and the View': Chance and Choice in Pale Fire," *Studies in American Fiction*, 4 (1976), 204. I am in basic agreement with Walker on the critical controversy over the novel as to whose voice—Shade's or Kinbote's—is the authoritative one. For Walker, the question is moot, since it is the drive to create correspondences *between* texts that forms the novel's main interest. But for dissenting views, see Julia Bader, *Crystal Land: Artifice in Nabokov's English Novels* (Berkeley and Los Angeles: Univer-

sity of California Press, 1972), p. 31, where she argues that Shade writes both poem and commentary, projecting Gradus, Kinbote, and himself as aspects of the artist's multiple personality. See also Page Stegner, *Escape into Aesthetics: The Art of Vladimir Nabokov* (New York: Dial Press, 1966), p. 129, who argues that Gradus, Shade, and Kinbote are all figments of Kinbote's imagination—projections, like Zembla, of a mind obsessed with chance and coincidence.

6. Vladimir Nabokov, *Pale Fire* (New York: G. P. Putnam's Sons, 1962), pp. 62–63. All future references will be to this edition and will be noted parenthetically in the text.

7. The familiar distinction is that of M. H. Abrahms, *The Mirror and the Lamp: Romantic Theory and the Critical Tradition* (New York: Oxford University Press, 1953). Nabokov's frequent comparisons of lamps, suns, and fire with the aesthetic act in *Pale Fire*, and his use of mirrors as distortive rather than purely reflective devices, place him in the tradition Abrahms defines as romantic and antimimetic.

8. This analysis of translation, exchange, and interpretive thievery is based upon Michel Serres' compelling "The Apparition of Hermes: *Don Juan*," in his collection of translated essays, *Hermes: Literature, Science, Philosophy*, ed. Josué V. Harari and David F. Bell (Baltimore: Johns Hopkins University Press, 1982), pp. 3–14.

9. Jacques Derrida, *Dissemination*, trans. and introd. Barbara Johnson (Chicago: University of Chicago Press, 1981), p. 89.

10. June Perry Levine, "Vladimir Nabokov's *Pale Fire*: 'The Method of Composition' as Hero," *International Fiction Review*, 5 (1978), 105.

11. Nabokov is notorious for his doubling and mirroring motifs; these are investigated for *Pale Fire* by Phyllis A. Roth, "The Psychology of the Double in Nabokov's *Pale Fire*," *Essays in Literature*, 2 (1975), 209–29.

12. Vladimir Nabokov, *Speak, Memory: An Autobiography Revisited*, rev. ed. (New York: G. P. Putnam's Sons, 1966), p. 25.

13. Claude Lévi-Strauss, *Structural Anthropology*, quoted in Terence Hawkes, *Structuralism and Semiotics* (London: Methuen, 1977), p. 50; Culler, *Structuralist Poetics*, p. 190.

14. For explications of this view and its thematic results, see Douglas Fowler, *Reading Nabokov* (Ithaca: Cornell University Press, 1974), p. 17; Bader, *Crystal Land*, pp. 4–8; Walker, "'The Viewer and the View,'" pp. 205–20; and Tanner, *City of Words*, pp. 33–39.

15. The term "misprision" I take from Harold Bloom, who defines it as the deliberate misreading of the poetic father or original by son or commentator, so that the latter may establish his own originality. *Pale Fire* might be seen as a parody of misprision, in which the swerving or clinamen of the son's text from the father's original becomes, in Kinbote's case, a wild careening, a comic chase after the elusive Gradus (shadows cast by the poetic father/double) in the text. Bloom's theory is clearly informed by a series of patrilineal metaphors that, themselves, deserve thoroughgoing questioning

as evidences of self-inscription. See Harold Bloom, *The Anxiety of Influence: A Theory of Poetry* (New York: Oxford University Press, 1973), pp. 19–45.

16. David Packman, *Vladimir Nabokov: The Structure of Literary Desire* (Columbia: University of Missouri Press, 1982), p. 89. Packman's book appeared as I was completing this analysis of *Pale Fire*; I share its views of several matters discussed here, particularly of the text's inculcation of its own temporality and its desire for immortality, reflected in the narrative line; see especially pp. 74–89.

2. *Travesty*

1. John Hawkes, *Travesty* (New York: New Directions, 1976), p. 11. All future references will be to this edition and noted parenthetically in the text.

2. Erving Goffman, *The Presentation of the Self in Everyday Life* (1959, rpt. Woodstock, N.Y.: Overlook Press, 1973), pp. 250–51.

3. For an extended discussion of the reader's entrapment in *Travesty*, see Charles Baxter, "In the Suicide Seat: Reading John Hawkes's *Travesty*," *Georgia Review*, 34 (1980), 871–85.

4. Rodolphe Gasché, "The Scene of Writing: A Deferred Outset," *Glyph*, 1 (1977), 170.

5. Heide Ziegler, "John Hawkes's *Travesty* and the Idea of Travesty," *Arbeiten aus Anglistick und Amerikanistik*, 7 (1982), 164, also discusses Papa's narcissism in a Freudian context and in relation to the Fountain of Clarity he discovers, which is a symbol for the transparent surface and medium of his own art.

6. Michael Leiris, *Manhood: A Journey from Childhood into the Fierce Order of Virility*, trans. Richard Howard (New York: Grossman Brothers, 1963), quoted in the frontispiece to *Travesty*, unpaged.

7. Paul Emmett, "The Reader's Voyage through *Travesty*," *Chicago Review*, 28 (1976), 175, suggests that Honorine is the center of Papa's vision in a more literal sense: *Travesty* is *her* dream; tired of Henri, her overbearing husband, and her jealous daughter, she fantasizes their deaths in the accident. While I do not disagree with the plausibility of this interpretation, I insist that Papa's plan "works" in that no single reading of these events is possible and that the novel travesties, while encouraging, all potential readings.

8. For an extended discussion of *Travesty*'s Poesque elements, upon which several critics have casually remarked, see Charles Berryman, "Hawkes and Poe: *Travesty*," *Modern Fiction Studies*, 29 (1983), 643–54.

9. Donald J. Greiner, *Comic Terror: The Novels of John Hawkes*, rev. ed. (Memphis: Memphis State University Press, 1978), pp. 263–75.

10. René Girard, *Deceit, Desire, and the Novel: Self and Other in Literary Structure*, trans. Yvonne Freccero (Baltimore: Johns Hopkins University Press, 1965), especially pp. 1–52.

11. For a discussion of Papa as artist, see my *John Hawkes* (Boston: Twayne Publishers, 1982), pp. 135–42. The present discussion of *Travesty* very briefly recapitulates part of my argument about the novel to be found there.

12. Jeffrey Mehlman, *A Structural Study of Autobiography: Proust, Leiris, Sartre, Lévi-Strauss* (Ithaca: Cornell University Press, 1974), pp. 83–84.

13. Even if parodically conceived, Papa's transcendent self-negation might be seen to parallel what Sartre refers to as "unreflected consciousness" or "consciousness in the first degree." See Jean-Paul Sartre, *The Transcendence of the Ego: An Existentialist Theory of Consciousness*, trans. and introd. Forrest Williams and Robert Kirkpatrick (New York: Farrar, Straus and Giroux, 1957), especially pp. 31–42.

14. John Kuehl, *John Hawkes and the Craft of Conflict* (New Brunswick: Rutgers University Press, 1975), pp. 3–27, discusses this opposition as fundamental to all of Hawkes' work from a mythopoeic perspective. See also O'Donnell, *John Hawkes*, pp. 20–23, 138–39.

15. Hélène Cixous, "Fiction and Its Phantoms: Reading Freud's *Das Unheimliche* (The 'Uncanny')," *New Literary History*, 7 (1976), 548.

16. For a crucial discussion of clothing and stitching imagery in an earlier novel by Hawkes, *Second Skin*, see Tanner, *City of Words*, pp. 219–29. Marc Chénetier, "'The Pen and the Skin': Inscription and Cryptography in John Hawkes's *Second Skin*," *Review of Contemporary Fiction*, 3 (1983), 167–76, moves beyond the metaphors of stitchery to parallel concerns of my own in *Travesty*: stitchery as a form of graphesis, revealing "the narrative strategy of the text as cover (*steigen*: to cover, as in 'steganography'), hiding (*kryptos*), retreat, escape and erasure" (168).

17. For a discussion of the development of Hawkes' canon as parallel to the movement from modernism into postmodernism, see Heide Ziegler, "Postmodernism as Autobiographical Commentary: *The Blood Oranges* and *Virginie*," *Review of Contemporary Fiction*, 3 (1983), 207–13.

18. John Hawkes, *The Blood Oranges* (New York: New Directions, 1971), p. 1, and *Death, Sleep & the Traveler* (New York: New Directions, 1974), p. 164.

19. John Enck, "John Hawkes: An Interview," *Wisconsin Studies in Contemporary Literature*, 6 (1965), 143–44.

20. Peter Brooks, "Freud's Masterplot: Questions of Narrative," *Yale French Studies*, 55/56 (1977), 296.

3. *LETTERS*

1. "Second Interview with John Barth," in Evelyn Glaser-Wöhrer, *An Analysis of John Barth's Weltanschauung: His View of Life and Literature* (Salzburg: Institut für Anglische Sprache und Literature, Universität Salzburg, 1977), p. 240.

2. Williams, *Marxism and Literature*, p. 37.

3. The first quotation is from Derrida's *Dissemination*, p. 161; the second is from his *Writing and Difference*, trans. and introd. Alan Bass (Chicago: University of Chicago Press, 1978), p. 205.

4. Manfred Pütz, in *The Story of Identity*, also discusses Barth's interest in the self and parallels in his fiction through *Lost in the Funhouse* between the formation of identity and the creation of narrative. Relying on Propp and Greimas, Putz is more programmatically structuralist than I in his view of this relationship, an approach that forces him to take the usual view of Barth's "later" fiction as dead-end enactments of reflexivity. As I hope to show, at least for *LETTERS*, Barth transforms a critical no exit into an opening that allows for the commingling of the traditional and the avant-garde, the reflective and the reflexive, as a means to literary production. In *City of Words*, pp. 254–59, Tony Tanner takes a similar view of the evolution of Barth's fiction through *Lost in the Funhouse*, citing a "corrosive doubt about identity and its relation to language" as the end product of Barth's efforts (254). Again, my intention here is different: to suggest that the doubtful relations between self, narrative, and history are problematic but ultimately productive of the represented historical world we inhabit, which Barth's *LETTERS* both parodies and celebrates.

5. One of the major critical debates over Barth's work focuses on the dichotomy between randomness and order, chaos and system, and on which of these terms he ultimately affirms. As I argue, part of the value of Barth's fiction is that it does not reduce these ontological categories to warring polarities but manages to create a narrative structure which imaginatively "contains" randomness and order, thus a true synthesis. Several readers of his most Hegelian novel, *Giles Goat-Boy*, support this notion of Barth's quest for synthesis, wherein "opposites are both distinctly themselves and certainly the same at the same time"; see Jac Tharpe, *John Barth: The Comic Sublimity of Paradox* (Carbondale and Edwardsville: Southern Illinois University Press, 1974), p. 79. Robert Scholes, in *The Fabulators* (New York: Oxford University Press, 1967), pp. 135–73, also argues for a synthetic reading of *Giles*. In opposition to this view, see Tanner, *City of Words*, who asserts that what emerges from the novel is not "synthesis but a constantly dissolving plurality of versions and combinations" (p. 247).

6. John Barth, *The Sot-Weed Factor* (1960; rev. ed. New York: Bantam Books, 1967), p. 524.

7. The term "modern formalist novel" is coined by Barth in Charlie Reilly, "An Interview with John Barth," *Contemporary Literature*, 22 (1981), 4, where it refers to *Tristram Shandy* as well as to *LETTERS*. "Modernism," for Barth, is clearly a matter of narrative strategy, not chronology. The concept of "replenishment" is articulated in John Barth, "The Literature of Replenishment: Post-Modern Fiction," *Atlantic*, 254, no. 1 (January 1980), 65–71.

8. Reilly, "An Interview with John Barth," p. 10.

9. John Barth, *LETTERS: An Old-Fashioned Epistolary Novel Told by Seven Drolls and Dreamers* (New York: G. P. Putnam's Sons, 1979), p. 280. All future references will be to this edition and will be noted parenthetically in the text.

10. Jameson, *The Political Unconscious*, p. 29.

11. For a discussion of the different responses "historical" and "literary" narratives encourage in their readers, see Wesley Morris, *Friday's Footprint: Structuralism and the Articulated Text* (Columbus: Ohio State University Press, 1979), p. 61. My discussion observes that *LETTERS* attempts to collapse the distinction between these kinds of narrative as well as the responses they encourage.

12. Northrop Frye, *Anatomy of Criticism: Four Essays* (Princeton: Princeton University Press, 1957), pp. 308–12. For a reader of Barth's fiction, the fact that Frye mentions a neglected anatomy of the eighteenth century, *Noctes Ambrosiana*, and that Barth's most self-conscious letter writer in *LETTERS* is Ambrose Mensch is a coincidence not to be passed over.

13. I refer to the "waterworks" section of "Ithaca," which shows Bloom's and Daedalus' return home as the narrative's "return home," its circulation back to the beginning. This process is enacted literally in *Finnegans Wake* as the end of the book circulates back to the beginning, the river of narrative (like all the rivers of the novel) flowing unto itself. In *Paradoxical Resolutions: American Fiction since James Joyce* (Urbana: University of Illinois Press, 1982), pp. 150–54, Craig Hansen Werner notes what he sees as Joyce's influence on *LETTERS* as a similar use of generational metaphors, but he does not notice these as indicative of narrative processes, nor does he discuss the resemblance between Barth's and Joyce's circulatory metaphors.

14. Barth discusses his fondness for "infinite narrative" in many places, e.g., John Enck, "John Barth: An Interview," *Wisconsin Studies in Contemporary Literature*, 6 (1965), 4. Barth's homage to *The Arabian Nights* is most apparent in the Dunyazadiad section of *Chimera*, the story of Scheherazade's endless story-telling (as a means of preserving her life and the "life" of narrative), told by her sister.

15. Reilly, "An Interview with John Barth," p. 12.

16. Serres, *Hermes: Literature, Science, Philosophy*, p. 42.

17. For a brief study of *LETTERS* as "organized complexity," as noise or excess transformed into a system, see Tom LeClair, "Avant-Garde Mastery," *TriQuarterly*, 53 (1982), 265–67; for an expansion of this idea in the context of another author, see LeClair's "Joseph McElroy and the Art of Excess," *Contemporary Literature*, 21 (1980), 16–37.

18. Edward Said has noted, in Valéry's comparison of Leonardo da Vinci to Napoleon, that both were compelled "to find the law of continuity between things whose connection with each other escapes very nearly all of us." If Barth's choice of Napoleon as the "common ancestor" to the writers

of *LETTERS* is accidental, he would no doubt enjoy the irony of the fact that the novel's "father" had a mania for historical connections. Cf. Said, *Beginnings*, p. 48.

19. Ibid., p. 12.

20. The parallels between the production of selves and literary texts are discussed by Steven G. Kellman in *The Self-Begetting Novel* (New York: Columbia University Press, 1980), especially pp. 1–12.

21. Said, *Beginnings*, p. 10.

22. The notion of the self as hieroglyph, as a sign of its own creation, is explored, particularly for Poe, in Irwin, *American Hieroglyphics*, especially pp. 123, 129. I am, again, indebted to Irwin's discussion for my analysis of self and signs in *LETTERS*.

23. Antonio Gramsci, *Selections from the Prison Notebooks*, ed. and trans. Quintin Hoare and Geoffrey Norwell Smith (New York: International Publishers, 1971), p. 353.

24. Roland Barthes, *S/Z: An Essay*, trans. Richard Miller (New York: Hill and Wang, 1974), p. 11.

25. V. N. Vološinov [Mikhail Bakhtin], *Marxism and the Philosophy of Language*, trans. Ladislav Matejka and I. R. Titunik (New York: Seminar Press, 1973), p. 36.

26. Again, the informing theory is that of Michel Serres, who suggests that the disruption of a system is essential to its renewal and increasing complexity (see Josué V. Harari and David F. Bell in the introduction to Serres' *Hermes*, "Journal à plusieurs voies," pp. xxvi–vii, and Serres, pp. 3–14). Serres creates a figure, the parasite, who performs this disruptive function, as static in a system of communication or as the act of the interpreter in a hermeneutic tradition. (Cf. Serres' recently translated *The Parasite*, trans. Lawrence R. Schehr [Baltimore: Johns Hopkins University Press, 1982].) J. Hillis Miller, "The Critic as Host," *Critical Inquiry*, 3 (1977), 439–47, adumbrates the figure of the parasite as implicated by both textual and interpretive strategies. In a similar context, cf. Barthes, *S/Z*, pp. 131–32, 145, where he contrasts the "noise" of narrative to an idyllic, two-way communication consisting of pure signs. Barthes asserts that the function of narrative is to create "defects" in communication which the reader parasitically "consumes." See also, in this regard, Anthony Wilden, "Order from Disorder: Noise, Trace, and Event in Evolution and in History," in *System and Structure: Essays in Communication and Exchange*, 2nd ed. (London: Tavistock Publications, 1980), pp. 395–412.

27. This concept of the self as "open" to the endless supplementation of documents accords with Michel Foucault's deconstruction of an author's *oeuvre*: it is not to be seen as a homogeneous "collection of texts that can be designated by the sign of the proper name" but as a "vast mass of verbal traces," an "endless confusion of so many languages" that would require an infinity to context and translate. Cf. *The Archaeology of Knowledge*, trans.

A. M. Sheridan Smith (1972; rpt. New York: Pantheon Books, 1982), pp. 23–24.

28. Homer Obed Brown, "The Errant Letter and the Whispering Gallery," *Genre*, 10 (1977), 587–88.

29. Some time after I had completed my analysis of *LETTERS*, Barth published his first work of nonfiction, *The Friday Book: Essays and Other Non-Fiction* (New York: G. P. Putnam's Sons, 1984). There, the reader may find several interesting glosses on *LETTERS*, some which affirm and some which diverge from my own view of the novel. Of course, given Barth's view of the Author, the phenomenon of "John Barth" exposing us to a critique of a novel (his "own") where his authorial self is anonymously present complicates the issues of authority and authorship that *LETTERS* explores at length. In the role of critic of his own unauthorized novel, Barth discusses *LETTERS* directly or indirectly in "*Western Wind, Eastern Shore*" (124–26); "The Spirit of Place" (127–29); "Getting Oriented" (130–40); "My Two Problems: 2" (144–50); "Algebra and Fire" (166–71); "Speaking of *LETTERS*" (172–80); "Historical Fiction, Fictitious History, and Chesapeake Bay Blue Crabs, or, About Aboutness" (180–92); and "The Self in Fiction, or, 'That Ain't No Matter, That Is Nothing'" (207–14). Also reprinted in this collection are the twin essays "The Literature of Exhaustion" (62–76) and "The Literature of Replenishment" (193–206), which inevitably inform any reading of Barth's fiction.

4. *Gravity's Rainbow*

1. Thomas Pynchon, *Gravity's Rainbow* (New York: Viking Press, 1973), p. 5. All future references will be to this edition and noted parenthetically in the text.

2. Thomas Pynchon, *V.* (1963; rpt. New York: Bantam Books, 1963), p. 285.

3. Scott Simmon, "*Gravity's Rainbow* Described," *Critique*, 16 (1974), 55.

4. Clifford Geertz, *The Interpretation of Cultures: Selected Essays* (London: Hutchinson, 1973), p. 20.

5. See Lawrence C. Wolfley, "Repression's Rainbow: The Presence of Norman O. Brown in Pynchon's Big Novel," *PMLA*, 92 (1977), 873–89, for a psychoanalytical discussion of repression in Pynchon's world as that which gives rise to culture while leading to its death. In Wolfley's view, *Gravity's Rainbow* is largely "about" the conflictual processes of cultural repression and the escape mechanism that fiction creates.

6. Tanner, *City of Words*, p. 153. See Edward Mendelson's important "Gravity's Encyclopedia" in George Levine and David Leverenz, eds., *Mindful Pleasures: Essays on Thomas Pynchon* (Boston: Little, Brown, 1976), pp. 161–95, for a discussion of encyclopedic narrative that locates *Gravity's*

Rainbow within the tradition of the anatomy and thereby provides a crucial definition of the novel's generic capacities.

7. "Molecular hermeneutics" is the coinage of Joel D. Black, "Probing a Post-Romantic Paleontology: Thomas Pynchon's *Gravity's Rainbow*," *boundary 2*, 8 (1980), 245; the second part of the quotation is from Black, p. 239. I am indebted to Black's illuminating discussion of the influence of romantic mythology upon Pynchon, particularly the connection between digging in the earth and the quest for truth.

8. Bernard Duyfhuizen, "Starry-Eyed Semiotics: Learning to Read Slothrop's Map and *Gravity's Rainbow*," *Pynchon Notes*, 6 (1981), 5–33, discusses the desire of the novel's reader to discover its significant patterns, and Pynchon's intention of thwarting that desire. Duyfhuizen's intentionalist interpretation is important in its understanding of a dynamics of reader response for the novel, though I think he reduces *Gravity's Rainbow* too much to a series of deceptive ploys on Pynchon's part that inspires in the reader a kind of reified skepticism concerning readerly processes of interpretation.

9. The phrase "caries into cabals" comes from *V.*, p. 139, where, interestingly, a dentist, Dudley Eigenvalue, reflects that an individual tooth is not subject to a "conspiracy" of the several cavities that invade it, yet there are men like the novel's quester, Stencil, "who must go about grouping the world's random caries into cabals."

10. Indeed, social anthropologists have recently begun reading cultural wastes in order to understand the power structures and value systems of a given society. A lively and illuminating analysis of this endeavor is provided by Michael Thompson, *Rubbish Theory: The Creation and Destruction of Value* (New York: Oxford University Press, 1979), especially pp. 77–102.

11. Explanations for the connection between life and death in the novel based on Norman O. Brown's *Life against Death* and Herbert Marcuse's *Eros and Civilization* have been made extensively by Pynchon's critics. For the former, see Wolfley, "Repression's Rainbow"; for the latter, see Joseph W. Slade, "Religion, Psychology, Sex and Love in *Gravity's Rainbow*," in Charles Clerc, ed., *Approaches to* Gravity's Rainbow (Columbus: Ohio State University Press, 1983), pp. 153–98. I am not detracting from these useful readings by suggesting that they fall into the trap which every reader of Pynchon and every interpreter of culture must fall into—the creation of an explanatory fiction which reduces what is, essentially, a dynamic, groundless relational process.

12. This "narrative" process, again, is brilliantly discussed from a post-Freudian perspective by Brooks, "Freud's Masterplot."

13. Charles Russell, "Pynchon's Language: Signs, Systems, and Subversion," in Clerc's *Approaches to* Gravity's Rainbow, pp. 251–72, also discusses the problem of language in the novel as a double process that embodies repressive or deathly movements while subverting them. Russell's excellent semiotic analysis is parallel to my own at several points in the discussion of Pynchon's view of language, though he is less concerned than I am with the

language of culture in *Gravity's Rainbow* and more interested in the essential theme of repression versus freedom from language systems. Consequently, he reinforces the view of Pynchon as an ironic pessimist in this regard, while I maintain that *Gravity's Rainbow* is more concerned to perform a cultural phenomenology. In *Ideas of Order in the Novels of Thomas Pynchon* (Columbus: Ohio State University Press, 1983), Molly Hite proposes a view of Pynchon's language similar to Wolfley's, Russell's, and my own, as a dialectically repressive/disseminatory process (pp. 33–45). Her discussion of *Gravity's Rainbow* sees the novel as a form of secular theology, figured as upsurgings of moments of transcendence or disruption within a paradoxical, "open" cosmic order. Thus, her approach is, ultimately, based more in metaphysics than in epistemology.

14. The pervasive and important mathematical imagery of *Gravity's Rainbow* and its many associations are observed by Lance W. Ozier, "Antipointsman/Antimexico: Some Mathematical Imagery in *Gravity's Rainbow*," *Critique*, 16 (1974), 73–90, and "The Calculus of Transformation: More Mathematical Imagery in *Gravity's Rainbow*," *Twentieth Century Literature*, 21 (1975), 193–210.

15. Miller, "Ariadne's Thread," p. 68.

16. Tony Tanner, *Thomas Pynchon* (New York: Methuen, 1982), p. 77.

17. Mendelson, "Gravity's Encyclopedia," pp. 167–71.

18. Interestingly, if "only" coincidentally, Derrida's conception of "heliotropes" parallels Slothrop's flowering rhetoric here. For Derrida, who studies metaphors of sun and flowers in classical philosophy, these "roots" of language and their scatterings always reveal the operation of language as a gathering toward and dispersal from an absent center. Cf. Jacques Derrida, "White Mythology: Metaphor in the Text of Philosophy," trans. F. C. T. Moore, *New Literary History*, 6 (1974), especially pp. 29–60. I am also indebted to Derrida's larger discussion of dissemination in "Plato's Pharmacy," in *Dissemination*, pp. 61–171. For an analysis of how this process is related to a Hegelian concept of consciousness, see Eugenio Donato, "The Ruins of Memory: Archeological Fragments and Textual Artifacts," *MLN*, 93 (1978), 575–96.

19. Frank Kermode, *The Genesis of Secrecy: On the Interpretation of Narrative* (Cambridge, Mass.: Harvard University Press, 1979), p. 47. See also pp. 23–47, 125–45, for the development of this concept about narrative.

20. Joseph W. Slade, "Escaping Rationalization: Options for the Self in *Gravity's Rainbow*," *Critique*, 18 (1977), 27–37, discusses the self in the novel in light of psychologistic, existential models of wholeness and disintegration rather than as a language element.

21. The "questing function" is a familiar figure in Pynchon's fiction, represented by Enzian, Slothrop, and others in *Gravity's Rainbow*, by Oedipa Maas in *The Crying of Lot 49*, and by Stencil in *V.* The self defined as an information sorter is informed by communications theory, which defines an operator in any communications system that both retards and facilitates the

flow of information. I am suggesting that this *is* the work of interpretation in *Gravity's Rainbow*. For Serres, again, this is the function of "the parasite"; cf. his *The Parasite*. Anne Mangel, "Maxwell's Demon, Entropy, Information: *The Crying of Lot 49*," *TriQuarterly*, 20 (1971), 194–208, usefully discusses the "Maxwell's Demon" of that novel as the figure for this parasitic labor. See also John O. Stark, *Pynchon's Fictions: Thomas Pynchon and the Literature of Information* (Athens: Ohio University Press, 1980), pp. 60–69.

22. Sanford S. Ames, "Pynchon and Visible Language: Ecriture," *International Fiction Review*, 4 (1977), 170. Ames' Lacanian reading of *Gravity's Rainbow* is all too brief but highly suggestive in its discussion of the novel's semiotics.

23. In *Pynchon: The Voice of Ambiguity* (Urbana: University of Illinois Press, 1981), Thomas H. Schaub suggests that Slothrop is an embodiment of an archetypal situation in Pynchon's fiction, that of ambiguity or uncertainty, which becomes a mode of meaning (and survival) opposed to the polarities of systems and antisystems, order and randomness—a situation, finally, in which Pynchon's fortunate reader comes to dwell (see especially pp. 103–38). My analysis suggests that Schaub's reading unproblematically validates ambiguity as a somewhat existential mode of being without questioning its status as produced by a semiotic system of signs and countersigns.

24. Wolfley, "Repression's Rainbow," p. 876.

25. The process of acculturation captured in *Gravity's Rainbow* is hardly contemporary or revolutionary; it is, as the novel's archaeological figures would have us believe, at the roots of consciousness, the ongoing dialectic of our cultural self-knowledge. The mythological, religious, and historical consequences of this process are illuminated by Herbert N. Schneidau, *Sacred Discontent: The Bible and Western Tradition* (Berkeley and Los Angeles: University of California Press, 1976), especially pp. 1–49. Juri M. Lotman and B. A. Uspensky discuss this process as "the necessity for continued self-renewal, to become different and yet remain the same, [which] constitutes one of the chief working mechanisms of our culture," in "On the Semiotic Mechanism of Culture," *New Literary History*, 9 (1978), 226. Bakhtin perceives this process, in terms particularly applicable to *Gravity's Rainbow*, as a movement between "heteroglossia" and "stratification": "Alongside the centripetal forces, the centrifugal forces of language carry on their uninterrupted work; alongside verbal-ideological centralization and unification, the uninterrupted processes of decentralization and disunification go forward." See "Discourse in the Novel," *Dialogic Imagination*, p. 272. For a psychoanalytic reading of this cultural process, see Juliet Flower McCannell, "The Semiotic of Modern Culture," *Semiotica*, 35 (1981), 287–301. See also Jacques Derrida, "Freud and the Scene of Writing," in *Writing and Difference*, pp. 196–231, for an adjacent discussion of this dialectical process as a sign of consciousness inscribed.

5. *Wise Blood*

1. O'Connor's description of Hazel as a "Christian *malgré lui*" occurs in the preface to the second edition of *Wise Blood*. The readings of the novel that follow O'Connor's lead in viewing it, theologically, as presenting a tortuous quest for salvation include, among many others, Miles Orvell, *Invisible Parade: The Fiction of Flannery O'Connor* (Philadelphia: Temple University Press, 1972), pp. 69–75; Kathleen Feeley, *Flannery O'Connor: The Voice of the Peacock* (1972; rpt. New York: Fordham University Press, 1982), pp. 56–69; and Leon V. Driscoll and Joan T. Brittain, *The Eternal Crossroads: The Art of Flannery O'Connor* (Lexington: University Press of Kentucky, 1971), pp. 33–58.

2. Frederick Asals, *Flannery O'Connor: The Imagination of Extremity* (Athens: University of Georgia Press, 1982), p. 35.

3. Flannery O'Connor, *Wise Blood*, 2nd ed. (1952; rpt. New York: Farrar, Straus and Giroux, 1962), p. 55. All future references will be to this edition and noted parenthetically in the text.

4. Orvell, *Invisible Parade*, p. 76.

5. John Hawkes, "Flannery O'Connor's Devil," *Sewanee Review*, 70 (1962), 403, 396.

6. My use of the terms "hermeneutic" and "antihermeneutic" in this discussion is a general one that indicates a quest either for meaning or (in Hazel's case) for nonmeaning authorially encouraged or discouraged. For a discussion of O'Connor's fiction that employs a more formal and specific application of hermeneutic theory, see John R. May, *The Pruning Word: The Parables of Flannery O'Connor* (Notre Dame: Notre Dame University Press, 1976).

7. Paul de Man, "The Rhetoric of Temporality," in Charles S. Singleton, ed., *Interpretation: Theory and Practice* (Baltimore: Johns Hopkins University Press, 1969), p. 192.

8. Carol Shloss, *Flannery O'Connor's Dark Comedies: The Limits of Inference* (Baton Rouge: Louisiana State University Press, 1980), pp. 11–20, discusses O'Connor's fictions as anagogies from a different view: she is concerned about how O'Connor controls the novel's meaning through the use of the anagogical mode as a matter of pluralistic intention, while I am concerned to show how O'Connor's anagogy becomes a form of authorial domination. For a discussion of the generic and interpretive constraints of anagogy, see Frye, *Anatomy of Criticism*, pp. 115–28.

9. Claire Katz, "Flannery O'Connor's Rage of Vision," *American Literature*, 46 (1974), 54.

10. Ludwig Binswanger, "The Case of Lola Voss," in *Being-in-the-World: Selected Papers of Ludwig Binswanger*, trans. and introd. Jacob Needleman (New York: Harper and Row, 1967), pp. 284, 311, 305.

11. Interestingly, Eugene Minkowski, Binswanger's fellow worker in the school of *Daseinanalyse*, describes a patient who "consumes" the world in

ways similar to but much more dramatic than Lola's. Minkowski's patient suffers from a "persecution complex," in which even the smallest of the world's objects seems an incarnation of hostility to him: there was a "'residue politics' (*politique des restes*) as he called it—a political system that had been instituted especially for him. Every leftover, all residue, would be put aside to be one day stuffed into his abdomen—and this, from all over the world. Everything would be included without exception. When one smoked, there would be the burnt match, the ashes, and the cigarette butt. At meals, he was preoccupied with the crumbs, the fruit pits, the chicken bones, the wine or water at the bottom of glasses. The egg, he said, was his worst enemy because of the shell—it was also the expression of the great anger of his persecutors. When one sewed, there would be bits of thread and needles. All the matches, strings, bits of paper, and pieces of glass that he saw while walking in the street were meant for him. After that came nail parings and hair clippings, empty bottles, letters and envelopes, subway tickets, address-bands, the dust that one brought in on one's shoes, bath water, the garbage from the kitchen and from the restaurants of France, etc. Then it was rotten fruit and vegetables, cadavers of animals and men, the urine and faeces of horses. 'Whoever speaks of a clock,' he would tell us, 'speaks of the hands, cogs, springs, case, pendulum, etc.' And all this he would have to swallow . . . In these conditions, it is not difficult to understand that the smallest thing, the most minute act of daily life, was immediately interpreted as being hostile to him." See Eugene Minkowski, "Findings in a Case of Schizophrenic Depression," in Rollo May, Ernest Angel, and Henri F. Ellenberger, eds., *Existence: A New Dimension* in *Psychology and Psychiatry* (New York: Basic Books, 1958), pp. 127–38; the quote appears on p. 128.

12. Jacob Needleman, "Introduction to Binswanger's Existential Psychoanalysis," in Binswanger, *Being-in-the-World*, p. 142.

13. For a brief discussion of three modes of interpretation—the empirical, the "surprising," and the infinite—based upon Binswanger's thought and informative of this discussion of O'Connor, see my "Ludwig Binswanger and the Poetics of Compromise," *Review of Existential Psychiatry and Psychology*, 17 (1983), 235–43.

14. Katz, "Flannery O'Connor's Rage of Vision," p. 57.

15. I discuss the implications of the "gap" or "space of interpretation" and the reader's role in chapter 7.

16. Flannery O'Connor, *Mystery and Manners: Occasional Prose*, ed. Sally Fitzgerald and Robert Fitzgerald (New York: Farrar, Straus and Giroux, 1961), p. 21.

6. *The Franchiser*

1. William H. Gass, foreword to Stanley Elkin, *The Franchiser* (1976; rpt. Boston: David R. Godine, 1980), p. xiv. All future references will be to this edition and noted parenthetically in the text.

2. Sharon Cameron, *The Corporeal Self: Allegories of the Body in Melville and Hawthorne* (Baltimore: Johns Hopkins University Press, 1981), pp. 5–6.

3. Bakhtin, "Epic and Novel," *Dialogic Imagination*, p. 17.

4. See Tom LeClair's important article, "The Obsessional Fiction of Stanley Elkin," *Contemporary Literature*, 16 (1975), 146–62, for a discussion of how the verbal pyrotechnics of Elkin's heroes belie their "obsessions," defined as "subjective, strange, and extreme . . . characterized by a narrow focus on fixed ends, by intense desire and extravagant means, and by the lack of relations and options" (146).

5. Again, Brooks' essay, "Freud's Masterplot," is crucial to my understanding of narrative "ends" in *The Franchiser*.

6. Julia Kristeva, "Word, Dialogue, Novel," in *Desire in Language: A Semiotic Approach to Literature and Art*, ed. Leon S. Roudiez, trans. Thomas Gora, Alice Jardine, and Leon S. Roudiez (New York: Columbia University Press, 1980), pp. 78–79.

7. Entanglement

1. Frank Kermode, "Novels: Recognition and Deception," *Critical Inquiry*, 1 (1974), 115.

2. William Faulkner, *Absalom, Absalom!* (1936; rpt. New York: Random House, 1964), p. 261. For a discussion of the reader's role in this novel, see David Krause, "Reading Bon's Letter and Faulkner's *Absalom, Absalom!*" PMLA, 99 (1984), 225–41. As will be seen, I do not agree with Krause that the reader's relation to the text is "writerly," nor can the distinction between the "reader" and the "writer" be as unproblematically collapsed as Krause thinks they can be.

3. Faulkner, *Absalom, Absalom!* p. 316.

4. My characterization of the reader as solipsist is countered by Linda Hutcheon, *Narcissistic Narrative: The Metafictional Paradox* (Waterloo, Ont.: Wilfred Laurier University Press, 1980), especially pp. 1–17, 138–52. While I would agree with Hutcheon that there is always a "tension between involvement and self-awareness in the act of reading" (150)—a tension I have labeled "passionate doubts"—I disagree with her view that the effect of "metafiction" is to collapse the distinctions between author, text, and reader. While this is the *stated* enterprise of, particularly, "surfictionists" like Raymond Federman and Ronald Sukenick, I propose here that the effect of reading such superficially self-conscious or disruptive fiction is to, in a very contrived manner, widen the gap between reader and text, insofar as that gap defines the difference between the reader as witness to and as producer of textual operations.

5. These are the definitions assigned to the reader in the following well-known arguments. For a discussion of the reader as an observable construction of the text, see Wolfgang Iser, *The Implied Reader: Patterns of Communication in Prose Fiction from Bunyan to Beckett* (Baltimore: Johns Hopkins Uni-

versity Press, 1974) and *The Act of Reading: A Theory of Aesthetic Response* (Baltimore: Johns Hopkins University Press, 1978). The discussions of the reader's subjective response are many, but a twentieth-century history of the subject might be formulated by a reading of I. A. Richards, *Practical Criticism: A Study of Literary Judgment* (1929; rpt. New York: Harcourt, Brace, 1935); Norman Holland, *5 Readers Reading* (New Haven: Yale University Press, 1975); and David Bleich, *Subjective Criticism* (Baltimore: Johns Hopkins University Press, 1978). The reader as participant in a community of interpretation has been one of the themes of Stanley Fish's reader-response theory, particularly in *Is There a Text in This Class? The Authority of Interpretive Communities* (Cambridge, Mass.: Harvard University Press, 1980). The theory of the reader as scientist, observer, or truth seeker finds its contemporary defender in E. D. Hirsch, *Validity in Interpretation* (New Haven: Yale University Press, 1967). For an array of positions see Jane P. Tompkins, ed., *Reader-Response Criticism: From Formalism to Post-Structuralism* (Baltimore: Johns Hopkins University Press, 1980), and Susan Suleiman and Inge Crosman, eds., *The Reader in the Text: Essays on Audience and Interpretation* (Princeton: Princeton University Press, 1980).

6. Private communication.

7. Barthes, *S/Z*, p. 44.

8. William Golding, *Free Fall* (New York: Harcourt, Brace, 1959), p. 8.

9. Gabriel Josipovici, *The World and the Book: A Study of Modern Fiction* (London: Macmillan, 1971), p. 149.

10. Herbert N. Schneidau, "The Word against the Word: Derrida on Textuality," *Semeia*, 23 (1982), 5–28, studies the discomforts implicit in the reading of any fiction: "its most noteworthy quality . . . is to seem to be straining with signification while at the same time presenting so many aporiae, so many 'undecidable' readings, that we can never feel quite comfortable with the understandings we have, even of those texts on which we may spend a lifetime's effort" (23). Given this "generic" quality of reading, the contemporaneity of contemporary fiction may be assessed by the degree of hermeneutic discomfort it elicits. Of course, once again, this contemporaneity is hardly chronological; it is a mood or spirit that pervades *Tristram Shandy* as well as *Gravity's Rainbow*. In our time, contemporaneity is more a matter of quantity than of quality—a point that must be viewed in light of Hegel's notion, adapted by Barth in *LETTERS*, that an increase in quantity eventually leads to a qualitative change.

11. William H. Gass, *Fiction and the Figures of Life* (1970; rpt. Boston: David R. Godine, 1978), p. 75.

12. Robert Coover, *Pricksongs & Descants* (1969; rpt. London: Picador, 1973), p. 62.

13. Richard Macksey, "The Artist in the Labyrinth: Design or *Dasein*," *MLN*, 77 (1962), 242.

14. Italo Calvino, *If on a Winter's Night a Traveler*, trans. William Weaver (New York: Harcourt Brace Jovanovich, 1981), p. 254.

15. John Barth, *Giles Goat-Boy* (1966; rpt. New York: Fawcett, 1967), pp. 724–25.

16. Ibid., p. 721.

17. Scholes, *Fabulation and Metafiction*, p. 99, cites this same passage and notes that the librarian contributes to the making of the text, while reading the book we read. Scholes goes on to say that the effect of the passage is to tell us that "Barth is a fabulator, and he is gently and wittily reminding us of that, reminding us that our world and this one are different, different," but he leaves matters on this general level; in reciting the passage, I am interested in investigating, more specifically, the "difference."

18. Gayatri Spivak, "Translator's Preface" to Jacques Derrida, *Of Grammatology* (Baltimore: Johns Hopkins University Press, 1976), p. xx.

19. De Man, *Blindness and Insight*, p. 17. Gerald Graff, *Literature against Itself: Literary Ideas in Modern Society* (Chicago: University of Chicago Press, 1979), pp. 173–75, also discusses this passage from de Man, but in a very different context, as a nonempirical statement about the nature of fiction.

20. Jean-Paul Sartre, *Being and Nothingness: A Phenomenological Essay on Ontology*, trans. and introd. Hazel E. Barnes (1956; rpt. New York: Washington Square Press, 1966), p. 129.

21. Georges Poulet, "Phenomenology of Reading," *New Literary History*, 1 (1969), 56–57.

22. Vološinov [Bakhtin], *Marxism and the Philosophy of Language*, p. 26.

23. Wallace Stevens, "Sunday Morning," in *Collected Poems* (New York: Random House, 1982), p. 70.

24. Barthes, *S/Z*, pp. 5–6.

25. Merleau-Ponty, *Phenomenology of Perception*, p. 140.

26. Iser, *Implied Reader*, pp. 284–85.

INDEX